THINKING IN SYSTEMS
AND **MENTAL MODELS**

Think Like a Super Thinker.

Primer to Learn the Art of Making
a Great Decision and Solving
Complex Problems. Chaos Theory,
Science of Thinking for Social Change

MARCUS P. DAWSON

TABLE OF CONTENTS

Part 1. Thinking in Systems

Part 2. Mental Models

PART 1

THINKING IN SYSTEMS

INTRODUCTION

In systems thinking, we take a gander at the entire system as opposed to attempting to separate it into its parts; that is, we turned out to be sweeping in our thinking instead of reductive. By taking a gander at the entire, we are increasingly fit for seeing interrelationships and patterns after some time. We likewise start to understand that the introducing issue might be symptomatic of more profound problems inside the system; thus, we begin searching for the main drivers. In doing as such, we move away from appointing fault and spotlight on the desired results.

Systems thinking is proactive and round, rather than linear thinking, which will, in general, be receptive. There are 3 main systems thinking ideas worth noting: reinforcing feedback, balancing feedback and delays, enhancing or amplifying feedback loops are what drives fuel development, or creates a system decrease. They wind up or down, though they rarely occur in confinement. Growth and decrease are both limits. A simple case of a reinforcing loop is how profitability of an organization can influence development, which therefore affects budget prizes, which appears at ground zero to influence efficiency. This loop can move either a positive way, or a negative course stops at a distinct containment point at the end of the day.

Balancing or settling feedback loops are those that endeavor to look after balance. These systems are goal situated and will do whatever is essential to reach or keep up that goal. Driving a car is a balancing loop since the aim is to reach the desired destination. The driver will take the steps necessary to reach that destination in a sheltered and proficient manner. We're knocking towards a balancing loop in organizations when our efforts to make a change take us back to where we started. We are experiencing protection against change as the current system is striving to maintain a specific objective. In any event, that goal may not be self-evident; we may discover that we need to reveal the mental models that keep that system set up before we have any desire to evolve it.

Delays are inescapable in any system yet are regularly not perceived. Delays cause flimsiness in systems, and vigorous activity to make up for delays will probably cause organizations to overshoot or undershoot. To delineate, how about we utilize the case of an indoor regulator.

Nowadays, with vitality costs heading through the rooftop, a large number of us have developed the propensity for setting the indoor regulator back around evening time to save vitality. It is enticing to turn the heat on those unusually chilly mornings higher than would normally be appropriate in the first part of the day, yet not at all like a stove burner, turning the temperature up higher will not deliver more heat. There is a delay from when the fever reaches its actual temperature when the groom arrives. If the heat is set to be higher than would generally be appropriate, then the room will overheat at that point. We set the heat back to chill the room in response to that, yet then the temperature drops excessively low and we set the heat up again by and by. This could always continue if we weren't fit to make a profit from our activities. Developing patience against climate delays and not responding too quickly to changes in the system is essential in system thinking.

What Are the Attributes of Systems Thinkers?

A systems thinker is one who:

- Sees the entire picture.
- Changes viewpoints to see new use focuses on complex systems.
- Searches for interdependencies.
- Thinks about how mental models create our fates.
- Focuses and offers a voice to the long-term.
- "Goes wide" (utilizes fringe vision) to see complex cause and effect connections.
- Finds where unexpected results rise.
- Brings down the "water line" to concentrate on structure, not fault.
- Holds the strain of Catch 22 and debate without attempting to determine it quickly.

Systems thinkers are the individuals who consider some fresh possibilities. They understand that there are no correct answers, just different ways to similar results. They know that convenient solutions will, in all probability, lead ideal back to where they began from and therefore developed patience with the possibility that cause, and effect are not firmly related in time and space. They understand that things may deteriorate before they improve; however, they have figured out how to take the long view. In doing as such, they can tap the creative collaboration that exists in organizations.

How Do Organizations Apply Systems Thinking?

There is an assortment of ways to actualize systems thinking inside an organization, and every organization must discover what fits well inside the organizational culture. However, there are vital aspects of systems thinking to consider. The following is one conceivable methodology that incorporates these key aspects:

- Occasions: Begin the act of systems thinking by recounting the tale of the present circumstance. It is imperative to hear many points of view, however, don't hop to arrangements right away. It might be essential to give a handy solution with the understanding that it is a stopgap measure that isn't intended for long-term arrangements. In the interim, investigate the idea of the occasion or issue in more prominent detail.

- Patterns of conduct: Track the circumstance over some time. Search for trends and patterns that go underneath the surface. Return ever, if you have the information. Those patterns are key indicators for the system.

- Systemic structure: The patterns and patterns you've found look for interrelationships. Search for feedback balancing and strengthening and identify system delays. Disclose the mental models driving those patterns.

- Mental models: Creating new mental models to make system change. Be tolerant - delays will occur, and things could deteriorate before they show signs of improvement. Track the effects of the changes and assess them. Decide whether there are unintended outcomes and choose which tweak requirements.

For the fact that this may seem like a moderately direct procedure, it is a long way from it. There are numerous difficulties in actualizing systems thinking, the greatest of which is conventions or potentially propensities. Patterns of conduct are difficult to perceive and significantly harder to change, and we regularly feel strain to act quickly with almost no systemic data. Finding the harmony between taking care of the present and making what's to come is never simple.

What Are the Advantages of Systems Thinking?

Systems thinking is the string that ties the other four controls of organizational adapting together. Organizations participating in systems thinking can:

- Develop new ways of taking a gander at old issues.
- Incorporate new data all the more effectively.
- See interrelationships and cause and effect all the more obviously.
- Develop patience with executing change and enduring delays.
- Step away from habitual pettiness toward shared obligation.
- See the entire as opposed to the parts.

Although each of the above benefits can set aside an extreme measure of ace effort, the interest in developing system thinkers is worth the time and effort. At last, organizations rehearsing systems thinking will most likely step up to that subsequent degree of thinking to tackle issues and create their desired fates. They will have more prominent command over their fortune and be progressively deft in reacting to environmental changes. What better way to remain one step in front of the challenge?

CHAPTER 1
WHAT IS SYSTEMS THINKING?

There are two fundamental ways in which to respond to an ever-changing world: when events happen, you can react, or, with knowledge of how events work, you can be a participating actor instead of a passive reactor. When a machine breaks down, we respond by trying to fix it. With systems thinking, you begin to develop an ability to predict when and why the machine will break down, therefore giving yourself an edge in terms of strategic planning and decision making.

What is a system? At its most basic, a system is the holistic sum of the interdependent parts which interact with one another to a specific purpose. The crucial point here is that of interaction and interdependence: without these, you merely have a loose collection of parts, not a system. For example, a kitchen in and of itself isn't a system because not all of the parts interact with one another, and it doesn't have one clear overarching purpose; whereas, an oven is a system, in that all of its working parts must interact in order for it to operate for the purpose of cooking food.

Instead of looking at the surface of things, systems thinking asks that you look deeper into how these structures are created and how they interact with one another. We may be cogs in a machine, as the old saying goes, but we can become cognizant of how those cogs work together, thus building a better machine. The whole is greater than the sum of its parts. Therefore, understanding how systems work is of great advantage to anyone trying to assess and solve challenges. By reframing your perspective – you are no longer looking at a broken machine but a damaged system – you are better equipped to understand that each part is significant in its own way, while the whole working together is significant in the highest way.

There are several key terms to understanding systems thinking, and these are all explored in greater depth throughout the reading. First, the concept of interconnectedness requires that we recognize that all parts are dependent on one another and to the larger system. Think of the term "ecosystem" to illuminate the concept of interconnectedness: this consists of not only the animal life forms but also the plant material, the environmental structure (air quality, water access), the spatial requirements, even the microscopic bacterial components that create good soil and clean water, for example. When one of these things goes awry, the entire system is compromised.

Second, the idea of synthesis is key to systems thinking. Synthesis is, essentially, recognizing the interconnectedness of a system and being able to study both the whole and its component parts – as well as understanding how they work together. This leads to an understanding of the third key term, emergence: when synthesis is working well, we see an emergence of positive outcomes. Basically, when everything works together seamlessly, we get the Goldilocks effect: it is all "just right." Disruption within a system invariably impedes the emergence of desired goals.

Fourth, to harness the energies of a system, you must get to know how feedback loops work. Top-down styles of thinking and of management no longer respond nimbly and successfully to challenges: if the communication is only going in one direction, then the system gets bogged down in routines, misinformation, and mistrust. Feedback loops can occasionally work against us, as in a reinforcing loop. This is like a recording getting stuck, repeating the same line over and over again. If we are only telling ourselves one story, then it becomes dominant, and the system gets out of balance.

Understanding how feedback loops work is an exercise in old-fashioned rhetoric – understanding cause and effect. When we understand causality, our fifth term is about being able to ascertain how the parts in the system interact with one another – and what emerges from that interaction – then we begin to gain a perspective on the relationships with different elements within the system. This leads to smarter planning and better decisions, ultimately.

Last, the term systems mapping describes the tools that allow us to view how our system is working (or why it is not working and, thus, how to fix it).Thus, systems thinking employ a plethora of diagrams and charts in order to help you look at the system as a whole, understanding how each part affects each other part.

Systems mapping opens up a world of possibilities for problem-solving. We will look at various archetypes of typical ways in which systems function, and more importantly, how they become dysfunctional over time if we don't examine how the dynamic works. This allows us to look beyond mere events to the patterns of behavior within the system itself that lead up to them. It's a powerful mechanism wherein we become active instead of reactive to events as they occur.

When we examine the enormous problems that we encounter in the world, we must acknowledge that there is no such thing as a simple fix. Often, people will use the phrase "systemic racism," for example, to describe a nefarious problem that isn't limited to one arena of the social sphere, or one isolated event, or even to one time or place or institution. The system itself is arranged in such a dysfunctional manner that the problem crops up at various times along various fault lines until the underlying system itself is addressed. When we practice systems thinking, what we are doing is exploring the context within our connections with others and with organizations, understanding and respecting the perspectives that each actor within the system brings, and trying to define the scope and scale of what might be needed to begin to make improvements. This kind of thinking enables us to tackle the large-scale problems facing our world today, learning and depending on one another within the institutions that we foster.

Systems thinking is crucial to problem-solving, because no problem exists in isolation, all are part of a larger system of interacting networks.

CHAPTER 2
WHAT DOES IT INVOLVE?

The word "systems thinking" can mean different things for people. It is important to note. The discipline of system thought is more than a set of instruments and methods – it is also a theory that underlies it. Many beginners like causal loop charts and control flight simulators are drawn to technologies in the expectation that these technologies will assist them in coping with persistent business problems. Structures thought, however, is also the sensitivity of the systemic existence of the environment in which we live; the understanding of the role of the process in creating the conditions we face; knowledge of the powerful laws of structures which we do not understand.

Thinking technology is also a diagnostic tool. Like in the medical profession, accurate diagnosis accompanies successful treatment. In this sense, system thinking is a systematic method for a more thorough and reliable analysis of issues before acting. This helps us to ask informed questions before we conclude. Systems analysis also requires shifting from events or data to behavioral overtime trends and processes underlying these trends and events. We will extend the options available, and create more meaningful, long-term solutions for chronic issues by identifying and modifying systems that are not well served (including our mental models and perceptions).

Generally, the viewpoint of systems thinking requires curiosity, insight, compassion, preference, and courage. This approach requires the ability to look at the situation in more detail, realize that we interconnect, realize that an issue often includes multiple solutions, and championship approaches that might not be common.

When to Use?

Problems suitable for systems-oriented intervention have the following features:

- The problem is relevant.
- The problem is persistent, not one-off.
- The issue is well known, and its history is well known.
- People have tried to solve the problem unsuccessfully before.

How Do We Use System Thinking Tools?

Diagrams of Causal Chain. Recall, first, that less is more. Start small and simple; add additional elements to the story if needed – present part of the plot. The number of elements in a loop will be dependent on the needs of the story and the individuals using the diagram.

A concise explanation may be sufficient to encourage conversation and provide a new way of seeing a problem. In other cases, you can need more loops to explain causal relationships.

Keep in mind also that people always assume that a diagram will contain all possible variables in a story; this is not generally true. In other cases, external factors do not change, change very slowly, or are irrelevant to the problem.

You can complicate things unnecessarily by sharing this information, especially those that you have little or no control over. Many of the most successful loops show links or interactions between parts of the organization or program that the community has not been identified.

Ultimately, don't ask if a loop is "right." Ask yourself then if the loop correctly represents the narrative the community wants to tell. Loops are brief explanations of what we consider to be a current reality; they are "correct" enough if they represent that viewpoint.

Types of Thinking

Convergent Thinking

When you break down the term convergent thinking, you come out with two pieces: convergent can mean a variety of ideas coming together to form one specific conclusion. Thought is obviously what we have been talking about throughout this entire book.

When you put the terms together, convergent thinking can be defined as a problem-solving technique that enables a variety of different people from different backgrounds and occupations to come to the best conclusion about a bright, well-understood question. This thinking strategy is used to develop a fast, logical answer to a problem. By using convergent thinking, a group can solve problems at a quicker pace as long as they can agree on a solution. This train of thought can be considered lacking in creativity, but it is efficient. Therefore, while it has cons, it also has pros.

This type of thinking is suitable for obtaining straightforward facts, such as the sky is blue, and the Earth is round.

Convergent thinking is used in any standard IQ test. It is also used when there is only one correct answer to a problem. We can say that math problems will utilize a lot of convergent thinking. These tests evaluate things such as pattern recognition, logical flow of thought, and your capacity to solve problems. Multiple-choice questions are also a way to test convergent thinking.

Divergent Thinking

Divergent thinking is defined as a problem-solving strategy which allows a person to see multiple correct answers to a problem and determine which one will work the best. This type of thought process involves creativity and enables you to look at various things at once. You use divergent thinking when you are brainstorming ideas for a paper or free-writing. Through divergence, a person is able to take one approach or statement and branch off to make several different conclusions about that statement. All of these conclusions can be considered correct, and the findings will vary depending on the person.

There are 8 elements of divergent thinking:

1. Complexity: This is your ability to theorize many different ideas that are multilayered.

2. Risk-taking: This is important when considering your ability to set yourself apart from others. Those who venture into the unknown are generally the ones who make new discoveries and find new answers to questions.

3. Elaboration: This is taking one idea and building off of it. For example, Hershey's Chocolate has grown from a simple chocolate bar to several different types of chocolate in various forms which allows for a more enormous amount of productivity.

4. Originality: This is why it is so incredible to see several different people use divergent thinking to come up with an answer to a problem. People will utilize many different trains of thought to come up with new ideas.

5. Imagination: This is important in creating new products and developing new ideas. This also will connect to originality.

6. Flexibility: Your ability to create varied perceptions and categories. This is how we get several variations of the same thing.

7. Curiosity: To create new ideas, you must come up with further questions and inquiries.

8. Fluency: The ability to stimulate many ideas to have many different solutions in case one works better than the other.

People who think divergently share traits such as an inability to conform, persistence, curiosity, and readiness to take risks. There are no personality traits associated with those who engage in convergent thinking. This means that all people engage in convergent thinking. There are no tests to determine divergent thinking.

The two different thinking styles can be compared in several different ways. Studies show that divergent thinking and convergent thinking can affect mood. When prompted to use divergent thinking, a positive atmosphere was triggered, increasing productivity. When prompted to use convergent thinking, a negative attitude was triggered. Different thinkers generally score higher in categories that test word fluency and reading ability.

Divergent thinking is necessary for open-ended problems with even the smallest bit of creativity. Things like sleep deprivation can decrease your ability to think divergently. However, sleep deprivation hardly affects convergent thinking.

Let's look at some examples.

An example of a question that would require convergent thinking would look like this:

Who was the first president of the United States?

a. George Washington

b. Barack Obama

c. Thomas Jefferson

d. Abraham Lincoln

There is only one real answer to this problem – George Washington. This type of problem would not require any critical thinking and is merely asking for a recitation of your memory.

An example of a question that would require divergent thinking would look like this:

Who was the most influential president of the United States?

There is no one right answer to this question. As long as you were able to gather sufficient evidence, you could choose any president that you wanted. This question requires creativity and would call for originality, as long as you weren't copying off of the person next to you. If you chose a president who maybe did not have a significant impact, you would be taking a risk that could benefit you in the long run as long as you played your cards right.

So how does this all play into critical thinking?

I said before that convergent thinking does not require any critical thought. This remains true. You would utilize convergent thinking when acquiring information. An excellent example of a convergent thinker is Sherlock Holmes. He used deductive reasoning to solve a slew of crimes. He was able to take in all of the details of a crime scene and make connections to come to one conclusion and answer the question of who committed the crime. This sums up the description and analysis portion of our critical thinking model.

Once you delve into the evaluation portion of our model, you are making the transition to divergent thinking. Divergent thinking would take the answer of who committed the crime and ask more questions about it. For example, once you figure out who committed the crime, you will want to know why the crime was committed, what crimes could be engaged in the future, etc. Through divergent thinking, we can create profiles and answer questions about future crimes, which lead to more efficient problem-solving. This is where you will begin to see that critical thinking is more of a cycle than a step-by-step process. You can pick up at any point in the critical thinking process and continue onward around and around.

CHAPTER 3
LINEAR THINKING VS. LATERAL THINKING

The philosopher and psychologist Edward de Bono, who coined the concept of lateral thinking, referred to the aforementioned type of reasoning and thinking as linear thinking when compared with his own concept of lateral thinking. In general, they are linear in that they follow a straight line of reasoning. This has its advantages in that its way of thinking is much easier to understand and instruct others, but it comes with some serious limitations. Think back to the example with Galileo. The existing geocentric view of the solar system set some kind of artificial limitation on the way people think about it, with the idea that the Earth was the center of the solar system and the universe. Had Galileo stuck to linear thinking, that fundamental underpinning would not have been in question.

Lateral thinking seeks to take a different route to the conclusion by approaching the problem from a different angle than when used in linear thinking and the rest of the pages will illustrate several different ways of doing so.

You might have learned the phrase, "What you see is what you see." It means that our perception restricts our capacity to understand this.

None dispute that a person who never experienced love in their lives discovers establishes or retains a first-class relationship with great difficulty. Similarly, if you have grown up in extreme poverty, it takes a lot of personal transformation before you can survive comfortably in wealth.

This paper examines the parallels between the spiritual "thinking force" paradigm and the "thought style" practice of science and organizational growth. Working with these thoughts brings us on the path we're most likely to get it.

Some History of Little Information

I will start our analysis of mind power with mental models and a little context. As an ancient magical practice, alchemy, of which you could learn the ability to change the lead in gold, deals with the ability to transform an environment heavily laden by the development of our thoughts into an experience full of possibilities and riches.

Turning the poor to the positive by the force of our minds was a theme that regularly appears in human history. The most current and popular method was the film "The Secret" and the emergence of some excellent teachers, including Jerry and Esther Hicks.

People working with the power of the mind draws on the premise that the "subconscious" can also let us be in contact with the life-force of the world. By meditation and other mechanisms that open up the mind to more than our narrow awareness, we have exposure to concepts that lead your life in fresh and unpredictable ways.

Jerry and Esther Hicks introduce the empathy to this combination to tell us that our' emotional direction' also helps us to realize whether or not we are on the road to peace and lightness of our lives.

Mental processes can be traced back to Kenneth Craik's research in 1943 by suggesting that the human mind constructs a small model of nature that it uses to predict events. He also indicated that a visual model could construct through our experience, creativity, or the standards of life that we live in times of life.

Ironically, conceptual representations are closely related to visual images and can be symbolic. Have you ever stared at a drawing of the concept of someone and instantly "seen it?"

This is the mental model's strength a famous expert described them as: "The picture we have in our minds is only a model for the world around us." No one in his mind imagines the planet, policy, or nation society at large. He only has chosen principles and interactions and uses them to represent the real structure.

The report explains: "Mental models are profound ideas and generalizations, or even pictures or photographs, which affect how the environment is perceived and how we behave."

"What's similar to both is the belief that we cannot alter them until we understand the limits of our thoughts or mental models."

Once we are conscious, our ability to act on new ideas is much improved.

Bring Everything Together.

How Valuable Are These Ideas?

If we communicate the force of thought or a visual pattern, our first step is to accept our life's limits because of our way of thinking. Like we couldn't picture the experiences that we led so comfortably with people all over the world 30 years ago.

We will open ourselves up to the possibility that our opportunity for existence could be much more significant and much more thrilling than we can imagine today. Professional on human nature would warn us that we are inferior to our highest potential if we stitched in items that don't feel good.

People who work for client mental models often say that if we can't go beyond what we know, we can ever step up to the new opportunities around us.

My concern is, what if large groups of people started to build their lives for this planet seriously?

What if, instead of dwelling on environmental destruction, we focused on building Paradise on Earth?

What if we conduct studies into those things that create wellbeing, rather than spending trillions on our knowledge of safety?

And if those of us who work to create a linked society were not the exception but the norm?

What kind of future do you expect for your kids and grandkids?

How can we focus our mental models or our mind's power to build just that?

CHAPTER 4
THE CREATIVE THINKING

Creativity is not solely about being an artist. Product managers need to be creative just as much as musicians, ballet dancers, or sculptors. Creative thinking is a crucial skill for all product managers to succeed in today's dynamic, complex, and inter-dependent global business environment (Gundry et al., 2016).Creating new products, developing countermeasures to problems, planning research projects, improving processes, and creating product education workshops all require creative thinking skills. Generating and implementing new ideas is critical to the success or failure of the organization (Bergendahl & Magnussion, 2015). Due to the complexity and volatility of today's business environment, it is critical to developing new ideas continually (Sinfield et al., 2014).

Most people greatly underuse creativity based on the conditioning processes of society, educational systems, and business organizations (Nolan, 1989). Most adults feel they are not creative; however, their creative abilities have just atrophied – they are not lost. Learning creative thinking tools and techniques, practicing, and creating an environment where critical judgment is suspended, and speculation encouraged to form the foundation for creating innovative products, services, and processes.

You need to become skilled at developing new ideas at any time and any place, then putting those ideas into practice to develop innovative solutions. Search for new possibilities and actively use the information around you (de Bono, 1992). Explore new ways of thinking and challenge firmly held assumptions (Zaltman et al., 1982). Most importantly, discover and exploit opportunities to create competitive advantages and innovative solutions; do not wait for opportunities to appear (Gundry et al., 2016). The objective of creative thinking is to develop new and better ways to do things (de Bono, 1992).

When developing new ideas, focus on "what could be" and "what if," rather than "what is." Challenge tradition and current concepts, and do not be afraid of being wrong (de Bono, 1992). Ignore "killer phrases" which stifle creativity; for example, "It won't work," "We tried that before," or "It's not practical" (Biech, 1996).

Do not allow the status quo to handcuff you and suppress creativity (Brandt & Eagleman, 2017). Not innovating is the biggest risk to poor performance (never doing anything new or never seeking alternatives) (Nolan, 1989).

Move beyond basic business housekeeping activities (e.g., cutting costs, improving quality, enhancing customer service) and develop new ideas to drive future growth (de Bono, 1992). Focus on areas that have no obvious problems and identify ways to improve these "perfect" areas of the organization (de Bono, 1992). Break things that are working fine. Focus on areas that you are not interested in or that cause you discomfort; face challenges head-on and continually improve (Trott, 2015).

Create new ideas individually and then develop the ideas collectively with a cross-functional team (Carucci, 2017). Research has shown individual ideation to result in a higher quantity of quality, effective, and useable ideas when compared to group ideation (Schirr, 2012). The goal of creative thinking is to create many ideas (divergent thinking). It is not about judging ideas: you do that during critical thinking (convergent thinking).

Do not try to develop new ideas ad hoc or you will be wasting time – the most effective way to develop new ideas is with a deliberate, structured, and systematic process.

Using a systematic process for creativity may sound counterintuitive; however, research has shown that when using a systematic process, participants developed a higher number of ideas than when using ad hoc methods (Schirr, 2012).

James Webb Young (1960) identified a five-step creative process to develop new ideas.

1. Gather materials
2. Digest the information
3. Ignore the information – let it incubate (e.g., go for a walk, go to a movie)
4. An idea will appear out of nowhere
5. Apply the idea to the real world

Graham Wallas (2014) identified a similar process.

1. Preparation
2. Incubation

3. Illumination
4. Verification

Young and Wallas both noted that new ideas are typically combinations of many unrelated items. Developing creative ideas requires you to "connect the dots" from many different sources and experiences, aligning and combining unrelated areas. As your ideas incubate in your unconscious mind, the ideas expand and elaborate until a creative breakthrough emerges (Morris, 1992).

Most "new ideas" are the reconstruction of things you already know or have experienced. For example, smartphones combine the telephone, camera, internet, and voice recorder into one simple device. The snowmobile is a combination of a tractor, motorcycle, and snow skis. Continually exploring a variety of subjects and exposing yourself to new experiences is critical to connecting unrelated "dots" to create new innovative ideas. Connecting disparate areas of study provides an endless supply of ingredients for new ideas. When you ask questions, experience new things, and develop a thorough understanding of the topic, this will allow you to create new ideas and develop innovative solutions to develop new opportunities.

The challenge of creative thinking is balancing structure and flexibility, divergent and convergent thinking, individual and group ideation, productivity and creativity, and art and science (Carucci, 2017). It is about overcoming mental blocks such as there is only one right answer, the idea is not logical, or you have to follow the rules (Jorgenson, 2018). You must work hard to overcome society's rigid, rule-driven, constraining systems (Ackoff & Rovin, 2005). Most of us have been "domesticated" to think logically and negatively, not searching for alternative ways to do something, but finding the weakness of new ideas.

Creative thinking is exploring new ideas and exploiting existing ideas. It is difficult to get people out of their comfort zones and to move beyond the status quo (old habits die hard); however, for continued growth, you must become comfortable developing new ideas and challenging long-held beliefs – you must become comfortable with being uncomfortable. Adapt to change and reimagine the world (Brandt & Eagleman, 2007). Most importantly, do not overanalyze or judge your new ideas. Also, do not dismiss or abandon a new idea until you have given it sufficient time to develop.

Definitions

Four key terms in creative thinking are imagination, creativity, innovation, and invention. These terms are often loosely used and can cause confusion.

Creativity is developing new ideas: coming up with something new and original (Jorgenson, 2018). It is applied imagination: taking your wild thoughts and developing new ideas (Robinson, 2017). It is a continuous process of discovering and solving problems. Creativity is the capacity to find new and unexpected connections and find new relationships: a mindset that anything is possible (Prince, 2012). Mindlessly following rules does not lead to creativity. Creativity is about challenging or denying assumptions that constrain you from achieving what you want to accomplish (Ackoff & Rovin, 2005).

Good ideas are a dime a dozen. It is only after a new idea is translated into a reality that it becomes valuable: an innovation (Nolan, 1989). Innovation is the process of implementing creative ideas and introducing something new (Robinson, 2017). It is figuring out how to take a new idea and turn it into a product or service (Jorgenson, 2018).

Invention is creating something new that has never been developed. Merriam-Webster's online dictionary (2019) defines invention as "to produce (something, such as a useful device or process) for the first time through the use of the imagination or of ingenious thinking and experiment."

New and improved ideas are the foundation for future success. Building the skills to develop new ideas any time and any place is critical for developing new products, devising effective marketing campaigns, or planning new product launches to confuse and surprise your competitors. An organization focused on continuous improvement will constantly be on the lookout for areas of opportunity where new ideas can transform the business.

Society

People are creative, constructive, and exploratory beings, so why does creativity seem so difficult (Norman, 2013)? Why don't more people develop great new ideas? Unfortunately, creativity is often discouraged by our educational systems and business organizations. Also, society values adult practicality, consistency, and rigidity, diminishing our creative abilities and the desire to look beyond the obvious for alternative answers (Prince, 2012). Society values logic and judgment over imagination. As we mature, we undergo a conditioning process that suppresses our creativity (Basadur, 1995). As we get older, the learning curve decelerates, resulting in less time to explore, learn, or play (Schulz, 2011). Childhood playfulness is discouraged as we grow older and become engaged with formal society.

Most of our creative skills atrophy due to societal influences, attitudes, behaviors, and thought processes (Basadur, 1995). The educational system is a main cause of the lack of creativity in adults and organizations. In formal education, we learn what's acceptable and what's not (von Oech, 1998). Teachers typically have an expected, acceptable answer for questions or problems (Ackoff & Rovin, 2005). We are taught how to solve problems rather than look for opportunities. Throughout our schooling, we are taught to find the one right answer, not to look for alternatives. Children are continually taught limitations instead of searching for a large quantity of different options (Prince, 2012). It is important to continually challenge the establishment and "color outside the lines."

Also, the educational system awards students for following the rules, rather than developing many new ideas and thinking originally (von Oech, 1998). Rules and the insistence on conformity puts a chokehold on children's innate, natural curiosity (Ackoff & Rovin, 2005). As adults, we too often accept workplace norms without question. Yes, it is important to follow a variety of rules in order to survive in society (e.g., do not scream "fire" in a public place, stop at a red traffic light, raise your hand when wanting to speak); however, if you never challenge the rules or discard your "sacred cows" you will never be able to see the benefits of alternative ideas (von Oech, 1998).

There are benefits to conforming to societal norms; for example, cooperating with others and learning by observing how others react (von Oech, 1998). However, you need to challenge the status quo and live with a revolutionary mindset to create innovative products and services. You need courage, confidence, and persistence to achieve your dreams (Ackoff & Rovin, 2005).

Another reason for lack of creativity is that the majority of people haven't been taught how to develop new ideas. Most people use ad hoc methods when new ideas are needed. However, creative thinking is a skill, and like other skills such as ice skating, cooking, or singing, it is developed by learning the basics and then practicing. Unfortunately, the majority of schools never teach structured methods for ideation. Most people struggle through life, trying to "think up" new ideas.

Finally, your own beliefs may prevent you from seeking new ideas (von Oech, 1998). Your schooling, religion, and community influence how you think and perceive the world. These "mental blocks" prevent you from proactively changing routine or moving beyond what is familiar (von Oech, 1998). Creativity is a skill and mindset. Learn the tools and techniques and adopt a mindset that strives for seeking multiple perspectives and a large number of possible alternatives.

CHAPTER 5
THE VALUE OF SYSTEMS MODELS

Identify leverage points: Just as the small movement of the captain's wheel can change the course of a half-million-ton oil tanker, complex systems may contain points of high leverage. System models and simulation tools allow the exploration of a system's sensitivity to changes in various parameters. A large sensitivity to parameter value indicates potential for high leverage. Often, in complex systems, the location of high leverage points may not be intuitive. Using system models to identify high leverage points is the primary method of finding unanticipated solutions! Also, prior system behavior, identified in the course of gathering model data, may give subtle clues to points of high leverage.

Recognize modes: Systems models afford the user the chance to characterize the basic modes of the system. For example, are certain variables exhibiting exponential growth, approach to an asymptote, or perhaps oscillation? Comparing model behaviors to the observed data from the real system can help in understanding the nature of the system relationships. Further, the model may expose potential behavior of the system that had not been anticipated. Thus, the model may help avoid unexpected results.

Communicate: Models are very valuable to communicate and teach. Simulations can be a very impactful tool to illustrate an effect on managers and colleagues. If the simulation can be interactive and provide instant feedback to questions, all the better. Simulation models can also be excellent learning tools when used as management flight simulators. Some of you may have participated in strategic role-play using one of these simulation tools.

The process: There's great value in the process of building a systems model. This process will entail doing a series of interviews with managers in the organization, collecting historical system performance from corporate databases, and so on. This model-building process will help to identify feedback loops, delays, areas of important heterogeneity, etc., that may produce emergent effects. So this process of gathering data and thinking deeply about it may provide valuable deep insights and be one of the prime benefits of building a model.

Generative: System models based on deductive reasoning may be able to provide support for your ideas about why a system is behaving as it is. Scientifically, we would say one is trying to build support for a hypothesis. This has been described by Epstein and Axtell (1996) as generative science. Their argument is that if you can build a simulation using the characteristics of the real world and your simulation produces behavior that is consistent with what you see in the real world, then you have supported, but not proven, your argument about the system mechanisms.

Emergence

Emergence has been mentioned but not precisely defined. While there isn't an agreed-upon definition, here is a working definition:

Emergence: A phenomenon where an interaction among objects at one level generates new types of objects at another level. The emergent characteristic requires a new descriptive category at another level.

An illustrative example is in statistical mechanics, where laws of gases, such as Boltzmann's law, emerge from the interactions of the gas molecules. Descriptions at the micro-level (molecules) versus the macro-level (gasses) require different constructs. Similarly, temperature is an emergent property of the motion of atoms. While an entity, which is a collection of atoms, has temperature, a single atom has no temperature.

System scientists might debate if emergence is subjective or objective. Philosophically, this may equate to an epistemological versus ontological viewpoint. I take a broad subjective view on this topic in that an unanticipated result from an interaction of entities can be considered an emergent effect. No matter the definition or viewpoint, emergence is a powerful concept that will serve us well in business analysis.

CHAPTER 6
THE ICEBERG MODEL

How Do I Truly Immerse Myself in a Culture?

In the past, traveling is a luxury for the comfortable rich and the adventurous street-smart. In the recent decades, though, traveling has become more accessible. In fact, it has become a worldwide trend, with tourists flocking to tourist destinations, vacationers taking breaks from their lives back home, and backpackers exploring the world.

The internet and social media greatly influenced the spread of this travel bug. You can now see real-time posts of those who would like to broadcast their travel, while those who prefer to narrowcast would just send pictures to their loved ones via private messaging apps.

It is now easy to be in a foreign land, and communicate our whereabouts to the other side of the globe. It keeps us grounded and secure. It assures our loved ones of our safe travels. Staying connected is good.

At the same time, we must make that conscious effort to connect to the places that we are visiting. Think of the last time you went traveling, whether locally or internationally. Can you truly say that you were able to immerse yourself in that place, in its people, and their culture?

Were you able to enjoy the must-eat food, the must-see places, and must-do activities in that place? Good if you did. You touched the tip of the iceberg. Did you also take time to dig deep and try to understand the history and underlying reasons behind those foods, places, and activities?

The cultural iceberg model shows us that like an iceberg, below cultural manifestations is a deep cultural anchor. Once we go below the surface, we can have a deeper appreciation of a culture. We understand its customs and social styles. It keeps us from making a mess and hurting social sensibilities when in a new place.

To exercise your ability to understand cultures, start at home with your own bailiwick, your own culture. Examine the surface cultures or what you can see from the outside, such as arts, food, social structures, events, language, etc. Then examine the forces behind each. What do your practices say about your culture? What is the worldview behind your culture? What is your notion about life and death, about people within your society, about family and relationships, about the self and its role in society, about people from other cultures?

With a profound understanding of your culture, you may be able to see the dynamics of other cultures better, which in turn may make you appreciate your own culture more.

Each level of Iceberg Model offers a more profound understanding of this system being analyzed, in addition to increased leverage for altering it.

- Event: over the surface represents one occasion.

- Pattern: beneath the A degree of evaluation, surface shows patterns of trends or events.

- Construction: underwater below the Degree of this trend is the base that supports and generates behaviors' higher up, that the construction.

- Emotional Model: the level Down, psychological models impact the arrangements we put in place and how we realize the top areas of the iceberg.

How Can It Affect Your Research?

Systems thinking can help enhance your research skills in many different ways.

Decisions

Systems thinking helps you Assess why people act in certain ways or why things happen. Therefore, if you are studying psychology or sociology systems, at the diploma level, it helps you have a step back to make well-informed decisions and expand your suggestions.

Problem-Solving on Your Research

Systems thinking enhances your creative problem-solving skills. By thinking 'outside-the-box,' you will expand your capability to rejuvenate and to innovate thoughts.

Deeper Studying and Thinking

Realizing how systems operate Time, create your own learning habits, and in the context of larger systems, you are going to delve into thoughts.

Rather than thinking of a single Angle, you discover five angles of a topic that you have never thought about earlier.

Stray From the Standard

Backing away from conventional, a new outlook is offered by ways of thinking. Thus, when writing essays or Missions, systems thinking injects fresh ideas and expands your framework of thought.

CHAPTER 7
FOUR STEPS TO SOLVE ANY PROBLEMS

Solving problems in any area of life involves going through a set of steps, what we commonly refer to as a model. We have many other models, and if an existing model does not work for you, you can create your own model.

The goal here is to help you create a personalized problem-solving model; you can think of this model as an improved version earlier, and you can use it to solve problems in any situation. Let us jump right into it.

The IDEA Model

The model we are discussing is the IDEA model. The name is an acronym that stands for the following:

I: Identify the problem

D: Develop solutions to the problem

E: Execute the plan

A: Assess the outcome

By implementing each of these steps when you are facing a problem, you will be able to solve the problem in a more efficient manner. We shall spend some time looking at each of these steps in detail so that you can grasp the efficacy of the process.

Step 1: Identify the Problem

Identifying the problem is the first and most important step when you are facing an uncomfortable situation of any kind. The goal of this step is to help you clearly define the issue.

Whenever you face any issue, the first thing you need to do is ask yourself a simple question: "What is the problem?"

It is useful to write down or type out your problems. Let us use the example of Matt and assume that the problem you are facing is that of organization. In this case, you would type/write.

"What is the problem?"

You would then think about it deeply and perhaps come back with an answer such as the one below:

"I have so much to do and very little time. I feel hurried and stressed."

Now that you have stated the problem clearly, where do you go from here? Do you create solutions right away? Creating solutions immediately is what most people do, and unfortunately, this approach is usually inefficient. Attempting to solve problems without having enough information leads to partial solutions that do not solve the problem completely.

Solving problems is like treating a sickness. If a doctor only treats the symptoms of an illness like malaria, the fever may go away, but the illness persists. The same applies to problems: you have to diagnose and treat the root of the problem.

Getting to the root of a problem involves probing and digging deeper into the underlying issue. To help you do this, the nature of the question changes from that of "What" to that of "Why?"

Asking yourself "why" questions and answering them as clearly as possible will bring the underlying issues to the surface. These underlying issues are the primary target and the very things you need to solve in order to overcome a problem situation.

Once you have answers to the 'what' question, you continue the self-querying by typing/writing the following questions:

"Why is this a problem for me?"

"Why do I feel hurried and stressed?"

"Why do I have very little time?"

Once you think through these questions, you may develop answers such as:

"Because I have to balance work and study."

"Because I have no plan."

"Because the material looks like too much to cover so rapidly in very little time."

As you can see, why-related questions help bring the underlying issues to the forefront. If you decide to start coming up with potential solutions at this point, your solutions will not be premature. Nevertheless, prodding a bit more could serve you well.

Prodding further involves asking more "why" questions. The idea is to keep questioning the answers you uncover until you arrive at the root cause of the problem. We call the process the Root Cause Analysis, a process frequently used by many top executives to solve problems in business. If it yields results for them, it will work for you as well.

If we continue using our example, we would continue asking questions:

"Why do I have to balance work and study?"

The answer to this would probably be:

"Because the business world is moving fast, and my knowledge can easily become obsolete."

The answer to the question,

Why don't I have any plan in place?

Could be:

"Because I haven't sat down to create one."

Asking,

"Why does the material look like too much?"

Might yield:

"Because I have not set priorities on what to study first."

If you approach the issue in this manner, you will clearly identify the problem and get to its root cause. Once you do, you will have enough data and can move on to the following step of the problem-solving model:

Step 2: Develop Solutions to the Problem

At this point, having laid out the main problem in the clearest way possible by dint of conducting a "root cause analysis" to pinpoint the underlying cause(s) of the problem, another step is to start looking for solutions to your problem. At this point, finding solutions will be easier because you will not need to come up with solutions from a magician's hat, solutions that are based on conjecture because you have no clue as to the nature of the problem's source(s). Since you have identified the root cause(s) of the problem, you will come up with solutions that address those root causes. This greatly increases your odds of solving your problem.

The first thing to do is look at the root cause(s) of the problem. After that, you start working out potential solutions to effectively address each root cause of the issue. You then repeat this process for each of your root causes.

In some cases, as you come up with solutions to root causes, you may find that only one solution applies to each case. If this happens to you, be happy, because solving your problem will probably not take much effort.

For instance, in the example we have just talked about, you may look at the root cause of not creating a plan to guide your study. It does not take a genius to figure out that there can only be one solution to this root cause: create an actual plan.

Unfortunately, many of your problems will be complicated in nature and a simple look at the root cause will make it clear that multiple solutions are necessary. When facing a problem that requires multiple solutions, you will have to work a bit more diligently in order to select the best possible solution for each root cause.

To illustrate how to do this, we shall use our initial example:

Look at the root cause that suggests you have not set priorities related to what to study first. The obvious answer here is to set priorities. However, you can establish your priorities in a number of ways; it is, therefore, possible to come up with multiple solutions here. The issue then becomes a matter of selecting the best choice to implement.

The good news is that selecting the best solution is not as challenging as it sounds. We have various methods you can use to arrive at an effective solution faster.

Tips: How to Select the Best Solution

Here is how to select a solution specifically suited to an issue:

1. Weigh the pros and cons

Weighing the pros and cons is the easiest way of sorting through a list of possible solutions. With this strategy, you simply list out the advantages as well as the disadvantages of each solution you have at your disposal. After doing that, you simply select the solution that offers you the highest number of advantages, provided it fits your end goal.

2. A weighted rubric analysis

If the term weighted rubric analysis sounds complicated, do not fret; the concept is simple.

Using a weighted rubric is about understanding the most critical factor in whatever you are doing. It is about understanding the main objective you are trying to achieve. Once you identify that one main objective, you assess every choice on that basis.

For instance, let us say that knowing how to use business accounting software like a pro is your main priority. In this case, as you select from a list of suggested study plans, you concentrate on the plan that emphasizes mastery of business accounting software over anything else. The plan that emphasizes that goal best becomes the best solution.

3. A SWOT analysis

Lastly, we have the SWOT analysis method. This method of arriving at a decision is especially popular in the corporate world. In case you are not familiar with SWOT, it is an acronym that stands for:

S: Strengths
W: Weaknesses
O: Opportunities
T: Threats

These four factors provide a framework you can use in decision-making in a business or anywhere else; you can use it to arrive at decisions concerning your personal and social problems as well. A SWOT analysis is especially useful if you have a good idea of your end goal; to use SWOT effectively, you must be clear on what you want to achieve. What outcome are you envisioning? Once you have that in mind, using SWOT becomes easier and you are likelier to select your best possible solution.

After identifying the best possible solution for the underlying root cause of the problem, you then have to marry this solution to a goal. A goal helps you clearly define what you would like to achieve, holds you accountable, and increases the chances of successfully executing your plan.

Step 3: Execute the Plan

Now it's time to make a decision. Look at your list of options, and pick out the ones that are most practical and helpful. There may be one obvious solution, or some might work in combination.

Put your solutions into practice.

Have faith in yourself and make the commitment to try out one of your solutions.

Step 4: Assess the Outcome

What did you do? To know you successfully solved the problem, it's important to review what worked, what didn't and what impact the solution had. It also helps you improve long-term problem solving skills and keeps you from re-inventing the wheel.

Improving Problem Solving Skills

Once you understand the four steps of problem-solving, you can build your skill level in each one. Often we're naturally good at a couple of the phases and not as naturally good at others. Some people are great at generating ideas but struggle implementing them. Other people have great execution skills but can't make decisions on which solutions to use. Knowing the different problem solving steps allows you to work on your weak areas, or team-up with someone whose strengths complement yours.

CHAPTER 8
SYSTEM ARCHETYPES

Archetypes are universal patterns that influence how you interact with life – patterns that appear repeatedly and are recognizable in yourself and others. Understanding archetypes can help you quickly gain a sense of a person's character, attitude, beliefs, and behavior. Archetypes are essences that contribute to a person's identity, but they are not personality traits: instead, they provide a sense of who someone is through their behavioral patterns. Archetypes provide a model for how you see the world and interpret experiences; they provide insight into why a person behaves and feels the way they do. Archetypes are groups of beliefs, feelings, and attitudes that operate in the collective unconscious, and outside of your awareness and consciousness. They direct and motivate your behavior through your personal unconscious.

You see and experience life and your relationships through archetypal patterns. Childhood experiences play a significant role in shaping the archetypal patterns you instinctively adopted to gain power and ensure your survival. These archetypes go on to develop and influence you throughout your life. Archetypes are deeply rooted patterns of behavior and as such, they can be difficult to see within ourselves.

Your "archetypal map," which is based on the collective unconscious, your personal unconscious, and the interpretation you give to these experiences, influences how you see and interpret events and situations in your relationship and the world. No two people will interpret an event the same way. Each of us has a set of filters, and how you filter and interpret information is based on your experiences. For instance, twenty people in a restaurant may witness an argument between a couple and every person will have a different recollection and interpretation of the incident. You may have seen two people arguing over the price of the meal and it made you extremely anxious because it brought up fears of abandonment in your relationship. Another person who recently left a violent relationship may have seen the male as aggressive and hostile. Yet another person may have thought the woman was antagonizing her partner, badgering him into a fight. This person may recall the argument this way because he perceives his partner as a Needy Nag (another of the power archetypes).

Your current situation, how you feel, and your dominant power archetype together comprise a map to provide meaning to events and situations in your life. Learning how to interpret this map will allow you to have a greater understanding and control over your interactions with your partner.

Archetypes organize experiences and influence how you perceive and interact with the world. They help you understand why you are attracted to or repelled by certain partners and patterns of behavior.

Limits to Growth

Nothing can grow forever; at some point, the system will fight back and intervene to regulate exponential growth.

A fierce forest fire will continue to widen until fuel runs out.

Overfishing will cause the stock to collapse.

A virus can continue to spread until people are left out to infect.

Successful high-growth products will ultimately saturate market demand and reduce future growth.

Growth of an oil-based economy could collapse without cheap oil availability.

Tragedy of the Commons

The Tragedy of the Commons is an economic theory that describes how people often take advantage of natural resources without considering the good of a group or society as a whole. When a number of people consider only their own welfare in this way, it leads to negative results for everyone, as the natural resource becomes depleted.

Escalation

The escalation archetype refers to behavioral patterns where the actions of one party are perceived by another party as a threat, and the second party reacts similarly, further increasing the threat.

Eroding Goals

This archetype refers to reducing your level of goal. When actors in a system fail at achieving what they set out to do, they reduce the bench-mark, constantly reducing the level of their goals.

Addiction

Sometimes, an individual want to decide for dramatic and difficult change such as making rapid changes in lifestyle, staying away from an addiction, making resignation for a long-term job, staying away from your loved one and so on. It is essential to reach the point where he or she wants to start the action of breaking. There is a requirement for lots of activation energy to reach the breaking point or to start the action of breaking.

Seeking the Wrong Goal

If you perform any stupid activity, you will not utilize the regret minimization framework as an excuse. You should consider the right timing, your recent level of competence, environmental factors, and other types of forces. You will have to be flexible in adopting several conditions. You should be determined to achieve your goal in life. The principle of the regret minimization framework will allow you to think anything considering different situations and make the decision for yes or no easily. If you have confidence that you can follow an excellent strategy, you can make your decision for yes. You should know the risk when you are taking the challenge. You can avoid regret when you are smart about your superior strategy.

Exponential Successful

Following the principles that led you to success in the past, maintaining traditions and choosing proven roads will at best allow you to get the results that you have had in the past.

Race to the Bottom

In the beginning, you probably set goals for yourself that ignited a fire within you. What happened? Did you lose sight of those goals, or did you allow the Fire Within you to become extinguished? To increase your productivity, to adopt positive habits, you need to get to the bottom of why you began in the first place. What was that passion or that fire that got you going and made you set the goals that you set for yourself? Try journaling so that you can get reacquainted with why you began the journey that you are on. Figure out why you started, how you came to this point in your life, and focus on getting back to that point. This is going to help you set positive habits in your life that are going to allow you to succeed.

Rule Breaking

Leaving several paths open for discussion will distract you from devoting full attention to any one of them. It will take a lot longer to rule out or decide on any one path if you can't find the concentration to focus on just one. Simplify, and concentration will be easier.

The archetypal perspective is also a precondition for the recognition of discontinuity in domains other than those described by physics, for although the numerous expressions of this principle have often been recognized in modernity, from atomic electron transitions and phase transitions to scientific revolutions and psychological breakthroughs, the underlying coherence of these specific manifestations has been difficult to assert based on modern assumptions of the particulate division of entities in all domains (though one might notice that the modern assertion of this very principle of atomicity across scale paradoxically violates its own premise). However, by means of the archetypal perspective, the emerging mode reveals the separation of entities asserted by rationality to be the expression of one archetype, describable as the senex, which organizes boundaries and limits of all kinds, while the novel world view admits all the archetypes delineated in premodernity into its conceptual pantheon. The root of the word "rationality" itself is "ratio," meaning the quantitative calculation of proportional difference. Although it is often necessary to analyze, reduce, separate, and differentiate processes in order to understand phenomena, it is often equally necessary to perceive the efficacy of qualities across scale, including discontinuity, which makes possible sudden leaps to novel domains of ingression such as the paradigmatic Promethean discovery of fire, and all of the subsequent discoveries that ensued, from the archetypes themselves to quantum field theory.

Fractality is also predicated upon archetypality, as archetypes are the initial potentialities that the fractal dynamic expresses, not only in mathematical sets and their aesthetically dazzling visual representations, which seem to have been waiting in the nature of process to be discovered and synthesized by Mandelbrot half a century ago but in the broader definition of fractality.

CHAPTER 9
CHAOS THEORY IN SYSTEMS THINKING

Chaos Theory is concerned to explain non-linearity in the development of systems. Analyses that are based upon a single cause seeking a single effect are linear. Non-linearity represents unpredictable change. Change, in turn, means that a system is dynamic. Lack of change denotes a system that is static. Systems rarely operate in a steady-state and progress in a linear fashion. A linear system is deterministic; its outcomes can be predicted from the initial conditions; cause and effect. However, it is much more common for the form of a system to change unpredictably. A tree, as a system, will develop from seed to seedling, from sapling to maturity, old age, limb loss and die back. Its general form or genotype will be largely predictable, but its specific shape or phenotype will not. Indeed, every tree, although similar within species, will be different. No two trees, dogs, cats, cows, landscapes, cloud formations, snowflakes in a snowstorm or people on earth will be the same. A car will run well when new, but over time, paint fades, rust will invade, bearings will wear out and parts will fail. No two old cars, even of the same make and model, will be the same. A perusal of quality and prices of stock of secondhand car dealers will suffice to prove this point. Similarly, a human will change over his/her lifetime as youthful strength and agility may decline, but thinking and rational capacity may increase until all sub-systems break down in old age. Therefore, systems do not move through time with precisely the same shape as when they commenced. If they did their progress would be linear. But systems development is non-linear. The development of Chaos theory helps to explain non-linearity.

Chaos does not represent disorder. Rather it explains that there is order in what at first sight appears to be disorder. Each tree in the forest is different representing disorder, but the differences lie within predictable bounds as each one is recognizably a tree. This represents order in the seeming disorder. The characteristics of Chaos are:

- Sensitivity to initial conditions (as mentioned above in relation to system creation) which leads to unpredictability.
- Mixing in which adjacent points may end up in completely different positions as the system progresses.

- Non-linearity as the output of one system becomes the input to the preceding one.
- Feedback is a major driver of Chaos.

The concept of increasing order within a system may be traced to Descartes. Descartes held that the ordinary laws of nature would bring about order and that an external guiding hand was unnecessary.

A feature of systems is wholeness. But paradoxically within the wholeness lies further complexity as systems are formed of sub-systems. While these sub-systems are 'whole' they, in turn, are components of the larger system. And not only are they components of the larger system, but they often do not have a viable independent existence and are in themselves composed of further subordinate sub-systems. For example, the trunk of a tree is an essential component of the system that is a tree but, once removed, ceases to function independently. The sub-system of the tree trunk consists of subordinate sub-systems of, Bark to provide protection, Phloem to supply sap from leaves to branches and roots, Cambium to provide new cells for the phloem, Xylem to move water and minerals up the tree to the leaves and Heartwood that consists of old Xylem and provides support and strength. Each of these can be analyzed down the level of the individual cells that comprise them. The same analysis may be conducted with the liver of cow or the gearbox of a motor car. They exist in themselves but are, in turn, comprised of further sub-systems. The origins of the word system can be clearly seen: 'systema' is Latin for a whole consisting of several parts. A system, therefore, is group of components that interact to form an integrated entity or whole.

An economy is a system as it takes in raw materials, transforms them by production processes into goods and services and distributes them for consumption. Therefore, the analysis of the Economic System involves the study of the production, exchange and consumption of goods and services. The foundation structure of the economic system may be depicted in terms of its broad sub-system components of production, exchange and consumption.

Economic System Comprises Production, Exchange and Consumption

But like the tree trunk, each of these component sub-systems is, in turn, comprised of further subordinate sub-systems. Production requires raw materials such as mineral ores and agricultural crops as inputs. Production also requires raw materials to be processed into production materials that can be used in production processes. Examples are iron ore into steel, oil into polymers and bauxite into alumina. Production methods are also essential, and these have not been constant. Examples are the factory, interchangeability of parts, scientific management, lean and six sigma manufacturing. The importance of production methods cannot be underestimated, and the quotation commonly attributed to H. Nelson Jackson, "I do not believe you can do today's job with yesterday's methods and be in business tomorrow" is salutary. Finally, production requires energy. Energy is also required to power machines and move semi-finished parts between manufacturing processes. Examples of successive forms of energy include atmospheric, steam, and internal combustion engines and electricity.

Exchange does not occur of its own. Goods and services must be brought to market. Therefore, sub-ordinate sub-systems in the form of transport are required to move goods (especially consumer goods) from the place of production to the marketplaces where exchange can be conducted. Exchange is also facilitated by the sub-ordinate sub-systems of retail, finance and communication. Each of these sub-ordinate sub-systems has undergone substantial development. Transport has progressed from canal to railway and intermodal containerization. Retail has progressed from corner stores to department stores supermarkets and malls. Finance has developed from the joint-stock bank, central currency issue, fractional banking, central banking, Bretton Woods and floating exchange rates. Finally, market communication has benefited in turn from the Penny Post, telegraph, telephone, internet/intranet, e-mail and mobile phone.

Consumption, as pointed out by Adam Smith, is the "sole end and purpose of all production." Satisfying consumption is the goal end purpose or Telos of the economic system. All production and exchange take place to meet the needs of consumption. Consumption is enhanced through the innovation of new goods and services that offer a productive advantage to the consumer i.e. same goods at a lower price or goods that provide an increased personal benefit or superior performance at the same or a lower price. Such personal productivities enhance the human condition. Although there has been and still is a plethora of consumer goods and services, they may be viewed as a series of waves. First came mass-produced clothing (the eponymously named Manchester) then household goods such as pottery, china tableware, cutlery, stoves/cookers, bathroom and kitchen sink basins pedestals and baths. Another wave was automobiles, followed by household electrical products and latterly personal digital computing and communication devices.

Advancement of the human condition in the three options earlier provides the motivation for consumers to adopt. New consumer goods offer improvements in the standard of living. Goods and services that offer a productive advantage are 'new' in the sense that they provide an enhanced or differentiated benefit. Entrepreneurs are motivated to innovate new consumer goods and services for monetary rewards as well as to achieve at Abraham Maslow's hierarchical levels of Ego or Self-actualization. A more productive consumer product will provide a competitive advantage to its buyer. A productive improvement, therefore, creates disequilibrium as buyers of the new product have an advantage over those who have not. This disequilibrium acts to motivate others. Productive improvement provides both a competitive advantage to the producer but also provides the purchaser with a surplus equal to the productivity. This surplus can be expended in increasing the size of the market (purchasing more of the same), deepening the market (purchasing variants of the product e.g. big car and a small car, TV in bedroom as well as living room) or broadening the market (purchasing different types of products).

However, distribution and exchange are not just a link between production and consumption but are organic within all sub-systems as production entities distribute and exchange raw materials, production materials and parts, installations, accessory equipment and operating supplies while financial institutions exchange by borrowing funds from one another and consumers trade finished goods. Therefore, it must always be borne in mind that distribution and exchange linkages exist both between and within production exchange and consumption.

Economic System Showing Subordinate Systems

A further characteristic of systems is direction. Systems are said not only to be teleological (from the Greek telos or purpose) or goal-seeking but to have direction. This is akin to the system 'Attractor' as described by Ashby in 1947. At first glance, the purpose of an economic system appears to be to satisfy consumption, as it is in classical economic theory.

CHAPTER 10
THE PHENOMENA OF CHAOTIC BEHAVIOR

In order to analyze a fractal, you first get an overview of the complete structure, you then move down the levels of the structure until you get to the smallest segments. If you think you looked small to large, you are wrong. Evolution has taught humans to look general before getting too specific as a survival mechanism to ensure we don't miss anything large like a spewing volcano, before we worry about whether or not we might stub our toe on a rock. Even if you don't realize it, you saw the big image first. Perhaps you didn't notice it was a fractal until you looked deeper into the image for the detail, but you saw the big picture first, whether you like it or not. This instinct is fundamental and should be applied whenever you are trying to learn something. Big picture first, fills in the detail after. One more time for those of you like me who don't do anything without being stubbornly prodded.

Bifurcation

How do you create co-chaos? First, you make chaos. Patterned chaos, that is. Best way? Start with bifurcation. Splitting in two. Forking. "You take the high road, and I'll take the low road." "She lived on the morning side of the mountain, and he lived on the twilight side of the hill." In bifurcation, a single behavior splits into two related, yet different behaviors. Like this: suppose you're looking out the window, and you see a flag-draped in lank folds on a flagpole. The flag is not moving.

But now the wind comes up, and you watch the flag flap. It collapses with a buckling motion. It flaps again. Buckles again. For at least this moment, the flag's behavior is alternating between flaps and buckles. It is bifurcated. This event is important. Leon Glass and Michael Mackey point out in from Clocks to Chaos: The Rhythms of Life that bifurcation is a universal trait of patterned chaos. Whenever bifurcation occurs, patterned chaos is likely to follow. That patterning is predictable in its general form, but not in its exact details.

1. Bifurcation Puts Forks in the Road

Okay, you're still watching the flag out the window. It exhibits bifurcation by forking from a steady state of lank inaction into two alternating behaviors that dance between either flaps or buckles...at least for this moment.

Of course, if the wind increases, the flag might start flapping briskly without collapsing into a buckle...or it might end its motion and just drop back into the original static condition of lying lankly draped against the flagpole.

In order to chart the two behaviors happening right now, you draw a little bifurcation tree (b-tree) to represent the flaps and buckles. First, you make a dot. Then you draw it upward as a line that represents the original steady-state of the pole's lank, motionless flag. You count this single line or trunk as Period 1.

Then, you fork the trunk upward into two branches, with the two behaviors of flaps and buckles. Both branches sit on a horizontal plane. This horizontal level holding the two branches in Period 2 can be read across the b-tree as a horizontal period 2 window...or for short, just hp2.

Periods 1 & 2

However, instead of graphing the bifurcation of flag behaviors upward as tree branches, you could also chart it downward into wells of attraction. Period 1 represents the original steady-state of that lank, motionless flag on the pole. Its lank droop exists in one static well, so there is just one attractor point. But on the right, there are two attractor points, because flap and buckle sit in separate wells.

Wells of Bifurcation

Bifurcation can actually graph the cycles of organisms. For instance, if a bird or bee population is stable, it exists in one static well as Period 1, where the number of births in the flock or hive consistently just about equals the number of deaths. Its population rate sits calmly in a single well of attraction. But the population may bifurcate into two wells or basins of attraction as Period 2. For instance, maybe the young die off from an illness, but the adults don't.

Biologists chart population shifts in all sorts of living things: weeds, trees, bobcats, deer, elephants, snakes, rats, fish, and all manner of insects. Sometimes a population – of animals, insects, viruses, or even baking yeast – can develop a period-doubling pattern that keeps on forking up the b-tree.

For instance, in wheat bread dough, the traditional yeast used to make it rise will double every 20 minutes at 33° centigrade. As the yeast population doubles repeatedly, the dough keeps on rising...but only so long as the yeast continues to have food. When the yeast eats it all up, the bread stops rising.

That's why bread recipes will contain the carbs of wheat, honey, or sugar; the yeast needs to eat it while rising in a warm environment. By contrast, a sourdough starter that's kept in a refrigerator can stay alive for years by suppressing its appetite with a cool temperature and just kneading in a bit more flour occasionally to feed the yeast. I've done that myself.

An animal population can also keep on multiplying, given enough food and health. Witness all the begets in the Bible. Witness the human population statistics over the last two millennia. But it could instead develop the rhythm of a 4-beat or 2-beat cycle, or even drop back into a monotonous, steady-state of just one static point in a single well, with the number of births and deaths in the herd, flock, or city staying just about equal. That's zero-population growth.

Okay, look at what is happening now with our flag. As the wind grows stronger, the flag starts an intricate little dance. The flapping on the left branch elaborates into either a sharp crack, or alternately, a hollow boom. Meanwhile, the buckling on the right also begins to fork – into a twist around the pole, or alternatively, a shudder.

The flag has now developed four different but related behaviors!

Periods 1, 2 & 4

So now, the graph forks upward to show the four distinct behaviors in Period 4. The left branch of flaps has bifurcated into two higher branches of cracks and booms. The right branch of buckles has bifurcated into twists and shudders. All four behaviors interplay in a rhythm of cracks, booms, twists, and shudders. This higher level of forking is read horizontally across the b-tree as a horizontal period 4 window (hp4), since it holds four branches.

The depiction of this flag dance is a simplified event. Only a high-speed camera could register all the distinct, separate positions that occur when the wind moves a flag. Your eyes don't have stop-action vision, and it would all happen so fast that you could not easily discern all its distinct motions.

Thus, I'm just giving you a simplified bifurcation model here. It's easier to study movement in multi-colored liquids. They shift more slowly and visibly than air. Easier still to track slow-moving solids that may alter at a glacial rate.

For this dancing flag, let's double the behaviors once more by branching upward into a third level of activity. At this new, higher level of the b-tree, a horizontal window across the tree holds eight different periods of related behaviors: snaps, beats, bams, pops, hums, crinkles, shivers, and shakes.

Periods 1, 2, 4 & 8

In this b-tree, the trunk at first forks into the 2 branches of Period 2 that can be read across horizontally as the events in a horizontal period 2 window (hp2). Then it forks again into the 4 branches of Period 4 that can be read as its hp4. It forks yet again into the 8 branches of Period 8 that can be read as its hp8.

Thus, each time the b-tree's branches bifurcate, they multiply by a factor of 2, so that each new level of growth doubles the past period's number of branches. That's why bifurcation is also called period-doubling.

2. A Horizontal Period 3 Window Tracks Patterned Chaos

A b-tree can keep on forking upward until it is filled with many dark branches crisscrossing each other. Then, the b-tree has forked so often that it no longer shows the clean, black lines of countable branches. Instead, those sharp lines seem to have blended into blurry strata. The forking has doubled again and again, cascading until, in the upper part of the graph, the layers of twigs all jam into a dark blur. To a casual eye, it's random chaos.

Bifurcation Tree With a Horizontal Period 3 Window (hp3)

However, not all of the branching is completely obscured in this b-tree. Occasionally a branch doesn't sprout, so sometimes a window may even hold an odd number of branches. Luckily! Why is it lucky? We'll investigate the significance of the hp3, for something grand comes of it.

If enough twigs ever do reduce down to just three branches in a gap, then above that hp3, the events are redefined. The branches above that hp3 are no longer tracking mere random chaos. Instead, they are now tracking patterned chaos. It may still look random, but it's not. Above that hp3, the branches hold recurring, deterministic patterns in their multiplicity of events. No matter how dense that twiggy welter, it will never again lapse into true random chaos. Instead, it is now fractal, patterned chaos.

James Yorke and Tien-Yien Li in 1975 proved that if a b-tree develops the hp3, then the branching events above it are no longer tracking mere random chaos. Instead, they are tracking patterned chaos. York and Li reported their findings in a famous article in American Mathematical Monthly. That article is packed with heavy math, but for our purposes here, the title sums it up: Period Three Implies Chaos.

There are other, more elaborate routes to patterned chaos. Yorke himself admitted that there's more to chaotic behavior than just the horizontal periodic window (hp3) in a b-tree. He called it "just one leg of the elephant, so to speak." Nevertheless, for us, the hp3 on a b-tree opens the door that will lead to co-chaos.

The hp3 in a b-tree assures us that its dynamic kernel will allow events to drop back to that level, then sprout up again without losing their fractal mojo. Bifurcations can keep on proliferating above, then dropping back down to that hp3, but no matter how often they revert to that special, 3-pronged window, it guarantees that in the levels above, the twigs tracking random-seeming events will continue to iterate their dynamic chaos pattern with variations. Details may shift continually, but the hidden chaos patterning remains there.

Chaos systems churn out the way of the world. Emotional, social, cultural, economic, and political processes hold nonlinear chaos patterns, which means that we cannot identify the exact reasons for most events. Nor can we indicate reliably what will happen. Still, we are assured by the hp3 that something will keep happening. This universe keeps going instead of dying like a bad battery.

CHAPTER 11
HOW TO IMPROVE YOUR THINKING

We all have great potential within us, but we don't make use of it. Most of it lies dormant within us, or it is underdeveloped. Any improvement in thinking cannot take place if there is no conscious commitment to learning. You cannot improve your game in basketball if you don't put in some effort to do so and the same is true for critical thinking as well. Like any other skill, effort is essential for its development. As long as you take your thinking for granted, there is no way in which you can unlock your true potential. Development in your thinking process is gradual, and there are several plateaus of learning that you will have to overcome and hard work is a precondition for all of this. You cannot become an excellent thinker by just wanting to become one. You will have to make a conscious decision to change certain habits, and this will take some time. So, be patient and don't expect any change to occur overnight.

If you are interested in developing the skill of critical thinking, then you need to understand the different changes that one needs to go through in this process.

Stage 1: You are still unaware of the significant problems or pitfalls in your thinking. You aren't a reflective thinker. Most of us are stuck in this stage.

Stage 2: You start developing awareness of the problems in your thinking.

Stage 3: You try working on your thought processes, but not regularly.

Stage 4: You realize the need for regular practice.

Stage 5: You start noticing a change in the way you think.

Stage 6: You develop the ability to become insightful in your thinking.

You can progress through these stages by accepting the fact that there are specific problems in the way you think, and you start putting in conscious effort to improve yourself.

Making Use of "Wasted" Time

All human beings tend to waste time. That is, we fail to make productive use of all the time we have at our disposal. Sometimes we flit from one form of diversion to another, without actually enjoying any of them. At times we get irritated about matters that are clearly beyond our control. At times, we don't plan well, and this causes a butterfly effect of negative consequences that could all have been easily avoided by simple planning. How many times have you been stuck in the rush hour traffic when you could have easily avoided this by leaving an hour earlier? Apart from all the time that we waste doing nothing, we start worrying about unnecessary things. Sometimes we regret the way we functioned in the past, or we just end up daydreaming about "what could have been" and "what can be," instead of putting in some effort to achieve results. Well, you need to realize that there is no way in which you can get all the lost time back again. Instead, try focusing on all the time that you have at your disposal now. One way in which you can develop the habit of critical thinking is to make use of the time that would have normally been "wasted." Instead of spending an hour in front of the TV flipping through channels and getting bored, you can make use of this time or at least a part of it for reflecting on the day you had, the tasks you accomplished, and all that you need to achieve. Spend this time to contemplate your productivity. Here are a couple of questions that you can ask yourself:

When did I do my worst and best thinking today? What was it that I was thinking about all day long? Did I manage to come to a logical conclusion or was it all in vain? Did I indulge in any negative thinking? Did the negative thoughts just create a lot of unnecessary frustration? If I could repeat this day all over again, what would I change? Did I do something that will help me in achieving my goals? Did I accomplish anything that's worth remembering?

Spend some time answering these questions and record your observations. Over a period of time, you will notice that you have a specific pattern of thinking.

Internalizing Intellectual Standards

Every week select any one of these standards and try to increase your awareness of the same. For instance, you can focus on clarity for a week, then shift towards precision, and so on. If you are able to focus on clarity, observe the way you communicate with others and see for yourself if you are clear or not. Also, notice when others aren't being clear in what they are saying. Whenever you are reading, see if you are clear about the content you have been reading. While expressing yourself orally or while writing your thoughts down, check for yourself if there is some clarity in what you are trying to convey. There are four simple things that you can make use of to test whether you have some clarity or not. You have to explicitly state what you are trying to say, elaborate on it, give examples for facilitating better understanding and make use of analogies as well. So, you are supposed to state, then elaborate, illustrate and lastly exemplify yourself.

Maintain an Intellectual Journal

Start maintaining an intellectual journal where you record specific information on a weekly basis. Here is the basic format that you should follow. The first step is to list down the situation that was or is significant to you, emotionally. It should be something that you care about and you need to focus on one situation. After this, record your response to that situation. Try being as specific and accurate as you can. Once you have done this, then you need to analyze the situation and your reaction and analyze what you have written. The final step is to assess what you have been through. Assess the implications - what have you learned about yourself? And if given a chance, what would you do differently in that situation?

Reshaping Your Character

Select an intellectual trait like perseverance, empathy, independence, courage, humility and so on. Once you have selected a feature, try to focus on it for an entire month and cultivate it in yourself. If the trait you have opted for is humility, then start noticing whenever you admit that you are wrong. Notice if you refuse to admit this, even if the evidence points out that you are wrong. Notice when you start becoming defensive when someone tries to point out your mistake or make any corrections to your work. Observe when your arrogance prevents you from learning something new. Whenever you notice yourself indulging in any form of negative behavior or thinking squash such thoughts. Start reshaping your character and start incorporating desirable behavioral traits while giving up on the negative ones. You are your worst enemy, and you can prevent your growth unknowingly. So, learn to let go of all things negative.

Dealing With Your Egocentrism

Human beings are inherently egocentric. While thinking about something, we tend to favor ourselves before anyone else subconsciously. Yes, we are biased towards ourselves. In fact, you can notice your egocentric behavior on a daily basis by thinking about the following questions:

What are the circumstances under which you would favor yourself? Whenever you feel like you are egocentric, think what a rational person would say or do in a similar situation and the way in which that compares to what you are doing.

Redefining the Way in Which You See Things

The world that we live in is social as well as private, and every situation is "defined." The manner in which a situation is defined not only determines how you feel, but the way you act, and its implications. However, every situation can be described in multiple ways. This means that you have the power to make yourself happy and your life more fulfilling. This means that all those situations to which you attach a negative meaning can be transformed into something favorable if you want it to. This strategy is about finding something positive in everything that you would have considered to be negative. Try to see the silver lining in every aspect of your life. It is all about perspectives and perceptions. If you think that something is positive, then you will feel good about it, and if you think it's negative, then you will naturally harbor negative feelings towards it.

Get in Touch With Your Emotions

Whenever you start feeling some negative emotion, ask yourself the following:

What line of thinking has led to this emotion? For instance, if you are angry, then ask yourself, what were you thinking about that has caused the anger you are feeling? What are the other ways in which I can view this situation? Every situation seems different, depending on your perspective. A negative aspect makes everything seem dull and bleak and, on the other hand, a positive outlook does brighten things up. Whenever you feel a negative emotion creeping up, try to see some humor in it or rationalize it. Concentrate on the thought process that produced the negative emotion, and you can find a solution to your problem.

Analyzing the Influence of a Group on Your Life

Carefully observe the way your behavior is influenced by the group you are in. For instance, any group will have specific unwritten rules of conduct that all the members follow. There will be some form of conformity that will be enforced. Check for yourself how much this influences you and the manner in which it impacts you. Check if you are bowing too much to the pressure that is being exerted and if you are doing something just because others expect it of you.

You don't have to start practicing all the steps at once. Start out slowly and try following as many as you can. Initially, you will need to put in a conscious effort for critical thinking to work and, over a period, these skills will come naturally to you.

CHAPTER 12
SITUATIONAL PRACTICAL PROBLEM SOLVING

Solving problems demand you think objectively, like a scientist. You must see the real thing – that is the actual circumstances – firsthand, if possible. SPPS is based on going to the problem area and seeing it directly without depending on someone else's opinion or perspective. If someone brings you a problem and you believe the information they bring you, then you're accepting their view without seeing it yourself. This is second-hand information. Besides, one person's view may be accurate as far as it goes, but a single viewpoint is less likely to be comprehensive than multiple viewpoints. This can lead not only to identifying the wrong problem but selecting the wrong "root cause" and developing the wrong countermeasure.

I use the term "countermeasure" in this writing in place of "solution." The word solution lends itself to the belief you found the ultimate answer to the problem, a permanent answer you never have to think about again. In SPPS, there are no solutions, only countermeasures. Therefore, countermeasures are steps to always improving.

It is important to realize that problem solving is necessary to simply maintain the current level or status. Continuous improvement is necessary to improve this level or status. The SPPS process puts you on track for improving operations and even allows for maintenance and prevention.

A Logical Step-By-Step Approach

SPPS is a logical step-by-step approach to problem-solving. It emphasizes direct observation ("go and look for yourself") and common sense. You should look at what is actually happening versus what should be happening. This sounds deceptively easy, but it is a skill that demands practice. SPPS shows you how to clarify and break down large, vague and complicated problems into smaller problems or pieces, so you can identify the specific, actionable problems they contain. In so doing, SPPS reveals cause and effect relationships that lead to identifying the root cause.

SPPS is a simple, common-sense approach that demonstrates how management and employees can solve problems quickly and together, without spending a lot of valuable time studying them. Often problems can be solved at the lowest level of the organization, in minutes or hours, without meeting in conference rooms for days or weeks to discuss them. In this way, SPPS saves time and money.

Mastering SPPS requires an understanding that when you first start out, you cannot always depend on your experience. That sounds counterintuitive, but the point is you must separate your past experiences from the problem at hand to avoid preconceived notions and jumping to conclusions. Once you've mastered this skill and achieve an objective clarification of the problem, then you can use your experiences to develop effective countermeasures. Too often, our observations are colored by our experiences, which leads to misidentifying the real problems.

Analysis of the root causes is against our human nature. We are inclined to take short cuts and to go for the quick fix. We would rather try and fix the problem right away than try to understand why the problem began in the first place. SPPS teaches the lesson that spending 80% of your time identifying the real problem and 20% of the time fixing the problem provides optimal results.

How Problem Solving is Taught in Japan

To appreciate the distinctiveness of SPPS, it is helpful to look briefly at its origins, and how problem-solving is taught in Japan. Early in my career, it was typical for me to see a problem report submitted by a team for my checking and provide them feedback rather than going and seeing the problem firsthand.

After one such instance at Toyota, I asked my Japanese mentor-trainer Hiro to look back at the problem-solving report with me. The problem involved team members who weren't able to hear the overhead crane warning alarm when it passed over them. Hiro quickly scanned the report, asked me some questions, and suggested that maybe the problem wasn't that team members couldn't hear the alarms. The real problem may be that team members were in an unsafe area and correcting the problem by focusing on the alarms wouldn't solve the problem. Hiro asked if I had been to the floor to look at the actual problem and talk to the team members. When I told him I had not, he suggested I go see the problem to gain a fresh perspective.

I did as he suggested and experienced what the team members were dealing with by "walking in their shoes." This enabled me to see what I couldn't imagine just sitting in a room trying to visualize the situation. What the team members said was true and they were in a safe authorized area. The noise was louder than the traditional alarm bells on the overhead cranes. The bells could barely be heard. Either the bells had to be louder or the noise reduced to solve the problem. I suggested the team members focus on what was in their control to improve the problem.

The fact that Hiro had a different perspective about the problem was enlightening. Of course, his perspective was based on opinion and he would have gone to the floor to observe firsthand. He did as all good Toyota Senseis' do.

I remarked to Hiro how Japanese trainers appeared to be experts at problem-solving and I asked whether they attended a special school. He laughed and said no, rather they learned the hard way. His supervisor in Japan taught him problem-solving by constantly asking him questions instead of giving him answers. Every time he brought the supervisor a problem and asked for help, the supervisor would just ask him questions.

One day in frustration Hiro asked his supervisor why he only asked questions and never gave him answers. The supervisor replied, "Hiro my job is not to give you answers. My job is to teach you problem-solving by asking you questions. If I give you the answers, then you won't learn anything about problem-solving. You will depend on me for the answers. Someday you will find yourself alone and I won't be around to assist you. In problem-solving, you don't have to know the answers; you just need to know what questions to ask to lead you to solve the problem. That is why I ask you many questions to get you to think and observe for yourself. I want you to be able to defend your position with facts, not guesswork."

Hiro explained this is the way problem solving is taught in Japan. It is taught on the shop floor it takes about seven years to master. Each team member is taught by his supervisor, who, in turn, was taught by his supervisor.

This writing has unique case histories. There is an emphasis on learning to think critically by focusing on mastering the skill of continued questioning to uncover the root cause. It is my way of passing on the problem-solving skills I learned from my supervisors. The case histories illustrate certain aspects of SPPS. The repetition of terms and processes here is there to teach SPPS. Think of this as your apprenticeship. I hope that long after you have forgotten the specific text, you will remember the stories and the points they illustrate as a tool to help you on the journey to successful problem-solving.

Why Do I Call It Situational Practical Problem-Solving?

You are probably wondering why I added the word "situational." After decades of teaching practical problem-solving, I discovered there were pieces missing in the method. I found the problem-solving process was most successful when sensitive to its context, with the ability to be flexible. I adjusted the process to accommodate these features, tested it in real-life situations, and the results were measurable improvements. Teams were better able to solve problems more accurately and quicker than before.

The word situational refers to using tools as needed for each specific problem. It is a commonsense approach. Do what make sense. If the answer is readily apparent, then do it. If not, conduct further investigations. SPPS can be used on all problems, from simple to complex. Don't get hung up on the tools or the problem report. What tools you use and when you use them can change from problem to problem.

I taught students whose rigid approach taught them you couldn't conduct a formal investigation until you first defined the problem. What they missed seeing was that from the moment you first recognize a problem, you are investigating whether you have a real problem or a perceived problem. Also, you are investigating your standard to add to your problem statement and whether you're within that standard. You are, in fact, conducting an investigation throughout all of the steps. Situational Practical Problem Solving should be thought of as a journey and not as a destination. It isn't unusual to retrace your steps throughout the problem-solving journey.

I've added the missing pieces and offered new tools to enhance the Practical Problem-Solving process, hence the word "situational" was added. Think of SPPS as a meandering river that sometimes circles around and crosses itself. The river isn't straight going from one town (step) to the other. Remember to ask yourself "what makes sense to do at this step?"

Five Fundamental Principles of SPPS

1. Be objective; think like a scientist. Think like a scientist who has a theory. The scientist is objective and deals with facts and not opinions. Set aside cherished preconceived notions. Don't begin problem-solving convinced you to know the answer before investigating what is actually happening. Keep an open mind like a scientist. It is just as important to disprove your theory, as it proves it!

2. Go see the problem or situation where it occurs. Usually, you can physically observe a problem or situation, not just "see" it in your imagination. Go yourself to the area where the problem occurs and see what is actually happening. Do not just sit in a room discussing the problem based on you and your colleagues' memories of what you can recall about the problem. If you fail to see the problem firsthand, you're practicing second-hand problem solving, which often leads to failure. Be hesitant of so-called experts on a subject, as too often they are not open-minded to accept new ideas.

3. Delay solving the problem until you understand it. Do not jump too soon into solving a problem. Identify the real problem first before you investigate its causes. Most people think they have a clearly defined problem when, in fact, they are operating on assumptions. This leads to solving the wrong problem or "solving" something that is not even a problem!

4. Establish a cause-and-effect relationship based on facts rather than opinions. Demonstrate a relationship between what causes the problem and the effect it has on the problem. The relationship must be based on fact (confirmed information) and not assumptions (opinions).

5. Continue asking "why?" until you arrive at the root cause of the problem. The root cause is the real reason for the problem. You should ask "why" until you identify it. If you fail to do so, the problem will likely recur or cause additional issues.

CHAPTER 13
THINKING STRATEGICALLY

Strategic planning, as a process for action, is an essential management tool. In many cases, it is ignored because its seen as something complex to implement. However, thinking and acting in a strategic way is key in your professional and personal lives.

Strategic planning, though, isn't always a popular tool among many people. Some are concerned about uncertainty and constant changes. Any form of planning might be seen as naive. Some believe that given how complicated it can be to implement, it takes too long to take action. Therefore, it is often perceived as outdated and cumbersome in facing everyday challenges.

However, installing strategic planning in your mental code can make things way easier for you. Thus, instead of opposing planning, you can put this instrument into practice. You can use it to manage your life as efficiently as possible. People who use strategic planning soon realize that this 'tool' isn't the most important thing, instead, the key lies in "learning how to think strategically."

The very first step is to convince yourself that working with a strategic criterion and using a solid methodology in your life can become a 'binding' element of action. Strategic planning can help you to reduce insecurity, stop living your life in a reactive rather than responsive manner, etc. Knowing what to do to make things happen will make your future be much more promising.

You'll be able to use risks as factors of controlled opportunity. People who incorporate strategic thinking into their everyday routine, develop the capacity and potential of knowing where they want to spend time. Furthermore, strategic planning can help you to make an effort only in the things that really matter.

How to Get Started

Like any system, strategic planning can help you to prioritize things. This is the key factor in this new line code. To get started, be aware that you need to learn to think strategically. First, let's focus on the ways in which you can sort out your ideas. In principle, observing the big picture of your everyday life is the very first step. It is useful to see the "general map" of your life. This is the best way to start implementing strategic planning.

For instance, your life might be composed of your work, your family, friends, and any hobbies outside of this. You can start considering how much time you'd like to invest in each of these areas. If work takes half of your time (as with many people), why don't you start thinking about the amount of time you need to allocate each week toward focusing on your hobbies, your family and friends, etc.? What is more, you can (for instance) decide that Saturdays will be devoted to spending some time with your friends, while Sundays will be entirely for your family.

Afterward, you need to be aware of all the elements that compose strategic planning.

Define Your Mission

As part of every logical sequence, which tends to achieve an action, one wonders in the first instance: "Who am I?" or "What is my reason for being?" By answering these questions, the first link in the chain is met. You get to define what is now known as the 'mission' in your new system. This summarizes the raison d'être for you. This has a great power of attraction, which mobilizes all the energies within you. Therefore, you'll be able to gather resources after an end.

Think about how institutions are created. Companies are means created to obtain specific purposes. Think of yourself in this way. Kindergartens, schools, universities, religious organizations, industrial companies, unions, clubs, foundations, etc. at the time of their creation. Therefore, start by defining what's your mission in this world.

Defining the mission will help you to 'land' the idea of your reason for being. If this purpose is not well defined, it can be difficult to move forward in any direction. Think of any renowned high achiever. What they all have in common is a sense of purpose and a mission to which they devote their lives.

Analyze the Status Quo

Once your mission is defined, you will have greater clarity on why it exists. You will follow a "potential analysis" task to know in detail what is happening with:

a. Your goals and objectives: What are they? Where are they? What can you do to reach them?

b. Yourself: What are your flaws and strengths?

c. Your environment: How do external factors impact you?

d. Your goals and objectives: No matter how big or small they are. Maybe you want to spend more time with family and friends. Or maybe you want to build and grow a successful business. For all these purposes, you must ask yourself:

   - Why do you want to achieve a given goal or objective?
   - How can you achieve them?
   - What are the specific steps you need to take so you can achieve them?
   - What do you need to achieve your objectives? Are they permanent or occasional needs?
   - Do your objectives all have the same characteristics?
   - How do they relate to each other?
   - What resources do you currently have to achieve them?

Pay special attention to this issue. There are many people who fail to achieve what they want because they weren't aware of all that I just mentioned. They might have very clear of what they want, but they are not aware of what they need to do to achieve them.

Once you're aware of your objectives, spend some time trying to define yourself as a person. This analysis process will take you to look at yourself on three levels. Thus, you'll need to answer the following questions:

   - What strengths do you have as a person?
   - What are your flaws and weaknesses?
   - What do you lack as a person to achieve your objectives?

This is crucial in the sense that you might recognize that you (for example) need to be more assertive or less socially awkward. Whatever they are, be aware of what you need to work on. Furthermore, you can see such flaws as areas of opportunity and growth.

Your environment plays a crucial factor in whether or not you achieve your goals, and how quickly you do so. This means determining how everything happening around you can affect you. In other words: What impact does the environment have on you? This method, at this step, suggests revising your environment on three levels:

- What opportunities can your environment offer you?
- What problems can the environment throw at you?
- What threats to your objectives may be out there?

However, I want to emphasize that other people can actively behave in a way that counters your goals and objectives. Think of a boss who constantly forces you to work extra hours and who prevents you from spending more time with your family, friends, or pursuing your hobbies.

On the contrary, some external elements can enhance you. Think instead of a different boss, someone who allows you, for instance, to from home once a week or someone who is more understanding of your needs and wishes.

Specific Steps Toward Your Objectives

Beware of all the little steps needed to achieve your objectives. However, be sure of which way they can help you to reach your overall objective. Some specific steps are to set strict deadlines to it and have a way to measure how much you've fulfilled them. Deadlines and measurable mechanisms can help you to achieve your goals by providing you with clarity at times when you might be doubtful.

You don't need to over-stress about this. For example, you might want to get more things throughout the day. A specific step could be to wake up earlier. Thus, you start from Monday to wake up at 6 am instead of 7 am. Your measurement mechanism, then, is to record every morning at what time you wake up. If you do so for 21 days, you'd have created a new habit. Therefore, you've taken a little step forward.

Another classic example is to lose weight. You can start by having an objective of losing 20 pounds. The following step is to that June 1st (the beginning of summer) you would have lost such weight. After making a mental note of that deadline, you can start weighing yourself every week and record your progress, alongside tracking your meals, sleep, hydration levels, and fitness activity. If you stop losing weight or you haven't lost enough weight to reach your objective, you can set things right at that moment—instead of waiting until it is too late.

Action Plans

Writing down action plans is the best way to ensure the fulfillment of your objectives. These are scheduled processes that need to be answered for each objective proposed:

- What is going to be done?
- Can you do it by yourself or do you need help?
- How will it be done?
- When will you take action?
- What resources are available to do so?

Defining your action plan for each objective you have is a vital part of optimizing your life and business. A high percentage of failures occur due to the lack of planned, coordinated, and prepared actions. Figuring out action plans takes time and effort. However, it's worth the work.

The extraordinary thing about all this is that the final outcome is a 'map' of your objectives. This way, you won't be walking through "unknown lands." This 'map' will allow your mental code to internalize every specific step needed.

Let's go back to our example of losing weight. Measuring your weight every week is only one step. Additionally, you can also incorporate measurable steps such as tracking what you eat, how much you work out, how many hours you sleep, etc.

Think Strategically

As you can see, the strategic plan protocol is nothing more than a sequence of very specific actions that require dedication, commitment, and perseverance. It is a thought protocol for action. Strategic planning is nothing other than the most comprehensive method to achieve whatever you want. In other words, it is a statement of commitment that ensures things get done. From then on, everything consists of following each of the programmed action sequences.

What to Do for Now?

Go through the system and define the following:

· Define your mission and the goals/objectives you want to achieve.

· Analyze your current situation and what prevents/enhances you from reaching your objectives.

· Define the specific steps you need to reach your objectives. Set deadlines and measurement mechanisms for each of them.

· Establish an action plan that you can work on today!

CHAPTER 14
THE PROBLEM-SOLVING PROCESS

"How do you solve problems?" That was my opening question for every interview I did here. I generally got a deer-in-the-headlights response or, during phone interviews, total silence. Most people didn't know how to answer. They said something like, "That's a really good question" or, "I never thought about it that way."

However, once they had time to think about the question, they described following a process, which I agree is the right approach. They just hadn't realized it's the process they have been following. Here's a recap of the various steps people shared with me.

Step 1. Define the Problem

Defining the problem may seem an obvious place to start solving it, but it's surprising how many people ignore this step or give it short shrift. Don't allow yourself to be distracted by symptoms. You must get to the root cause of those symptoms, which is the actual problem.

How the problem is defined has more impact than any other factor on how – or whether – the problem is solved. Everyone involved, from the head of marketing to the marketing assistants, must agree on what the problem is. I highly recommend taking the time to write out the problem in the form of a question. It's a surprisingly helpful exercise for aligning a small group of people.

For example, you might write down, "People don't know our company, so they're not comfortable buying from us" or

"Our clients don't believe what our sales team promises. How do we get that trust back?"

Be sure not to define the problem as a marketing problem.

There are no marketing problems; there are only business problems that marketing can help solve.

In step one, you also need to identify the one or two metrics related to the problem. Are sales down? If so, by how much?

Do you have a client retention issue? OK, how big is the problem? If the answer to such questions isn't clear, then you don't really have a clearly defined problem.

Step 2. Understand the Impact of Finding a Solution

What is the expected business impact of solving the problem? And, just as important, what do you expect to happen if the problem is not solved? This is the time to ask whether the problem is even worth solving. Although asking this question is counterintuitive, great problem solvers know when to step away.

If you sense that the effort required to solve the problem might exceed the value of the solution, have a conversation with your boss. You can frame it like this: "I've spent some time looking into this problem, and I suspect that the benefits of solving it won't be that great. I'm confident that I/my team can solve it, and here's what the effort would involve. I think that our time would be better used to focus on other things. Do you agree?"

Thinking through and communicating the costs and benefits of solving the problem is not only a way to be sure the company is using its resources (that is, you're and the team's time) well but also a way to find out how committed company leadership is to finding a solution. Clarifying the future beneficial impact of solving the problem also ignites the excitement of those tasked with applying their energy to solving it.

For example, if you're trying to solve a customer-acquisition problem, you need to outline the financial upside. Will a 5 percent increase in sales result in an additional $2 million in revenue per year? If so, all of a sudden, a marketing expense of $250,000 feels like more of a wise investment than an expense.

Without demonstrating the impact of solving the problem, your business problem might fade into the background as more pressing issues are addressed.

Step 3. Gather Data and Insights

It's easy to be distracted by useless data, so sift through it and understand it. And then determine if the information is helpful or immaterial.

If it's just anecdotal, for example, it could even be misleading. If you have access to technical resources, have them analyze the data with you.

A litmus test for evaluating data: "Does this data help us think differently? Will it take us in a different direction or lead to questions we haven't thought of asking?" That's the kind of information to look for. Fight the urge to look for data that support your preconceptions; they will just reinforce how you already think and won't help you think of other, perhaps better solutions. If instead, you examine data purely to learn, you'll move closer to a good solution.

Step 4. Develop Potential Solutions Using Problem-Solving Techniques

This is where the rubber meets the road. Developing potential solutions, usually the most challenging part of solving the problem, is more art than science. There's no guaranteed approach to developing solutions. However, you should be adept at a variety of techniques that will help you to develop potential solutions – including the five whys, root cause analysis, journey mapping, creative problem-solving, and Hurson's productive-thinking model. Part III, "Problem-Solving Techniques," goes into detail about each technique.

Step 5. Refine the Solution

Once you have a potential solution, another is to determine its viability. Pressure-test the solution to understand any weaknesses. Try to poke as many holes as possible in the idea, even kill it. For example, if your solution involves purchasing $500,000 in media, is your company likely to approve that spending? If you need the sales force to have upgraded marketing technology, would the company invest in it? If the idea continues to stand up to your pressure-testing, then you know you're on to something.

When you think a solution is sound, provide the context of the problem and share the solution with your team members and the heads of groups that would be involved in implementing it, saying that this is one of the ideas you're thinking about. Don't expect them to immediately say, "Yes, that's a great solution" – which isn't what you want anyway. You want them to ask questions and poke holes in the idea. Their feedback will be extremely valuable to you; it will indicate how workable the idea really is.

How you present the potential solution to others is important. Don't appear to be excited, or even enthusiastic. Instead, present the idea as if you're unsure it will work. To get honest feedback, I say, "I think I may have a solution, but it doesn't feel right. Would you let me know what's wrong?" Phrasing it this way gives others permission to disagree with the idea. Creating a comfortable environment in which people don't feel pressured to respond in any particular way is the key to refining the solution.

Step 6. Document and Socialize the Solution

After the idea has been pressure-tested and refined, you must do one more thing before implementing it: make sure that others are on board with the idea. This requires documenting it – that is, putting the idea in writing so that it can be referred to in the content-marketing process. Then share the solution with the appropriate stakeholders and decision-makers.

This is pretty basic stuff, but you would be surprised how many people just tell people about the solution without putting it in writing. When presenting it to leadership for approval, keep the problem overview and proposed solution basic. You should be able to describe it in a couple of sentences.

When presenting it to people who will be involved in implementing the solution, provide more detail, including the data you used, the people you consulted or otherwise worked with, and the process you and your team used to arrive at the solution.

Getting buy-in requires working within your organization's hierarchy by managing up (to leadership) and down (to the team you manage) as well as horizontally, to colleagues and other interested parties.

Step 7. Implement the Solution

Implementation can be tricky. Sometimes, it will be as easy as hiring a company, if you're one of those marketers who has the luxury of hiring an agency to do the content-creation work for them.

Even if you do have that luxury, it's not always smooth sailing – you still need to oversee researching vendors, check references, get internal signoff, and do many other tasks. Other marketers are faced with having to add the work to their own – and others' – plates.

Beyond creating and implementing the solution, you also need to think about how easy it will be to roll it out both internally, at your company, and externally, with customers. Sometimes your solution will be well received, and people will ask for it sooner. Other times, people are going to resist and slow things down because they don't understand or appreciate the value of the solution.

Sometimes you may be the only person involved in a solution. Other times, it may take a year to roll something out. For example, I once worked on a brand rollout that took about eighteen months to implement. On the other hand, I also worked at a company where the brand rollout happened literally overnight. Both companies were very large; they just had different approaches to change.

Step 8. Measure the Effectiveness of the Solution

Even though measuring the effectiveness of the content--marketing solution that's been implemented is the last step, you should have been thinking about it from the beginning, when defining the solution. Be as clear and specific as possible about how success will be measured, so that you're measuring what really matters. Don't just say that an increase in website traffic, for example, will be considered a success and a decrease in it won't be. Instead, provide specific percentages.

After implementation, share the progress of the metrics with your team, your manager, and any other leader who should know about it. Tell them when the results will be in and deliver the information when it's available. Once you've looked at the metrics and perhaps received feedback from customers or observations from your team members, you will know whether the solution is working and whether the implemented idea should be refined further. This ongoing optimization can take a good solution and make it better, or an underperforming one and make it viable.

CHAPTER 15
POWERS OF THOUGHT
TO GET WHAT YOU WANT

One hopes that at this point, the solution needs just a tweak or two. However, if the solution has not had the desired impact and you're unable to refine it so that it does, have the courage to walk away from the solution. Then start all over again to solve the problem, beginning with step one.

How to Use Your Powers of Thought to Get What You Want

You recognize you can do something if you use your mind to do it. But what does this maxim mean anyway? How can you imagine it?

Sometimes too much concentration can cause headaches. You get creative blocks, you get gaps, and at the end of the day, you throw up frustrated and cursed hands that have ever made up the saying. All of us have had emotional stress and breakdown experiences unless you are a Swami who meditates under a tree all the time. The mind shuts down, and you work with reserve adrenaline. You can leave this cycle and use your mind to satisfy your desires. The brain emits electromagnetic waves in defined patterns (usually in certain frequency ranges), and science has recognized that each wave pattern opens up a certain state for the body. Like those in control of deep meditation, they can sometimes go into alpha and theta states - states that are extremely good at learning and reprogramming the subconscious. Our subconscious mind, languishing in the niches of our thoughts, is the culprit here. It is simply a mindless servant of consciousness who does what he is told and responds to situations based on past responses and emotions associated with a particular event. Without getting too involved, there is a whole lot of information about why the subconscious does this - but all you need to know is that you have to reprogram it.

In one's daily work, one might focus one's attention on intellect, as it is necessary to do in order to write a work of philosophy, for instance. However, whereas the modern world view is often compulsively fixated in the rational habit of mind, for the emerging mode, rationality is a tool that one can employ in its appropriate domain of applicability and put aside for other activities in which other modes might be more productive. If one is attending a rock concert or a religious ceremony, one might choose to embrace the magic or mythical modes of relation in order to experience the full efficacy of the pounding drums or the solemn chanting. One common instance of this transition can be observed in the necessity of "getting out of one's head" in order to dance with any conviction. The Western dances popular during the earlier centuries that spanned the height of modernity, such as waltzes or quadrilles, can seem stiff, formal, and overly structured to a sensibility raised on the modes of bodily movement that have accompanied swing, rock and roll, soul, hip-hop, or electronic music in the twentieth and early twenty-first centuries. In fact, as I suggested, these forms of music and movement seem literally to have been training the modern body to overcome its addiction to mentality in the embrace of a more expansive mode. It is no accident that the "hip" countercultures of the twentieth century have often been associated with archetypal modes of thought.

The integrative method, which affirms the positive content of all modes, is exemplified in the conscious reembrace of archetypes by the rational mind individuated in modernity. And conversely, the emerging mode itself is apparently the expression of an archetypal impulse toward integration, synthesis, and reconciliation. In premodernity, this archetype was associated with the hieros gamos, or sacred marriage, closely related to the alchemical unio oppositorum, the union of opposites. For the explicitly rational modern mode, this quality appears to be expressed in sexual reproduction, in political and economic unions, and in the integration of races, cultures, and scientific theories, though the modern mind generally declines to acknowledge any deeper coherence among these integrative instances. However, it appears to be with the novel mode that the archetypal impulse toward the integration of seemingly incommensurable polarities becomes self-aware in its inclusive acceptance of all forms of thought and modes of relation that do not detract from the freedom of expression sought by other modes, a situation which recursively serves as evidence for the efficacy of archetypal thought in the practice of integration.

Reprogramming your brain into different states is now extremely easy thanks to the effort and technology that have driven this area of personal development. From yoga to technical sound to binaural beats, you can call on your brain's strength and ask it to trigger a specific brain wave that is linked to learning, intelligence, creativity, or even one that gets you out of a cycle of depression. Memory is the main tool for learning. Even if you're spontaneous and creative, you're probably using your memory. Let's look at other means to improve your memory. Use memory techniques (like "Every good boy deserves fruit" and "FACE" in music). Doing small jingles and acronyms is an effective way to remember things you absolutely must remember. Such small ditties often remain in long-term memory. If you research mnemonics on Google, you will find that some mnemonics are funny, others are politically incorrect, and others are a little rude. Funny, controversial, and rude things are easier to remember. For example, one way to remember the difference between stalactites and stalagmites is that "tights fall off." You can use mnemonics for everything from spelling and grammar to science and law. You can also use visual images and other associations to improve your memory. If you are considering images, try to create colorful, moving images as they are more vivid and memorable. If you can, choose images that are associated with strong taste or smell, or with certain sounds or places to make them more vivid. Let your imagination run wild! Note here that you are not one Worry about the arteries if you can remember the blood flow to the veins.

CHAPTER 16
NURTURING A CURIOUS MIND

When the impossible look easy, you can be sure that the plan behind it is covered with mental fingerprints. Usually, the correlation between the seeming ease of a task corresponds directly to the intensity and scope of the planning.

The cognitive ability to simultaneously think in opposing directions is a trait great leader possesses. Be it corporate tycoons, generals in the armed forces, or chess grandmasters. Each thinks many steps ahead about multiple variables, attaches a probability to the various potential outcomes, dissects the situation for its components and influencers, formulates action options, and creates both forward and contingency plans with confidence. I call it, having a "curious mind."

Most successful event strategists have curious minds, although they may not realize it or identify that in themselves. They instinctively dissect program elements into small parts, analyze them, ask questions surrounding them, consider what could go wrong, determine how to reduce risks, figure out how to handle challenges and then put it all back together and act. They know from experience that small details, when neglected or overlooked, can become huge problems in no time.

Near the beginning of the semester in the strategic planning course that I teach, I told my students that any gathering could be considered an event and, therefore, would require thinking through the details. To put their skills to a test, I asked them to plan a pizza party for the following week's class. They'd be graded on how well it unfolded. They all thought it was a guaranteed "A." After 15 minutes of class time, all 18 students agreed that they'd thought it through thoroughly and were done planning.

By the following week, pizza and soda were ordered, and supplies were purchased according to the plans they'd made. The person who'd picked up the six pizzas and the soda couldn't carry it all in one trip, so she delivered the first three pizzas and a couple of two-liter bottles of soda. Then she had to walk back to her car for the rest. (This campus is notorious for its scarce parking, so the trip to her car and back was a seven-minute errand.)

Once she returned and the boxes and bottles were opened, people began to serve themselves. They quickly realized they hadn't ordered enough non-meat options. This caused some grumbling and some mitigating pepperoni removal. They had plates, but they didn't have cups! And what about paper towels and spray cleaner to get the dripped pizza grease off the desks? They'd forgotten to buy those, too.

Fortunately, I had done this exercise before. Under my desk, I had a cooler with ice, cups, paper plates, paper towels, and cleaning supplies. When it came time to tally the expenses and divvy up the costs, they also realized they didn't have enough singles to make a change. I'd anticipated that also and brought a stack of one-dollar bills.

A simple pizza party proved to be full of elusive details and hidden costs. The students were surprised. They realized they could have anticipated and avoided these oversights with a bit more thought (and perhaps more pizza-party experience). They understood the lesson: There is more to a flawless event than meets the eye.

Event strategists draw on their experience and context awareness to determine what logistics to manage and how to make the event seem effortless. (That's our gift!) Planning events have been compared to ducks swimming: It appears graceful and effortless...until you look below the surface.

That's why I created the "Curious Mind Exercise." Because planning graceful, elegant events is anything but effortless. These exercises help strategists refine their critical thinking skills. Doing so is the equivalent of taking out a mental insurance policy.

You also must remember that you're not planning alone. It takes teamwork. And, frankly, the smarter the people around you are, the better you can do your job.

Here are examples of some of the exercises to help you pay attention to important details:

• Choose an object at random, something from your briefcase, your desk, or that's visible from your window. For two minutes, write down as many questions you can think of about that item. Now that your mind is limbered up, do the same exercise, but this time apply a strategic planner perspective.

- Consider a task you do without thinking, brush your teeth, tie your shoes, eat an ice cream cone, and write down every step necessary to accomplish the task. Test yourself by doing the task just following your list and see what you missed.

Mastering Strategy

Event strategists who aspire to become Master Strategists need to go another step beyond logistics and synthesize information at a much higher level. They have to anticipate the impact of disparate, apparently unrelated world events on their events. Here's a Curious Mind Exercise to work that mental muscle:

Choose a headline from the newspaper. For instance, take these headlines:

- "Gas Prices Expected to Rise due to OPEC Supply Cut."
- "World-Series Victory Parade Scheduled for Monday."
- "Three-time Olympic Gold Medal Winner Convicted of Drug Use."

What could these headlines have to do with events? If you put your curious mind to work on this problem using an event filter, you can broaden your perspective while keeping events at the center. This way, you can start to assess the relationships and potential points of impact. For instance,

- Gas prices rising can negatively affect attendance at an event for an external audience that may be driving to the event.

- Airlines impose fuel surcharges when prices either spike or remain gradually on the rise.

- Your transportation budget may need to be adjusted to accommodate a fuel surcharge, delays, or cancellations that you didn't anticipate.

- The parade may cause road closures that may make it impossible for attendees to get to your event (that was scheduled long before the city's World Series victory was even anticipated).

- Your external-facing event attendance may drop dramatically as a result of traffic or if your audience members are also baseball fans and get distracted.

- What arrangements can you make with hotels to substitute part of your room block if necessary to accommodate victory visitors in case your attendance suffers to avoid unnecessary room charges?

- You were expecting that Olympiad to make an appearance at your fundraiser event.

- What contracted appearances are being canceled and what kind of scramble is happening to find replacements?

- Where is that person's image appearing for promotional purposes, what is being done to remove it from collateral, and how much will it cost to replace it with the substitute celebrity?

You Don't Know What You Don't Know

Logistics is not just about executing a set of tasks; it's about thinking through an array of good and bad scenarios that could occur and developing multiple contingency plans to cover them. Ask questions – lots of questions – to help you figure out what, in a given circumstance, you may be missing or what could happen.

I often ask colleagues, clients, and interviewees, "What should I have asked you that I may not have?" or "What do I need to know that we haven't covered?" Keep front and center the adage "You don't know what you don't know." It helps to open your mind to the possibility that you have overlooked something critical.

When every program element ties back to the achievement of the overall event goal, any disruptions, hiccups, or flat-out epic fails are more than inconvenient, they can be costly mistakes that hit beyond the wallet. Putting an enhanced emphasis on details and trusting that no detail is too small, will work well in your favor, trust me.

CHAPTER 17
COMBAT MENTAL CLUTTER

One way to fight the mental clutter that can come by external means is to be ahead of the game. When you're prepared to regularly handle the expected, you'll also be better prepared to handle the unexpected. Being organized, setting a routine, and keeping close tabs on yours and your family's obligations will help you when things occur out of the ordinary. Planners, calendars, and learning to set and meet goals and deadlines are a great method for getting yourself and your family on track.

Creating a 'Command Center'

Whether you live alone or have a large family, there's a place in your home that becomes a focal point for daily preparation. If you can pinpoint that place, you can create a central location to organize your life. This could be a wall in the kitchen or living room, where you can hang a calendar or corkboard, some hooks for keys, purses, and backpacks, and to tack important notes and reminders.

For busy families, there are a lot of obligations between sports and other hobbies and pursuits, as well as schoolwork, school memos and permission slips, party invitations and registration forms. Having a central location with a visual calendar and memo board can help keep everyone on the same page and make sure that all obligations are met.

Color-coded systems are great for larger households, where everyone gets a different color on the calendar or whiteboard. If everyone in the household has an internet-capable device, you can back up your in-house visual system with a shared digital calendar. This can give you peace of mind knowing that you've got the information in at least two places. Making sure to have your calendar both on paper and online is important for everyone, not just families. Be sure to add commitments to your calendar when you set them; you don't want to put it off and potentially forget to mark things down.

A corkboard or whiteboard is a great way to keep your family organized because you can customize it for whatever your family needs most. You can hang sports and work schedules, shopping lists, school memos, and even give everyone their own part to organize their things. Adding hooks and bins nearby for backpacks, equipment cases, and bags, and other miscellaneous items can add an extra layer of organization for your family. Make sure your children have small assignment pads that they can notate homework or projects in; even though many schools are transitioning into digital classrooms and digital message boards, it's still crucial that your kids know how to write obligations down the 'old-fashioned' way.

If you are the 'master' scheduler for your family, make sure your own daily calendar reflects everyone's schedules. You can use a color system or whatever works for you to make sure you know who needs to be where at any given time, and what they have to have with them. To get started, make a list of everyone's activities and which day and time they occur. Then write down your work schedule and your partner's. Then, make a list of any upcoming obligations and what you or your children need to bring. To make a weekly schedule, start with Sunday, and markdown everywhere you all need to be that day and when. Do the same for each day of the week. When you find a scheduling conflict, mark it down on a piece of scratch paper. When you've gone through all seven days, you'll see where you need to make adjustments and arrange for rides and alternate transportation. You'll also have a comprehensive list of all the equipment and trappings your family will need to haul around that week.

Use each person's basket or hook to put out items at night for tomorrow. Older children can handle this themselves, but you should double-check with younger children just to make sure their clarinet is actually in the case, or their library isn't torn up. By showing children how to prepare for their upcoming obligations, you'll be planting in them the lifelong seeds of organization.

Planners, calendars, and memo boards are such a crucial part of keeping mental clutter at bay, and evening preparation is a helpful aspect. Pack lunches and lay out clothes for younger children, and encourage older children (and yourself!) to do the same. You can check the weather and anticipate what shoes and outerwear you'll need and if you should pack an umbrella. As noted, spending time the night before putting out whatever your children need to take to school and what you need to take to work can save time during the morning rush to get out of the house. Once you've gotten into the habit of evening preparation, you'll find your mornings will be much less stressful.

Setting and Sticking to Goals and Deadlines

Earlier, we talked about organizing physical spaces and how it's easier to do when you break the tasks down into simpler steps. The same goes for eliminating mental clutter. For every big project, there are smaller steps that lead to the final product; doing so can help you meet your obligations and achieve your goals.

Taking time to divvy up a project before you begin can help you stay on track and feel more accomplished over the course of the task. It's important to give yourself a visual representation of a timeline for a project. Think about what you need to do, and when you need to do it by. Be realistic about which parts of your project will be the most time-consuming and which will be easier to complete.

Make a list of the steps you need to get from beginning to end. If you can't figure out what order to complete the steps in, you can write them down on notepapers or cards and shuffle them around until you've found an order that makes the most sense. You can even teach this method to younger children to impress upon them the importance of goal setting and not procrastinating. Here's an example for an elementary or middle school-aged child:

Planning My Report:

Deadline: Two weeks

Week One:

- Read a few pages.
- Take notes on my favorite character.
- Take notes on my favorite scene.
- Draw a picture for the cover of my report.

Week Two:

- Write the outline for my report.
- Work on my introduction and conclusion paragraphs.
- Write the body of my report about my favorite character and scene.
- Ask mom to proofread my report.
- Correct my mistakes.
- Print out my report, add the cover, and hand in!

This may seem like an oversimplification, but you get the idea. For every large task, there are a number of smaller tasks that make it up. Being able to set and meet goals and deadlines is a surefire way to fight mental clutter before it begins. This goes for any task at hand, whether it's a home improvement project, a work presentation, or something hobby related. If you are knitting a blanket for a birthday and you know how many rows you need to complete based on a pattern, you can divide to find out how many rows to knit per day to finish the blanket by that date.

Procrastination is both a cause and an effect of mental clutter. When you wait too long to begin a task, you begin to panic and invite your brain to fog up before you can even get started. You can also start out in a mental clutter and take so long to get out of it that you end up procrastinating almost by default. That's why goals and deadlines are so important for staying focused and giving yourself milestones to achieve along the way.

People are prone to procrastination when they feel overwhelmed and uncertain about their preceding steps. By using careful planning and preparation, you can avoid the panic that comes with waiting too long to complete your work. Make and stick to to-do lists, and you will save yourself a lot of stress in the long run.

The Importance of Perpetuity

Paper calendars are seemingly going out of style, but they still have their uses- one of them being a perpetual date tracker. You can use a paper calendar or small daily date tracker to write down annual occasions like birthdays, anniversaries, and holiday gatherings. Set it aside in a safe place and use it as a reference to make sure you purchase greeting cards and gifts as needed. This can eliminate last-minute shopping trips and the panicked feeling that comes with realizing you missed an important occasion. By having a visual representation that you can refer to at the beginning of every month, you can add any necessary cards or gifts to your shopping list before it becomes an urgent matter.

Mental Clutter at Work

Being organized to avoid mental clutter doesn't only apply to your home and your family, but also to your work life. Be sure to keep on top of your daily calendar and planner so that you don't lose track of any important meetings. Break large tasks down into smaller steps, and don't be afraid to make lists and hang them where you can see them. This will keep you inspired to stay in control and complete the step in your project. Make sure that everyone involved in group projects knows their action items and their deadlines.

Create a routine at work, too, and make it a habit. Set times for checking and responding to email, make a to-do list every day or week, and don't let yourself get distracted when you are supposed to be focusing. Complete one task before moving on to another. If someone emails you while you're working on something else, finish the something else first; the email will wait. Unless it's marked urgent and was accompanied by either a backup text or phone call, it can most likely sit for a little while. If it was an emergency, you'd already have been given a heads up.

If you can, take your breaks away from your work area. Eat lunch outside on nice days. Take a brisk walk up and down the hallway. Stretch your legs and get your blood flowing a little bit to get away from your desk or workstation. You'll feel more refreshed when you get back to your tasks. Sometimes stepping away from a frustrating task and getting a change of perspective can boost your spirits and your energy.

Because life doesn't always go as planned, being prepared with ways to combat both the internal and external causes of mental clutter can go a long way towards helping you when unexpected situations arise at both home and work.

Checklist for Getting and Staying Organized

There are some basic supplies you'll need to start on your way to organizing your life at home and at work:

- Calendar.
- Date tracker.
- Corkboard or whiteboard (tacks or magnets).
- Hooks and baskets for each family member.
- Calendar application for the computer/phone (can be shared among family).
- Note paper or index cards.

CHAPTER 18
BEHAVIORAL ACTIVATION
& PROBLEM SOLVING

Here, you're going to pick up a couple more tools that will help you fight back against low moods and depression: Behavioral Activation (BA) and problem-solving.

Behavioral Activation (BA)

Depressed people often feel weighed down and apathetic. Even small, everyday tasks such as doing the laundry become daunting. Depression drains you of energy, leaving you asking, "What's the point in doing anything?"

As time goes on, you cut more activities from your daily life, which leaves you feeling even more depressed and worthless. Your motivation continues to dive. You start telling yourself things like, "I can't cope with anything," "I'll never get better," and "I don't enjoy anything anymore."

To break out of depression, you need to stop this cycle. The only way to regain control over your life is to deliberately engage in positive activity again, even when you don't want to. This strategy is known as behavioral activation, or BA. The first step is to think of activities you used to enjoy, as outlined in another exercise.

Exercise: Planning Positive Activities

Make a list of low-key activities you enjoyed before you developed depression. These activities could be as simple as watching a movie at home. Give yourself time to make your list because depression can make it harder to remember things.

Now plan when you can do three of these activities over the coming week. To begin with, 20 minutes is enough. Make a note of each session in your diary. It's just as important as any other commitment, so don't feel guilty about making time for yourself.

Don't expect to feel excited at this stage. Making this list probably felt like a chore. That's normal! The real progress comes when you follow through and keep a record, as explained in another exercise.

Exercise: Pre- and Post-Activity Mood Record

Before you start a planned activity, make a note of your mood. Give yourself a score of 1-10, where a score of "1" means "very little energy or motivation" and "10" means "very excited and enthusiastic."

When you've finished, write down your score. Any increase, even if it's just one or two points, is a step in the right direction. Sometimes your score might not change at all. If you feel as though nothing is making you feel better, it may even go down. That's OK. It just means you need to change your planned activity, or perhaps try again another time.

Choose Activities That Move You Closer to the Person You Want to Be

BA is more effective if you choose activities that are in line with your goals and values. For instance, if you want to be more sociable, setting yourself the goal of chatting with an old friend for 10 minutes on the phone would be a great BA goal.

Finally, make sure you are choosing activities you really want to do, not what you think you should be doing. For instance, don't set yourself the goal of cleaning the bathroom or doing the grocery shopping. Sure, these are important activities, but the point of BA is to help you re-engage with the things you enjoy.

You Don't Have to Look Forward to It, Just Do It Anyway

When you try BA, the little voice in your head might tell you unhelpful things like:

"This won't work. You never enjoy anything."
"It can't be this simple. It won't make you feel better."

"It might work for other people, but not for you."

The secret? Try it anyway. What's the worst that could happen? Even if you try an activity for 10 minutes and feel no different, you haven't lost out on anything. You can then try again another day or try another activity. If you feel motivated on some days but not others, you can rest assured that this is completely normal.

Progress isn't always linear when it comes to recovering from depression. Some days, you'll feel hopeful. Others, you'll feel defeated before you even start. The trick is to just keep going. When you complete your BA exercises, give yourself plenty of praise. You have every right to be proud!

Once you have some evidence that BA works for you, you can challenge these negative thoughts using the cognitive restructuring exercise outlined. Remember: you need to identify an unhelpful thought, look carefully at the evidence for and against it, and then come up with a healthier alternative thought.

When to Get Support

If you've tried BA exercises several times and they don't seem to be working for you, it may be a sign that you need further support from a therapist or doctor. Please don't think that you've failed. Sometimes, depression doesn't respond to self-help. If you feel very low or have no energy for even brief 10-minute activities, it's time to find a medical professional who can help you take the first steps to recovery.

Depression, Problem-Solving & Empowering Yourself

A little-known but very common problem in depression is having trouble making decisions. The good news is that you can sharpen your problem-solving skills. Problem-solving isn't always straightforward, and it can feel overwhelming when your mood is low. At the same time, devising solutions and putting them into practice is very empowering.

When you realize that you don't need someone else to come along as rescue you, your self-esteem will grow. This will help you feel good about yourself, which in turn will help lift your mood.

Seven Steps to Problem Solving

1. Work Out What the Problem Is

In some cases, it's obvious. For example, if you know that you need to choose a new school for your child, solving the problem is a matter of evaluating local schools and picking the best option. On the other hand, some problems aren't so easy to pin down. You might know that you are unhappy in a specific situation, but perhaps the details are a bit fuzzy.

For instance, if you know that you dislike going into work, you'll need to think carefully about the underlying source of the issue. What is it about the environment or the work itself that is making you sad or depressed?

Upon reflection, you may discover that the problem is, "I need to find a new job," or "I need to be more organized so that I can meet all my deadlines and have a less stressful time at work."

When you've narrowed down the problem, write it down. Well done! You're off to a good start.

2. Brainstorm a List of Potential Solutions

Let your imagination run wild. Put aside half an hour to make a list of every solution you can think of. Don't worry if they seem strange or unlikely. You don't have to show this list to anyone.

Get some outside input. Ask a couple of people you trust to help brainstorm with you. They will probably come up with some ideas you haven't thought of. When you are stuck in a depressed mood, your problem-solving abilities take a hit. It's easy to become locked into a single perspective.

If you have a serious problem, or you can't rely on anyone close to you to help out, get some advice from a specialist. Depending on your problem, this person could be a counselor, a helpline volunteer, or a religious leader at your place of worship.

3. Weigh the Pros and Cons of Each Solution

You can do this alone or recruit someone to help you.

For each solution, ask yourself:

- How much time will it take me?
- How much money will it cost me?
- Will I need any outside help? Will it be easy for me to get this kind of help?
- Will I need any special equipment, training, or resources?

- Are there any important long-term consequences I should think about?

4. Choose the Best Solution

If you're lucky, you'll have found a perfect solution. Unfortunately, in most cases, we have to compromise when solving problems. That's why writing out the pros and cons and talking to others is so important. Knowing that you have given the matter serious thought will make it easier to believe in your own judgment.

Remind yourself that no one makes the right choices all the time. However, we can all try our best to work with the information and resources we have available at the time. Don't fall into the trap of postponing a decision just because you're afraid of getting it wrong.

5. Make a Plan

Having found your solution, you now need to make a roadmap for the way ahead. Your goal is to draw up a step-by-step plan that leaves you feeling empowered rather than overwhelmed. Make each step as specific as possible.

For example, suppose your goal is to sell your house and move to a new town. One of your first steps is to find out how much your property is worth. It would be more helpful to write, "Schedule a valuation within the following 7 days," rather than "Find out how much I could get for my house."

6. Execute Your Plan

Start with the first step and go from there. Take it slow and steady. Even people who aren't depressed need to be patient and encouraging with themselves when solving problems. You might need to break your steps down further. No step is too small as long as it moves you further toward your goal.

Other strategies that might help:

- Planning a small reward for every step you take.
- Asking a friend or relative to give you some support.
- Working on a step for just 10 minutes at a time.
- Keeping a log of your progress so you can see how far you've come.

7. Evaluate The Results

You've reached the final stage on your problem-solving journey. You've implemented the solution. Did it work? If not, what could you do differently? Perhaps something unexpected happened, or you didn't get hold of the information you needed. We can all try our best, but there are lots of things in life that are beyond our control.

Even if things didn't quite work out as you hoped, give yourself lots of praise. You tried something new, and that's something to celebrate. Remind yourself that problem-solving is a skill. Like all skills, it becomes easier with practice.

Summary

- Behavioral Activation (BA) and problem-solving are two practical tools lots of people find helpful in overcoming their depression.

- BA involves identifying activities you used to enjoy and scheduling time in which to do them.

- It's normal to feel resistance when you try BA, but you need to just go ahead and do it anyway.

- Problem-solving reduces feelings of depression because it makes you feel more empowered to overcome whatever challenges life throws at you.

CHAPTER 19
CHANGE MENTAL PARADIGM

Paradigms are a large number of propensities that control all that you do. They are mental builds and convictions in your mind that give the 'satellite route' for your life. They are seldom of your own structure. Truth be told, if you resemble a great many people, your paradigms are a blend of others' sentiments, convictions, activities, and propensities, but then they have total power over your life. It's very a startling thought that you are enabling others to control your world, and you aren't even mindful of it.

Be that as it may, never dread. Since you realize these paradigms exist, you have the power tom change them and start making the existence that you truly need to live.

Paradigms are the explanation the vast majority (around 97% of the populace) feel stuck, and regardless of how hard they attempt to roll out an improvement, they simply continue getting similar outcomes again and again. You will never observe the perpetual change in the event that you don't change the paradigm.

It is really a straightforward procedure to change a paradigm. However, you should be submitted, and you should be steady.

We will discuss how to change a paradigm in 5 basic advances. Apply what you realize, and your life will change like you wouldn't accept. Having the option to change your paradigm or paradigms resembles beginning a fresh out of the plastic new life as a child. You fundamentally will start to fix all the negative programming that you have experienced in your life. At the point when that is finished, you will get results to show so rapidly it will stun you.

Figuring out how to change your paradigm is so natural once you have a solid comprehension of how one is made in any case.

Paradigms, or what is otherwise called molding on an intuitive level, are framed by the steady reiteration of thoughts to somebody on an emotional level when the thought is rehashed it enough eventually in light of the fact that fixed in the subliminal mind.

Everything in life is made on a mental level first. Your external world is just an unadulterated sign of your internal world.

All the misfortune, the negative encounters everything is a direct result of YOUR thoughts, your emotional thoughts that you engage in truly is devastating your karma and great encounters.

In the event that you tireless in this state long enough, you start being negative, and that is known as a paradigm.

Everybody needs to change their paradigms yet consistently miss the above idea totally. In the event that you need better outcomes monetarily or seeing someone as I'm certain the vast majority do, you need to figure out how to have the option to get to your intuitive mind where the paradigm is at present.

When you have done that over and again for 21 to 30 days in a row, that is the place the new programming happens, and you start to draw in better conditions to you easily as you likewise make a move towards your fantasies. So how about we begin on the 5 Steps to take to get you reinvented for success on a subliminal level:

5 Steps on How to Change a Paradigm

1. Identify What You Want to Change Mentally

In the event that you are deficient in a part of your life that you are not happy with. This is an extraordinary spot to understand that you have a paradigm that isn't working in support of you. It was made through steady redundancy of negative things around you, and what individuals have said to you. You, at that point, acknowledged these constraints on an emotional level and went directly to your subliminal mind.

Record a couple of territories that you need to transform yourself on a bit of paper. In the event that you don't care for your present condition of salary, at that point record that. Make a rundown of 5 to 10 things that are influencing you the most.

2. Turn Negative to Positive by Repeating

With your rundown you've made, you 're going to have to get another bit of paper right now and work out the direct inverse in the current state of your negative paradigms.

As you are composing these out, you need to state them for all to hear gradually and with feeling. Truly feel the energy of what it resembles to have that sort of salary. As you are doing this, you are getting to your intuitive mind right then and there.

It is through the steady redundancy of working these attestations out each day a couple of times for 21 days that will truly make a move mentally for you. You will start to see peculiar and astonishing things transpire that you won't have the option to clarify it. Simply understand that it is your present perspective on a subliminal level that is making things occur.

3. Write Out Your Dream in The Present Tense

Composing and envisioning with emotion is so powerful in your subliminal mind. What you will need to do is go to an extremely tranquil place and get yourself completely loose by taking in and out gradually for one moment.

When you feel loose, and things hush up, start to expound on how you need your life to be. For instance, "I am so appreciative now that I... and fill in the clear. Compose everything just as it is occurring in your life now. As you do that, you will truly feel it, and won't have any desire to quit composing. Write in detail as much as you can.

At that point, what you will need to do after your biography is finished is re-perused it a couple of times for all to hear gradually and with feeling. This is likewise programming your mind to pull in those conditions to you through occasions and individuals.

You will need to peruse your story and assertions once in the first part of the day, once toward the evening, and a couple of times around evening time before you hit the sack. Recall that the entirety of this should be finished with the feeling that it is as of now occurring in your life. That is the main way you will change your old paradigm.

Do this for 21 days in a row. Try not to skirt a day since that is to what extent it takes for the wiring in the brain to be changed. On the off chance that you skirt 1 day, you should begin once again. Steadiness is the key to having this work.

4. Understand Who You Are

What that way to you will be you are a Spiritual Being living in a physical body. You have no restrictions on your latent capacity, with the exception of those that are made by YOUR mind. You really can do and be anything you need.

You have to comprehend your connection with this incredible power and understand that you are similarly as extraordinary as any other person that is successful on this planet, and any individual who is recorded in the extraordinary records of history. Any individual who has ever accomplished anything with bewildering results comprehends that there is something exceptional about them.

They realize that they truly can do anything they need through ceaseless industriousness and never quit on their fantasies. On the off chance that you can consider you to be as satisfied on the screen of your mind, that is not disregarding any laws of the universe, and then you can do it.

5. Read Biographies of Successful People

Perusing accounts of successful individuals a couple of times each week, that you respect will assist you with continuing to have confidence in yourself and reinvent your paradigm. As you read tales about them on Wiki, consistently remember that you are the same as them, with the exception of their outcomes.

They simply figured out how to assume responsibility for their minds and utilized it to further their potential benefit well indeed. Both of you are as incredible as them as of now. They have a similar potential as you do now. They're communicating it through their new successful paradigm and their moves they are making to give helpful assistance to humankind.

CHAPTER 20
TRAIN YOUR BRAIN, IMPROVE YOUR LIFE

It occurs instantly and it is over before you even notice. Three seconds is all you need to establish an incredible first impression, at whatever point you meet people for the first time. It is actually all the time it takes for the other individual to frame an idea regarding you, in light of your looks, your habits, your clothes, and your body language.

Each and every time you meet another person, the very same procedure takes place. Unfortunately, you never have another opportunity to establish an extraordinary first impression. These first experiences practically set the pace for all the following relationship. This is the reason they are enormously significant, extraordinarily, if the individual you're meeting with has an influence in your profession or in your public activity. That is the reason you ought to consistently remember the significance of making a decent first impression.

When you read all the guidance that therapists and profession advocates give out concerning making an incredible first impression, you understand that a large portion of the things they state are identified with frame of mind and great habits and little is said about looks. However, somehow people rather improve their looks first.

The method of reasoning behind such a decision isn't clear, yet it, for the most part, includes a profoundly established conviction that it is practically difficult to change yourself. All things considered, it's taken you all your life to become what your identity is, and that what you are is a comprehensive thing, encompassing the good, the bad, and the ugly. Additionally, individuals give a valiant effort to change outwardly, trusting that it will likewise affect their inside. Young ladies get a typo and guys exercise on steroids.

What they don't understand is that despite the fact that they may get a shock of adrenaline from those outer changes, it may be a brief one. In the long run, the novelty will blur away, and they will return to being their prior selves. Some will most likely begin the cycle all over again.

It doesn't have to be that way, however. You have the power inside yourself to change and turn into a better individual than you are at the present time. You should simply give more attention to your brain. Truly, that very same organ that you have ignored for such a long time, which by the way, is liable for everything that goes on with your body. Your brain can rewire itself to reconstruct all your constraining convictions and your deepest fears, with the goal that you can begin working at full steam. Neurologists call this brain plasticity.

Brain plasticity is at its highest when you are a baby. From that point on, it step by step fades, however, it never vanishes. If you utilize your muscle, if you exercise it regularly, it becomes more grounded. Be that as it may, if you don't prepare your muscle at all, it debilitates and inevitably decays. The same occurs with your brain and its plasticity.

Research has shown that our brain produces electrical impulses when our neurons communicate with one another, which happens constantly. These driving forces are called brainwaves and range in recurrence relying upon the sort of activity that you are performing. Interestingly enough, neurologists have found out that external stimuli can have an impact in brainwaves, to the point that it is conceivable to actuate the brain into explicit perspectives. Along these lines, if you want to double your capacity to learn or build your profitability, brainwave training can give you a hand.

A great deal of brainwave training items has been created over the most recent couple of years. Of those, BrainEv, short for Brain Evolution System, is absolutely the best. It joins 3 distinctive brainwave training strategies to deliver quick, quantifiable outcomes. And you should simply listen to a sound CD for 30 minutes per day, six days per week, for half a year. You will begin getting results soon enough. Your memory and your imagination will build, your dozing/sleeping pattern will improve, you will be in complete control of your life.

As you can see, it is very possible to change. It has consistently been. Customarily, meditation was the chosen way, however, it took long periods of training before you'd begin to perceive any outcomes. BrainEv doesn't take that long and you can get results right away. Consider BrainEv a workout regime for your brain. It will make you feel extraordinary about yourself and will likewise assist you with looking great.

The habits we structure, regardless of whether bad or good, address our issues, soothe strain and nervousness and give adjustments. At the point when we get the result, we're motivated to repeat the conduct that provided it.

For instance, after dinner you and your life partner watch a most loved TV show (cue), you sit together on the couch and unwind (routine) and have one of your preferred chocolate bars (reward). You've currently made a feedback loop: when you consider sitting in front of the TV, you consider relaxation and chocolate!

This may not be an issue except if you're overweight, have high diabetes, or wouldn't fret being addicted to chocolate. However, what if you have a seemingly good, which like being a perfectionist?

That was the situation for my customer Suzanne. She was a solitary working mother who was worried and depleted. She was inclined to making a few subjective contortions (thinking blunders) every day, one of which was white and black thinking.

To support her, I showed her the "art of taking note." I asked her to start paying attention to her negative self-talk, her real signs that revealed to her she was beginning to encounter uneasiness, and what she accepted about herself. I likewise instructed her to see the reasoning errors she was making and gave her some unwinding strategies to calm herself.

By uplifting her mindfulness, Suzanne figured out how to get a grip on her uneasiness before it overpowered her. Rather than reacting to her anxiety cues the manner in which she had, she interfered with the feedback loop by testing her contemplations with positive counterstatements and profound breathing. This provided an enduring compensation of serenity.

Because Suzanne would not like to pass on her anxious propensities and her perfectionist ways onto her children, she was excessively motivated to change.

Breaking habits requires purposeful intentional practice to change the neural systems in our brain. The uplifting news is it very well may be done on account of the brain's neuroplasticity. Here are a few hints on the most proficient method to start the rewiring procedure:

Practice Self-Awareness

You can't change what you don't see, so start focusing on what you're focusing on a minute-by-minute premise. Listen to what you let yourself know. Is your self-talk, for the most part, negative and condemning?

Practice Gratitude

For people that will, in general, observe the glass half empty, gratitude is an extraordinary propensity to develop. I advise my customers to record in any event two things every day they can be grateful for. After some time, it starts to change your viewpoint in astounding manners.

Get Motivated

Breaking habits does require solid motivation on the front end. No one but you can choose, however, once you have, you should practice positive thinking in order to re-wire the neuro-networks in your brain.

Practice Being Intentional

In the course of the most recent decades, there have been seas of research about the neuroplasticity of the brain. That is an extravagant way of saying that the brain can rearrange itself by making new neural pathways to adjust, as it needs. When learning another task, making sense of an issue, or attempting to defeat an impediment, you need to center. The more you practice and focus on something, the better you get at it the new aptitude that you're attempting to learn or the issue you're attempting to settle. This activity of concentrated practice and redundancy shapes new neural connections in the brain as synapses that don't as a rule fire together, presently do. This is what us sharpen the new skill.

Brain science has given us so much new and energizing information. Change isn't just conceivable, it's profoundly likely if we follow a portion of the rules earlier. In case you're tired of replaying all the negative tapes in your mind, and tired of being stuck in the regular old dysfunctional patterns, attempt some of these procedures for at least six weeks and see what occurs!

CHAPTER 21
FALL IN LOVE WITH THE PROCESS

The final self-discipline habit is the one which is severely under-taught, especially in schools, and that is an attitude towards failure and adversity. The school can give an impression that someone will be a failure at everything if his or her grades aren't perfect, and it is one of the most destructive mindsets someone can drill into a young person.

It is not possible to have self-discipline and fear of failure at the same, these two cannot coexist. You should know right from the start that you are supposed to fail because that's how you learn to be committed and disciplined. With each failure, there is learning and evolving and gaining wisdom. The goal is not necessarily about reaching the goal, but about the journey and the growth and about who you become. Think about your favorite movie or a video game. How would you like it if someone cut out the whole journey and the adversity and skipped right to the end when the bad guys are defeated, and the day is saved? It just wouldn't have the same impact.

The journey isn't easy, and it is not for those who are afraid of failing. Failure is a sign of life and a sign of someone trying something. Someone who doesn't even try doesn't stand a chance. If you're not failing, you are not learning and there is a certain knowledge that can be learned only through failure. It is a good idea to have some form of failure journal where you record your failures and what you have learned so that you can refine your approach and use failure as a sharpening tool. By failing, you will learn better than you would by trying to make a perfect plan. Failure on its own is not a failure, true failure is not learning from mistakes and repeating them over and over.

Some weaknesses and some areas for improvement can only be revealed by failing. I'm not trying to say to have no plan, you should have enough information you need to start successfully and then go into the field and collect feedback. In Silicon Valley, they use something that is called minimally viable product, which is like a prototype which has just enough features to work properly and then based on that, they collect real-world feedback so that the final product could be as good as possible.

There was also an experiment where a group of CEOs' were put against a group of kindergarteners in a competition which consisted of building the tallest structure with a certain combination of Lego blocks under a time limit. Kindergarten kids went straight to work and started failing a lot while CEO's were standing in circle strategizing. When CEOs finally started to take action, the time limit was nearly up and the kindergarteners who were at it the whole time managed to win by failing their way to success. Trying to be a perfectionist will keep you in paralysis. Done is better than perfect.

Behind every successful person is a succession of failures, but most people don't see that because that's not as sexy as the success. Most of the great inventions around us exist because the creators didn't let failure stop them and they knew how to learn from what did not work. Thomas Edison didn't fail 10000 times when inventing a light bulb, he just found 10000 ways that didn't work. Failing early and fast can be a great way to see if you fit in somewhere or if a certain way is for you. One way to not fear failure as much is to be aware of the worst possible outcome and to realize that it's nothing to really write home about. The fear is quite often worse than the thing itself and after you have dealt with it, you will wonder why you were so fearful in the first place.

The reason why failing builds self-discipline is because you get used to doing hard things and those that aren't necessarily easy since that is what improves you. The only practice which counts is the one which takes place at the edge of the abilities and that means that there is the possibility of failing. This is the sweet spot, as going beyond too soon can cause anxiety and hinder progress. People do not learn effectively under stress.

The longer one delays learning how to fail, the more fearful and routine-bound that person becomes. That is one habit you do not want to allow to solidify for too long because it only becomes harder to break the longer you wait. When kids are learning how to walk or how to ride a bike, they have to fall over and over, but they get up and try again until they are successful eventually. Accomplishing something meaningful in life is not much different. Children aren't in their heads all the time and for that reason, they don't make up excuses and they don't come to the conclusion that something isn't for them after only one failure. I'm not saying that thinking is evil because our ability to be introspective and to have thoughts about thoughts is what allows humans to come this far, while other unconscious animals that only follow their instincts are still where they were thousands of years ago.

Children are by nature, massive action takers and are curious, but something happens during the upbringing and the education, which makes people more and more set in their ways and less curious. They are educated about the world in the driest and boring way and when they start telling people about their dreams, they are told to be more realistic and how their ideas would never work in the real world. It is necessary to not allow this to go on for too long since habits are harder to break the older they are. Fail small and early so that you wouldn't fail massively in another lifetime.

Once you get more and more used to failure, life stars to change for the better. You can't fail if you're only doing that which you're good at and what is comfortable for you. If you learn to love failure and to reframe it as learning and to become comfortable with it, then it is only a matter of time until you succeed. Failing is the price which is sometimes necessary to pay in order to truly thrive. Failure is only temporary and sometimes it is only necessary to succeed once in order to forget all you had to go through. You may want to try accomplishing something extraordinary, but you keep hearing that only 10%of people succeed. That doesn't necessarily mean that your chance of success is 10%, it just means that you can't act like 90% of people who stop at the first sign of failure. Failure may be painful, and it may never get easier, but persistence is a better measure of someone's character instead of the attitude at the time of success. Failure should make you only hungrier instead of stopping you. Failure is when your willingness and commitment towards a goal is truly being tested.

CHAPTER 22
MAKE LEARNING SECONDARY

You might not know this, but mastering your intention and your success mindset is essential to you accelerating your learning.

How so, you may wonder?

Let's start with mastering intention.

Mastering Intention

The world we live in today is an action-packed life where most of us think about what we can do, how we can do more, and what we can do.

As you might guess, this mentality has led many of us to always be busy jumping from one activity to another; and as you learned earlier, jumping from one distraction to another.

Be honest for a minute.

When was the last time you sat down and did nothing but just think? You probably don't remember, right?

Many of us are simply not intentional with our thinking; we just move through life in some sort of "autopilot" mode. We are never intentional in our thinking and this is maybe because we don't see it as an important activity – which it is. In fact, if you think being busy is productive, you should try intentional thinking; many great leaders throughout history created outstanding results through utilizing their thinking time, with good examples being Albert Einstein and Henry Ford. Henry Ford once said: "Thinking is the hardest work there is, which is probably the reason, so few engage in it."

Many of us don't really think about what we are doing; we operate on autopilot mode; i.e. reacting to what is happening in the environment we are in, as opposed to directing our thoughts so that we don't just react. For example, as a student, you can go to class to learn but end up playing board games with your classmates – simply because that is the activity that is happening in class and since you are on autopilot, you go with the flow.

So, what is the danger of you being on autopilot?

The danger is that letting the autopilot take over makes it hard to keep our limiting beliefs and impulses in check; we simply go with the flow, something that can easily make it hard to accelerate our learning.

How can you check these impulses then? The answer is through practicing intentional thinking.

What Is Intentional Thinking?

Intentional thinking is simply spending some time thinking, without interruptions from your phone, TV, your family, and friends. It entails you just thinking about your life, your current thought, your plans, goals, your problems, how to solve them, et cetera.

But doesn't that sound like a goal-setting process? Well, intentional thinking and setting a goal are two different things. Goal setting is about achievement, while intentional thinking is about awareness. For instance, setting a goal makes you want to score an "A" in math, but intentional thinking makes you want to understand math more.

How Does Intentional Thinking Impact Learning?

Your thoughts usually have the power to lead you to a path of success or a path of failure when it comes to learning.

Here is how:

When you are on autopilot, i.e. when you don't practice intentional thinking, you react to life. This means you follow just any thought that comes your way.

For instance, many of us have grown up being told that math is a hard subject that is only suited to those who are "gifted in math." If you don't practice intentional thinking, you could easily grow up believing what you were told and true to your belief, math becomes hard for you. This is because how you think about something dictates how you feel, which in turn creates like-minded actions.

On the other hand, when you tap into the power of intentional thinking, what normally happens is that you take control of your life by starting to live your life instead of letting life live you. This automatically brings light to your learning experience and this is because you become aware of your thoughts and you become willing to challenge them. If you take the just mentioned example, for instance, intentional thinking makes you question the notion that math is hard. This leads to you investigating and trying to find if there is any proof that math is hard. The probable outcome will be you finding out that the notion math is hard is just a myth.

That's how intentional thinking impacts learning; it makes you question all the myths that make learning challenging. This transforms you into an open-minded person, which is the right attitude to have when it comes to learning.

Ultimately, you end up deriving a number of benefits from being an intentional thinker.

1. Intentional Thinking Helps You to Develop New Perspectives

As you have learned, you have limiting beliefs that are buried deep in your subconscious that can limit the way you view learning, as well as the way you learn. One of the benefits of intentional thinking is how it lets you examine your limiting beliefs like math is hard; reading is boring; failing an exam means you are dumb, et cetera. Once you examine these beliefs, you come to the realization that they are not true. You get to know that math is not hard – it just requires you to be keen with how numbers work; reading is not boring – all you need is to work on your concentration, and failing exams does not mean you are dumb – it just means you didn't prepare enough to pass for the exam.

This gives you a new perspective of your limiting beliefs, which transforms you into a person who is more open to reality and less held up by limiting past ideas.

2. It Makes You a Solution-Oriented Person

When you know your limiting beliefs were just twisted lies, the other benefit you get is that you become a solution-oriented person. In short, you become open-minded to possibilities. For instance, you stop seeing math as a hard subject and try to find ways that can help math work for you. You could think of looking for a tutor or joining a math club, or you might decide to have an open mind toward math teachings. In simple terms, intentional thinking turns you into a person that tries to seek solutions to your difficulties when it comes to learning.

3. It Gets You Deeply Involved in Your Own Learning

If you are a student, intentional thinking can help you to get deeply involved in your own learning, which improves your understanding greatly.

How?

One way that you can use intentional thinking is by summarizing what you have just learned in class. The process of summarizing gets you deep into your learning.

4. It Helps You Connect Old Knowledge to New Knowledge

When you think about what you learn, you sometimes get to activate old knowledge that relates to your new knowledge, something which can greatly help you to understand a certain topic better.

For instance, if you are a trainee nurse learning how to handle a wound and you think intentionally, you might come across a memory created a few years ago where you attended a first aid seminar. With that memory, you can connect your new knowledge with the old knowledge and get to understand the topic you are learning better.

5. It Helps You to Be Organized

Intentional thinking can help you to think about your studies and plan for them. For instance, it can make you come up with a revision timetable where each day you focus on a particular subject.

So when you go to class and find the lecturer is absent, the first thing in your mind won't be to play board games simply because that's what is being done by your classmates but to study for the subject you have set out to study on that particular day.

How Can You Be Intentional in Your Thinking?

Being intentional in your thinking is very important, especially when creating good learning habits. Here is the perfect path you can use to set your intentions.

Step 1: Make a Ritual

Creating a ritual or setting your intention should be your first step. Choose a time – in the morning, if possible – where you can take five-minutes to set your intention. This can be immediately after you wake up or before you go out to school.

Step 2: Write Down Your Intention

For that five-minutes in the morning, think and write down your day's intention, preferably on a journal you can use to refer to again. Your intention should be specific, creative, and a high-level dream – you should aim higher than where you are currently at.

Try to see what you want to change. If you want to improve your concentration in class, you can say, "I will have a top-notch concentration in my classes." If you want to have a better understanding, you can set your intention to be, "I will try to use my imagination and senses to improve my understanding."

The process of writing these down connects your mind and your intentions, which automatically enhances them even more.

Step 3: Make Yourself Aware of Your Intentions

As you go about your daily activities, you should try to be aware of your intentions by thinking about them. The best way to do this is for you to set a few reminders on your phone each day to remind you when to revisit your intentions. The frequent reminders will help shift the pathways of your brain.

Step 4: Celebrate Your Achievements

Another step is setting and following your intentions is to celebrate your achievements. If you managed to concentrate for twenty minutes, which is ten minutes more than you usually do, celebrate that victory and also celebrate the fact that you are starting to be aware of your intentions. This will automatically motivate you to do more.

Step 5: Start Slowly and Be Patient

For you to fully master your intentions, it will take some time to adjust. So, it is advisable for you to start with a small intention like saying "I want to always be on time in class." Give yourself 20-30 days to adjust, then move to another intention. After making your intention a habit, you should take some time to reflect and appreciate your progress.

Now that you've learned how to set your intention, the focus will be on how to build a success mindset.

CHAPTER 23
HABITS THAT FOSTER PURPOSEFUL, CONFIDENT LIVING

Being purposeful with how you live your life means having the guts to believe that you can dream big, plan for it, and then do everything in your power to ensure that your dreams become your reality.

Purposeful living is about having inspiring goals that motivate and challenge you to be your best self. When every day of your life is rich in inspiration and motivation and dedication to the pursuit of experiences that resonate with your spirit, you become confident, peaceful, sure of yourself and your purpose, and more successful.

To become more purposeful with your life, exemplify the following habits:

Adopt the "What Can I Do" Question

Being purposeful is about being sure of what you want and having a plan that helps you achieve it. Deep inspirational goals and aspirations always keep the company of a plan.

Asking yourself the "what can I do question" in various situations and areas of your life allows you to challenge your mind to come up with solutions and plans that bring forth the actualization of aims, goals, and dreams. For instance, if you want a great relationship, "what can you do" to ensure that your aim becomes your daily life?

This question makes you more purposeful about your pursuit, and when you are purposeful, you are more assured and confident.

Take Daily Responsibility

You are the only person capable of deciding what you want, what you have to do to achieve it, and what it means to you. Take responsibility for yourself and of your life by taking responsibility of how you spend your daily time and life.

The more responsible you are with your time, resources, attention, intention, and effort, the likelier you are to be more successful, confident, and purposeful with how you live your life. You are also likely to be happier with yourself and with where you are in your life, which is on the path to daily personal development by 1% in major areas of your life.

Take One Thing at a Time

To achieve your aims and aspirations, of which you probably have many, you have to be responsible with how you use your time and resources. Instead of multitasking or pursuing many goals simultaneously, which is likely to lead to overwhelm, low motivation, and low self-confidence, pursue one goal at a time, solve one problem at a time, and handle one thing at a time in all areas of your life every single day of your life.

By narrowing your intention and attention, i.e. what you want and what you have to do to achieve it, which requires time, you become surer of the effort you must take to achieve your primary aim. This clarity allows you to be purposeful with your daily habits, time, effort, and overall wellbeing as you pursue your goals, aim, dreams, and aspirations.

Adopt the Now Mentality

Many of us know the changes we need to make our lives better but often fail to do so, instead opting to maintain the status quo. To become more purposeful and, therefore, more confident and self-assured, adopt the now mentality, the mentality that allows you to stop postponing yourself, your goals, aspirations, you are neglecting the very thing your psyche truly craves.

Whenever you set an intention, i.e. make the decision to do or improve something, also make immediate changes or take immediate action, the now mentality, so that you can create the momentum you need to achieve a critical mass and success in key pillars of your life.

Adopt the Habit of Intentional Practice

Becoming purposeful with your life becomes possible when you adopt that which you want to achieve as an integral part of your daily life. Adopting habit of purposeful practice allows you to become intentional of your daily pursuits and the results of these pursuits on your overall wellbeing, peace of mind, success, and confidence. Whether you are working on a spiritual, physical, or mental aspect of your life, make its practice an integral component of your daily life. Consistent practice is the difference between self-actualization and a life rich in discontentment and unfulfilled potential.

Tap Into the Power of Vision

Your vision is a representation of what you would like to achieve within specific areas of your life. When you have a clear vision of the achievements you would like to have under your belt or the kind of person you would like to be one, five, or ten years from now, it gives you the clarity you need to be purposeful with how you use all your resources including intention, attention, time, energy and effort.

Creating a vision board, a sort of master timeline that shows what you intend to achieve and the kind of person you want to become will prove very useful here.

Set Intentions

At the start of each endeavor or aim, have an intention, a desired outcome. For instance, at the start of the day, set the intention to be more mindful and purposeful with your decisions and actions.

Attaching intentions to all your decision, aims, endeavors, and daily undertakings allow you to reconnect with the present moment, who you are or want to become, and to determine whether the intention and attention given to the activity at hand are congruent with your desires or aims.

By choosing how you want to be, feel, or act, you become more purposeful, at peace and content, and more successful and confident in key areas of your life.

Practice Simplicity

Having a grand purpose or vision for your life is great but to achieve anything substantial and to move forward with poise and confidence, you also need to think small and infuse simplicity into your grand scheme because only by doing so can you curtail our tendency to overestimate what we can achieve within a given period.

Have a grand dream yes, but break it down into simpler steps that build-up to, and make it easier to achieve your chief aim.

When you are purposeful, you avoid feeling overwhelmed and instead become surer of your decisions and actions, knowing that their under-taking helps create the life you want to live and experience.

CHAPTER 24
VISUALIZATION AND CREATION
OF MENTAL IMAGES

Visualization is a simple mental practice of imaging as well as meditating. Some people confuse it with meditation, but it is a different thing altogether. As opposed to meditation, which guides our thoughts, visualization is linked to the creation of mental images in a conscious state of mind. The most amazing thing about visualization is that our brain places in the same category of practice and learning. It means that when we visualize certain images, we are actually practicing the same and also learning it. Experts believe that visualization is so important that it has proven to be affecting the development of our motor skills, such as playing football.

Benefits of Creative Visualization Techniques

Now that you have learned what creative visualization is and what kind of exercises you can do to master the art of visualization. There are many benefits to creative visualization techniques. Let's take a look at some of the benefits of visualization and the creation of mental images.

It Gives a Big Boost to Your Focus

What does meditation do to us? Apart from relieving us from our worries, it gives a major boost to our focus. When we shut our eyes and focus on the mental image of an object or an image which we were looking at for the past few minutes, we are actually challenging our focus. That's how we are able to better perform ordinary tasks such as studying and taking exams. When we are in the midst of a creative visualization session, we tend to forget our daily problems and concerns regarding our future. In this way, we can focus on the present situation.

The Happiness Factor

Creative visualization is a tough exercise. We have to go through lots of struggles to create clear images in our mind. When we achieve our goals, this brings us the much-needed satisfaction a sense of fulfillment. Our mind seems to be in our control when we direct it to create an image and see immediate results.

It Reduces Stress

Creative visualization is amazing if we use it to relieve stress. Creative visualization helps you ease out stress. You have to dedicate some time, focus on a single thing and keep calm. The greatest stress reliever is that you are not thinking about the past or the future, but only the present moment. In addition, you will only visualize a positive situation.

Creative Visualization Will Give You Self-Confidence

Another benefit of creative visualization is that it offers us self-confidence. The sense of accomplishment and experiencing positive situations will increase our self-confidence. Our self-confidence is directly proportional to the inflow of positive images in our minds.

Visualization of Abstract Ideas and Concepts

Abstract ideas and concepts are difficult to remember because they don't have a particular image associated with them. If there is one, it is very weak and cannot be used to create a mental image, but this doesn't mean that there is no way to visualize abstract ideas and concepts. Let's explore some of them.

Simple Shapes

Sometimes simple icons can help you visualize some dull abstract ideas and concepts. Once our eye recognizes the icon, we can relate it to the concept or idea in question. For example, if you have to remember a graph, you can visualize the lines on the graph and try to relate them to the idea behind the lines.

Overlapping Circles

This type of pattern is the best to visualize and combine two concepts. For example, you have to memorize three rules of administration. These three rules are maintenance of law and order, collection of revenues, and running day to day administrative business. You have to remember all the three concepts and then blend them to form a connection so that you may be able to write them as a coherent whole. The examination days are getting closer day by day. Draw three circles which should overlap one another and write the three rules inside them. Now visualize the image of the circles and try to form a connection between the three circles, such as how the three administrative rules can complement one another. That's how you can put different abstract concepts in the circles and create a mental image of the picture.

Mind-Mapping

Another popular technique is to do mind-mapping. That's how you can better connect the idea nodes and then summarize the concepts. Connect different abstract concepts and ideas in your brain and then try to create a mental image of the same.

XYZ Coordinate System

There is another way to visualize abstract ideas. This can allow you to build up mental models. You can create three coordinates and allocate them to each abstract concept, such as the three branches of foreign policy. Each axis denotes one branch of foreign policy. Write it down on a piece of paper, draw the axis for the coordinates, and then jot down the three branches of foreign policy.

Some Additional Exercises

1. This exercise is commonly known as the candle exercise. Take a quiet moment and close your exercise. Now imagine that on opening your eyes, a candle has appeared in front of your eyes. Try to know more about the candle.

- What is the size of the candle?
- What is its weight? Is it heavy or light?
- How much has the candle burned and how much has it remained behind?
- Has it already burned down or can you still see the flame flickering in the air?
- What is the exact distance between you and the candle?
- What is the color of the candle? Is it full white or is it shabby?

You can also take real lit candles and do the exercise on it. Focus your gaze on the lit candle for a few minutes, then close your eyes and try to see from your mind's eye. What do you see now? Can you see the intensity of the flame? Can you see an after-burn effect? You are not seeing the candle with your open eyes, but you can feel the effects with closed eyes. Once the canvas in front of your closed eyes stabilizes, you can start mentally tracing the shape of the candle with closed eyes. Gather the traces and try to create a mental image of the candle. Try diligently so that the image you are trying to create should true to the real image of the candle.

2. Another popular exercise is the Apple exercise. You have to repeat what you have done with the candle on an apple. This can be another step in your learning process. Try to visualize an apple and observe closely its soft peel. What color is it? Is it ripe or not? Then try to imagine yourself taking a bite out of the apple. Feel its taste. Try to sort out different effects such as crispiness, softness, juiciness, and sweetness. Try to compare these effects with different things. For example, you can match the sweetness of apple with that of honey.

You can take the visualization of the apple to another level. Imagine that you have taken a bite and now the slice of the apple is slowly moving through your body across your digestive system. Feel how your digestive system is interacting with it. Trace it with your vision to create a beautiful mental image of the travel of the apple. There are other options which you can go for, such as visualizing that a lady has arrived on the scene who is trying to take the apple and eat it. She finally picks it up and takes a bite. Try to hear the sounds produced due to that bite. Also, try to visualize the movement of her jaw and throat as the apple rolls into her mouth and then glides down the throat to her digestive system. Along the way, you can ask yourself the following questions:

Ask yourself if the apple seems real to you or not. Once you are convinced that you have mastered the art of creating simple mental images, you can move on to visualizing these simple objects in relation to the room or a table. Try to visualize if the apple is in the corner of the room or put on the side of the table or not.

Try to visualize where the apple is in the room? Is it near the door or is it under the table or is it in the fruit basket? It is more like an optical illusion. You will enjoy it.

3. There is another very interesting exercise for creating clear mental images. Try to think about numbers in your brain. Numbers are abstract facts and there is certainly no story attached to them. They are pure concept-based facts. For this exercise, I am taking number seven. When we think of number seven, the first thing which comes to our mind is a group of seven words, apples or birds. Seven exists when seven different birds come together to form a group. Or there are seven apples on a table. There are lots of ways of writing seven, but generally, what we can remember is the symbol from mathematics because we see it so many times on a daily basis.

The exercise is simple. We have to start visualizing numbers which come before the number seven and after number seven. Try to visualize them in the form of mathematical symbols. Go backward and then forward until the point you find it easier to remember things. When you find out that everything is going on smoothly, you are ready for the real challenge.

You have to skip numbers. Until now, you have visualized numbers in a consecutive order. Now you have to skip by one. For example, if you are visualizing seven, the preceding number to go for should be nine. Similarly, the after nine should be eleven and the list goes on. Similarly, in the backward mode, the adjacent number after seven is five and after that, the subsequent number is three. Keep skipping and keep building up a list of numbers as you go. Once you have reached the highest possible number, turn back from that point. Say, the highest number at which you were able to keep your concentration intact was 21, move back from there. Keep visualizing nineteen, fifteen, thirteen, and eleven and so on. That's how you are able to train your memory.

CHAPTER 25
HOW TO PRESERVE YOUR FOCUS

The focus is crucial, and accordingly, multitasking is a lie. When you multitask, what you're doing is you're essentially spreading yourself too thin and allocating your focusing power among different competing tasks. What do you think the net effect would be? You wouldn't have enough focus left to handle the most important items of the day.

Unfortunately, if you are wasting your focus on stuff that doesn't matter all that much, like email or social media, you won't have much left to tackle the heavy stuff. These are the items that produce 80 percent of your results. The good news is that you can set up your daily task schedule in such a way that you can preserve your focus.

Burn Through Focus Intelligently

When you are working on "big win" for the day, it will take a lot of your focus. Think of your focus as dollar bills. When you're faced with many different task options, each option requires payment in "focus dollars." You only have so many focus dollars to spend.

The first big item on your daily schedule should be a big win. This is going to burn up a lot of your focus dollars. If you follow that up with another big project, the rate at which you burn up your focus goes through the roof. You'd be lucky to have effectively taken out two big wins. This may seem like a victory, but in reality, it's a loss because you've neglected the other big wins on your daily agenda.

For most people, it's usually three to five wins. Still, if you're like the typical person and you spent all your focus taking out the first two big wins, there's nothing left for big win numbers 3, 4, and 5.

Alternate Between Light and Heavy Tasks

If you get used to this process, you get a nice emotional lift in between, and it becomes harder and harder for you to lose your focus. You would then be able to achieve more by knocking out substantial heavy stuff that accounts for 80 percent of your results.

Warning: It's very easy to misunderstand this step. A lot of people would use it as an excuse to check email, screw around on social media, or otherwise do "tasks" that are essentially worthless as far as your productivity is concerned. That's not the kind of light task that you should do in between heavy tasks.

Celebrate Your Daily Wins

Now that you've learned how to knock through difficult daily tasks, the following step is to allow yourself to feel good about the fact that you're able to do this. I've seen many otherwise successful people beat themselves up unnecessarily because they keep focusing on their grand objectives in the distant future.

It should be very clear to you by now that everything you do today builds up to a magnificent future. If you still can't see the difference, then you're doing something wrong. Go back to the steps; look back and practice them until it's very clear to you that your choice of daily tasks builds up to grand objectives and dreams.

Allow yourself to feel excited about your daily accomplishments. It's too easy to lose energy and feel that you are just going through the motions as you make your way to your grand objectives. If you don't allow yourself to feel good in the here and now, your grand objectives may seem so distant and remote that it simply becomes easier for you to give up. This happens to the very best of us. It doesn't matter how passionate you are when you start. It doesn't matter how methodical and systematic your goal-crushing efforts may be.

If you do not celebrate the fact that you crushed your daily tasks today, you inch closer and closer to losing all motivation. Ultimately, you end up losing interest or your passion. Either way, you end up at the same place; you end up quitting. As you probably already know, you only lose if you quit. This is why it's important to celebrate your daily wins. The fact that you took your to-do list and it went from three to zero items is a cause for celebration.

Now, a lot of people around you may think it's not that big of a deal. After all, they can knock out their to-do list as well. That may be true, but the big difference is you have methodically targeted big wins for your to-do lists. You have used the Pareto principle, or the 80/20 rule, to make sure that the things you focus daily have a high chance of leading to the big objectives you have set for yourself in the future.

In short, those people who are leading to feeling that they're doing the same thing as you are just knocking out unimportant stuff on their to-do lists. The chances are high that a lot of the items on their task lists don't lead to big wins. They don't have that big of an impact. I'm not saying that all the items on their lists are completely unimportant, but in light of the Pareto principle, you are in a better position.

Your actions are more targeted, and the payoffs you get for your activities are more significant. Allow yourself to feel excited about all this and feel good that you are using a systematic and methodical way to handle your task list items and purposely making a move to get closer to your ultimate objectives. This is a personal victory. Just compare yourself to how you started.

When you started, you had no clue, and you're just taking shots in the dark, not moving in any particular direction. You had vague hopes, dreams, and wishes, but there's not much energy behind them. Things were not well-defined, and it seems that the day's flow into each other with very little effect. You put in all this effort and energy (or so it seemed), and at the end of the day, you're nowhere nearer to turning your hopes and dreams into reality.

You are now in a completely different place because, for every single daily win you register, you get closer and closer to the big one. Pat yourself on the back. This is a big deal because you are moving with a sense of purpose. You're not just chasing your tail and going around in circles.

Treat yourself. When you knock out your daily to-do list, treat yourself to something special. Maybe there is a video on YouTube that you've wanted to watch. It costs nothing to watch stuff on video, but when you reward yourself, you're telling yourself that you did something significant. Turn this into a habit. As long as the treatment does not add pounds to your weight or erodes your sense of urgency and is free, knock yourself out. Just make sure that the treat always comes after.

What you're doing here is you're trying to create a positive association between your ability to obliterate your daily to-list with something that brings pleasure. The more you create a mental association between eliminating your task list and a sense of accomplishment with an increased level of self-worth, you tell yourself that you're capable of doing something that most people can't do. You're able to work in a purposeful and deliberate direction, and you're going places.

This is not bragging; instead, this is a very important investment in your mental reward system so you can find the drive every day to do what it takes to achieve your ultimate victory. You need to celebrate your daily wins and create this positive mental association with your tasks. Otherwise, you're making things much harder for yourself because, let's face it, on someday you don't feel like getting up. Sometimes you feel that the world is working against you and things don't seem to go in your favor. There will be those days.

The good news is that by allowing yourself to create a positive mental association between your efforts and daily task lists' completion, you produce an inner sense of personal power that is independent of your external set of circumstances. Compare this with the alternative. You don't want to be dependent on what's going on around you to feel good; that's how most people are, and that's why they struggle.

When you depend on people, forces, and situations beyond your control, ultimately, you are powerless because you can't direct those people. You can't make sure every single day that things line up in your favor. Nobody has that kind of power. It's much better to create an internal reward system that produces a positive link between work and your tasks.

Eventually, your tasks no longer intimidate you. They won't seem like work; instead, they are part of your daily ritual of celebrating who you are. Instead of being negative obstacles to something that's positive, they become part of a necessary process that enables you to prove yourself and celebrate your capabilities. Now, I ask you which picture would you rather have? I thought so.

CHAPTER 26
MENTAL TOUGHNESS AND RESILIENCE

A resilient person knows how to deal with hardship and stress. Resilience is the mental pool of strength that you can summon in times of need to overcome hardships without falling apart. A resilient person can handle adversity better than someone who is not. Everyone experiences setbacks at some point in their life. How you deal with the challenges that come your way plays an essential role in the outcome and long-term psychological consequences you will experience. Some of these adversities might be minor such as not getting the dress you want to buy, while others are devastating, such as typhoons and hurricanes.

Resilience pertains to a person's ability to handle setbacks and problems. A resilient person can use his strengths and skills to recover from problems such as natural disasters, job loss, divorce, financial problems, medical emergencies, and illness. They don't hide from problems or fall into despair. A resilient person faces challenges head-on. This doesn't mean that they feel less anxious or feel less distress and stress than other people. It only means that a resilient person is capable of handling difficulties in a manner that promotes growth and strength. The problems they are facing may boost their mental strength and resiliency even further.

Those who lack resilience may become overwhelmed by the challenges and setbacks they are facing. They may use harmful coping mechanisms and wallow in despair. Failure or disappointment might cause them to adopt dangerous or destructive behaviors. Those who lack resilience slowly recover from challenges and may suffer from more psychological distress than others.

Resilient people understand that problems happen, and that life has ups and downs. Resilience doesn't rid of stress or difficulties in life. Resilient people still experience the grief, sense of loss, and pain that comes after a misfortune. However, their mental outlook lets them overcome such emotions and recover. Resilience gives them the strength to deal with setbacks head-on, move on, and overcome adversity.

Resilience vs. Mental Toughness

Mental toughness and resilience are not the same. These terms are frequently used interchangeably. All mentally tough people are resilient. However, not all resilient people are mentally tough. The main difference between mental toughness and resilience lies in a positive aspect. Experiential learning helps a person develop mental toughness. This can be done through simply living through life experiences, targeted development, or coaching. The result might be different, but crucial in an environment where we experience challenges, setbacks, and changes faster and more frequently than before. It's important to have a positive mindset. By doing so, you can accept setbacks as a natural part of life. Mental toughness helps you succeed, and resilience helps you survive. You get a positive result, and this leads to better wellbeing and performance and development of positive behaviors.

Some people naturally remain composed even when faced with challenges, but these behaviors are not only innate traits found in a few individuals. Many experts say that resilience is common. People can learn the skills needed to become more resilient. Social support contributes to resilience. Mentally strong individuals tend to have their loved ones' support. Their support systems encourage them during times of trouble.

Other factors that contribute to resilience include the ability to create realistic plans and follow them, having optimistic opinions of themselves and their skills, being an excellent communicator, and managing emotions efficiently.

Traits of Resilient People

Resilient individuals can maintain control over their situation and think of ways to deal with problems. They also understand that life has many challenges. We can't avoid these problems, but we can stay flexible, open, and ready to adapt to changes. Here are the characteristics of resilient people.

Excellent Problem-Solving Skills

Resilient people can identify the solution to their problem that will lead to their desired result. Sometimes, people develop tunnel vision when they're in a dangerous situation. They fail to leverage opportunities or notice essential details. Resilient people are capable of rationally and calmly looking at problems and thinking of a successful solution.

Viewing Themselves as a Survivor

Resilient people see themselves as a survivor when dealing with problems. Don't see yourself as a victim. What you should do is look for ways to solve the problem. Stay focused on positive results.

Sense of Control

Resilient people tend to possess an internal locus of control. These individuals believe that their actions will affect the result of an event. Some factors are outside of your personal control, like natural calamities. However, you should think that you have the authority to make choices that will influence your situation, future, and skill to cope.

Support Systems

When you're dealing with problems, having a support system can make things easier for you. Talking about the problems you are facing can be an excellent way to express your emotions, gain new perspectives and look for solutions. Online support groups, friends, colleagues, and family members can be your support system.

How to Improve Resilience

Whether you want to improve your coping skills, or you are going through a difficult time right now, improving your resilience is essential. Here are some tips on how to improve your resilience.

Be Optimistic

It's challenging to stay optimistic when you are facing a problem, but you should maintain a positive outlook. Having a positive mindset doesn't mean that you should ignore the issue to focus on a positive result. A resilient person understands that problems are temporary, and he has the skills to fight these challenges. You may be in a difficult situation right now, but you should stay positive and hope for a bright future.

Know Your Purpose in Life

Knowing your purpose in life can help you recover from whatever adversity you are facing right now. Cultivate your spirituality and become more involved in the community. Participate in meaningful activities.

Accept Change

A resilient person is adaptable. By embracing change and learning how to be flexible, you will be able to respond better to a life crisis. You can use this chance to take a new direction. Some people can't adapt to sudden changes. A highly resilient person, on the other hand, can adapt to changes and succeed.

Having Confidence in Your Abilities

A resilient person believes in his ability to cope with life's challenges. According to research, self-esteem plays a crucial role in recovering from tough events and dealing with stress. You should remind yourself of your achievements and strengths. When negative thoughts pop up in your mind, replace them immediately with positive ones like you're good at your job and you can do what you want to do. Be more confident in your ability to cope with a crisis because this is a good way to build resilience and mental toughness.

Social Support

Social support is essential for a person's health and overall wellbeing. Having supportive people around you is particularly beneficial when you are in a tough situation. Talking about your situation with a family member or friend will not make your problem go away, but it lets you get positive feedback, shares your emotions, determine possible solutions to the problem and get support.

Set Goals

Resilient people can realistically see crisis situations and set sensible goals to solve the problem. When you find overwhelmed, you need to take a break to assess what you are facing. Think of possible solutions and split them into manageable steps.

Take Care of Yourself

It is easy to neglect your needs when you are stressed. A person who doesn't adapt well to a crisis situation often loses appetite, refuses to exercise, and lacks sleep. You should focus on improving your self-nurturance ability even when you are facing a problem. This includes making time for activities that you love. Doing so will help you boost your resilience and overall health. Moreover, you will be prepared to face any challenge that may come your way.

Develop Problem-Solving Skills

According to research, those who can think of solutions to problems can cope with setbacks a lot better than those who can't. When you face a new challenge, create a list of the possible ways to solve the problem. Try various methods and develop a reasonable way to solve common problems. If you practice your problem-solving skills regularly, you will be ready to face serious challenges.

Solve Problems by Taking Action

Resilience takes time to develop and maintain. Don't get disheartened if you are still struggling to handle problematic situations. You can learn to be resilient, and you don't need to develop a specific set of actions to be one. Resilience can differ significantly from one person to another. You can practice the common traits of resilient people and improve your current strengths as well.

CHAPTER 27
MEASURING SUCCESS IN QUANTIFIABLE TERMS

It is necessary to have a way of gauging your performance at work in quantifiable terms in order to know where you stand and find out what else needs to be done to improve the quality of your work. You can do this in two ways: one, by creating your own set of criteria to judge your own work, and two, by relying on feedback from others.

In doing your self-assessment, try to be as honest as you can. The whole thing is going to be an exercise in futility if you wouldn't answer in as honest a manner as possible. The point of this exercise is to examine the effect of your output in relation to your personal and professional goals and highlight its impact in terms of how it fits into the larger scheme of things.

After completing a task, ask the following questions:

- In doing this task, was I able to reach my desired end? If yes, what are some of the best practices I should keep in mind and sustain in the future? If not, what are the opportunities for improvement?

- How did my finished output help in helping others carry out their functions?

- How did it help in achieving the organization's goals?

- Am I happy with what I have managed to accomplish?

- Is there any other way that I could have done better?

- Am I ready for my subsequent task?

Just as important is the need to understand the feedback coming from others, notably from your superiors. Employee engagement increases if there is an open line of communication between you and the management, particularly on matters relating to your performance at work and your career path within the organization. Having an outstanding feedback mechanism is a good way of correcting mistakes, highlighting achievements, and improving productivity in the future.

In any feedback, it is important to consider both your strong and weak points. The value of your strong points should not be diminished, especially since they can be very useful as you move along your career path.

Your weak points, on the other hand, should not be relegated to the periphery either. You should focus on providing an enduring remedy to these areas for opportunity with the able assistance of the management. If there was any failure in the completion of your task, get to the bottom of it and understand how it can be prevented in the future.

Treating the Drive to Succeed as a Lifestyle Choice

Sporting a positive and enthusiastic outlook toward your job doesn't work like a pill that you have to swallow every time you feel pretty low at your workplace. It's not a one-time exercise that you can conveniently pull out of your system that can magically turn your job-related blues away. Rather, it's a mindset, a trait if you will, that you have to imbibe and keep in your mind at all times. It's something that you have to sustain and nourish as long as you can until it eventually becomes part of your way of thinking.

Integrating positivity into your life and making it an essential part of your lifestyle means that you have to learn to juggle the demands of both your personal and professional lives. Creating a sustainable work-life balance is something that you should strive for. Paying excessive attention to your career to the detriment of your personal life is just as bad as neglecting your professional life in favor of unsustainable personal affairs. You need to straddle the fine line that separates the two without sacrificing one or the other. Remember to always aim for holistic and inclusive growth.

Need to Regroup

As such, don't be ashamed to admit if you need time off from work. If you begin to suffer from chronic lack of motivation to the point that the quality of your job gets affected, then take a breather and seek some sort of an escape. Break away from the toxicity of it all and find time for healing. Don't feel guilty about needing to take a quick break because, at the end of the day, it's more beneficial in the long term if you regroup now.

Indeed, if you want to be on top of your game, it is necessary that you look after your overall physical, mental, and emotional well-being. It's great to have a willing mind, but you need to back this up with a healthy body. On this end, try to grab adequate sleep every night. Without sufficient sleep hours, you tend to be cranky and unpredictable. The last thing you want to be in the workplace is to the kind of person who can't pull it together.

Maintain an active physical lifestyle. The best way to do this is by allotting part of your schedule for working out. Exercising regularly does not only keep you in shape, it also helps in keeping your mind alert and focused. Enrolling at a gym, creating your own workout routine within the comfort of your own home, or engaging in sports are some of the things that you can do to keep your body in tiptop condition.

Supplement your active lifestyle with a proper diet. Some food items have mood-altering effects, so go for those that are packed with nutrients and energy to last you throughout the day. Always aim for moderation, though. Refrain from indulging in food items that contain excessive amounts of sodium, cholesterol, salt, or MSG. Studies show that you are likelier to feel better about yourself and confident in what you can achieve if your body is in good condition.

Continuous Learning and Development

A good way of keeping your enthusiasm and motivation alive is by choosing not to let up in your quest for greater personal and professional development. See, one of the worst things you can do is being complacent with your situation and being content with the status quo. If you choose to go this route sooner, you'll end up getting stuck in a predictable cycle that can suck up your energy and make you feel less motivated.

A better way to go is by being proactive in seeking ways to improve your knowledge and enhance your skills. This way, you get to constantly update your skillset and get yourself exposed to new trends within the industry that you are a part of.

Most companies, for example, have in-house professional development courses that you can avail of for free or at a discounted rate. If you want a more formal training, enrolling at the university for specialized courses is a good option, too. Seminars, conferences, symposia, trainings and other related events are also things that you can watch out for to supplement your knowledge beyond your usual responsibilities at work.

If you are still at a loss on how to proceed with your career, set up an appointment with a career counselor. For all you know, your problem with lack of motivation at work may be brought about by some unresolved issues from your end. Talking it out with a counselor and implementing behavioral changes may be the best way to go for a full resolution of your issues.

In sum, where you want to go with your career is something that only you can decide on. You have all the power in your hands to effect the necessary changes needed to keep you motivated and inspired to succeed in the workplace.

CHAPTER 28
MINI HABITS AND WHY THEY ARE IMPORTANT

Take a moment and imagine what it would look like taking only little steps at getting yourself better and then in the process making impactful changes and meaningful changes to your life. If this is the first time you are hearing of mini habits, then you have just enough to learn here.

The word mini habits are just what it sounds like. It gives us the idea that we can actually do numerous little things and watch it add up to great things. As I'm sure you've heard it said countless times, the little things in life are what really matter.

Do them consistently and religiously, and you will find that your life is way better and those around you will be happier.

Imagine reading about happenings around the world every day. Imagine how well informed and versed you would have become by the end of, say, a month or even a year. You would have accumulated more knowledge about things happening around you and will be more likely to partake in discussions about recent happenings. In short, you would have become a more interesting person.

This is not the only thing that your mini habits do for you, though. They go a long way to impact your body and mind and, in the long run, affect how quickly and permanently, you can switch old harmful habits for new and beneficial ones.

Now, let's look at the benefits of mini habits.

1. You create an atmosphere of success: When we set very large goals, we look to ourselves as being incapable of achieving these goals and we look to the goals as being impossible. What mini habits do for us is that they make it easier for us to reach our goals. When you set small targets, it's usually easier to meet them and also to accomplish them within a very short period as compared to when you decide to take on your task fully without first breaking them down into smaller, achievable bits.

Take, for example, instead of piling up your unanswered calls and telling yourself that you will return all calls eventually, why not return the last call immediately or after some reasonable time than allowing it to pile up. Better still, you could fix a time for when you want to return your call and stick to it if you are so busy when the call came in. If the task were bigger, such as writing an article or writing an essay for a competition, then you could fix a time limit for every task. Divide your work into smaller parts and make them look simple enough to achieve.

A fixed time limit for research; another fixed time for giving an introduction; another fixed time for writing the body of the essay or article and so on and so forth. With this, you quickly find yourself completing your Herculean task in no time. When you do these, it takes away the feeling of failure, which comes from having procrastinated what you ought to do and also the feeling of failure for not doing enough.

Another thing about these small tasks is that you get to start with the mindset of succeeding because you have your activities all planned out before you and it seems quite easy for you. Starting off with the mindset of succeeding could help you eventually succeed.

2. Mini habits help you change how you view your capabilities: When you accomplish the small things, then you start to believe that you can actually do better than this or better than you did your last time. You boost your confidence, and it gives you a better understanding of what you are better at and also gives you a positive sense of your abilities.

3. You find motivation: While it is very easy to come by motivation (almost everyone is a willing motivational speaker), it is very difficult to make use of that surge of power you get at that moment you get motivated. If it, in fact, comes by, it gets used up very quickly and then you are back to square one, doubting yourself and all the motivational speaker said. This is why mini habits are very important.

Your mini habits do not rely on your motivation to get things done; it relies on your willpower. As you move on, you begin to feel the joy of having started and almost reaching completion, you can then find the motivation to finish what you started.

With mini habits, you create a series of changes that you have always wanted to accomplish all along. It helps to build your ability to start bigger things and actually finish them. It's like wanting to stay fit, and you start with push-ups every day and stay true to the daily exercise. With time, you add more exercises to your routine, and just like that, you have developed a new habit that keeps you healthy and fit.

To summarize, this how mini-habits work. First, you pick a huge task you would like to do and pick a date you would want it finished. Another thing is to shrink these habits until they are very small. If you want to write an article, then start with 50 words every day. Do you want to know more about the happenings around you? Then read the news every day. Do you want to be fit? Start every day with a push-up.

Looks easy, right? It's actually very easy. It works, and it will be easy because our brains are wired to fall for the smaller things that do not require too much at a time. You see fifty-word poems and you jump at it. You can do that because you have built yourself to write every day. Let's go through ten daily mini habits you should keep up with to become a better person.

Compliment one person daily. Your compliment should, however, be genuine. No one is asking you to fake your real feelings just in the name of developing a new habit. You might as well be living a lie in your habit at the end of the day. Think two positive thoughts every day. Meditate for one minute. Name three things you're thankful for, daily. Write fifty words. Read. Do one push-up. Drink one glass of water. Go outside. And take 100 steps.

You can change basically any area of your life. It takes just one mini-habit at a time and then you are better off this month than you were the last month. Remove the pressure and expectations and simply allow yourself to start.

CHAPTER 29
TIME AND TASK MANAGEMENT

Having many tasks to handle within a short period of time is now part of the daily routine for most of us. Daily assignments or tasks at home seem to take most parts of the day, leaving little time for relaxation and fun. However, you can decide how you spend your time. Setting aside time for the most important activities first before the less important ones can lead to success and satisfaction. Most of us keep grumbling that the hours of the day aren't sufficient to complete daily tasks!

However, twenty-four hours is more than enough time to carry out the most important tasks in our lives. All you need to do is learn the art of time management. That way, you can always make time for the people who are dear to you as well as other important activities.

What then is time management? Time management is the ability of an individual to plan and control how he spends the hours in a day in a way that he can effectively accomplish his goals. He must manage time between various facets of life, such as work, family, social life, and time for fun. It is imperative to set clear goals and prioritize important activities in order to set aside nonessential tasks that are time-consuming and to monitor what actually takes most of the hours in a day.

A good work environment that encourages efficiency is important. Poor time management is closely related to procrastination, lack of self-control, or distracting problems. To overcome these behaviors, organizational psychologists encourage the concept of setting up a work atmosphere that enhances productivity and efficiency. But this environment differs from one individual to another. Some individuals prefer a neat desk, while others do better in a creative mess. These days, deadlines are also important for some people, giving them a set period to complete a task at hand. In order to meet up, it is imperative to turn off electronic devices and reduce or avoid e-mail correspondence.

Before rolling out some principles, let's consider the key points and questions below.

Questions to uncover assumptions about mental strength thinking:

- What is your best time-management strategy?

- Can time be managed?
- Do you believe it is possible to be motivated by the scarcity of time?

Baseless assumptions about time management:

- Other people manage my time for me.
- At work, the time ticks slowly but goes fast, and on the weekend, it goes too quickly to manage.
- Time management is simply a waste of time.

Mental-strength viewpoint about time management:

- I am thankful for all the time I have.
- I cherish my time at home and also enjoy my time at work.
- Managing activities helps me get the most out of every second of the day.

Outrageous questions:

- In a range of 1–9, 9 being best, how well are you managing your time?
- What do you think can be done to improve your time-management skills?
- What percentage of time during the day do you spend on unproductive activities?

Reflective questions:

- What assumptions keep you from managing your time more effectively?
- If you could choose a role model when it comes to time management, who would it be and why?
- Is it possible to manage your time a day before you go on vacation the same way you do during the workweek?

The Importance of Time Management

Why is time management important? Or improving your concentration and focus?

You may say, "I don't want to protect my time or put in the extra effort or be over concentrated." Sorry, but those are mere excuses because the effort will pay off at the end of the day.

Time management should make extra time for you rather than take your time. It is also about making sure that you spend your time on the most important tasks.

It should not take much effort, but it definitely requires self-discipline. But the outcome of time management far outweighs the efforts.

Listed below are life benefits of time management:

Reduced stress. Managing your time can directly lessen your stress level. For example, you will have a few surprises, a few tight deadlines, but less jumping from task to task and place to place.

Avoid time wasting. You waste less time on idle activities when you know what you need to do. Rather than wondering what to do, you can already be a step ahead of your work.

Boost productivity. When you are conscious of what needs to be done, you will be able to better manage your tasks. Yes, being productive is one of the major aims of time management. You will do more with less time.

Boosts your reputation. Your reputation as someone who manages time will precede you. No one will question whether you are going to show up, keep your word, or meet that deadline. At work and in life, you will be known as reliable.

More free time. We can't create more time, but you can make wise use of it by effectively managing your time. We can produce more leisure time in your life by trying out simple actions, such as changing your mode of transportation or getting your work done early.

Fewer reworks. Forgotten details, items, and instructions lead to extra work. Being organized can result in less rework and mistakes. You can ask yourself how often you have repeated a task or made an extra trip because you forgot something.

Fewer problems in life. How often do you create your own problems? Whether it is a forgotten appointment or a missed deadline, not managing your time results in increased life friction. Planning and preparing for your day can help you avoid creating your own problems.

More opportunities. Being in control of your time and work offers more opportunities. Luck favors the prepared, and early birds always have more opportunities.

Reduced effort. A popular misconception about time management is that it takes extra effort. On the contrary, with proper time management, your life will be easier. You will begin to apply less effort at things, be it finishing up a project or packing for a trip.

More time where it matters. The concept of managing your time comes from allotting your time to where it has the most effect. With efficient time management, you are allowed to give your time to things that matter to you most.

Helpful Principles on Time Management

Each principle is closely connected to the other one, so you need to examine each one thoroughly. It is also a stepwise guide to time management. These principles will help you become more time efficient.

Each task should draw you closer to your goals. The principles and importance of setting the right goals should be meaningful and important to you.

For example, just learning football cannot be the goal itself. Rather, your goal should be to be able to kick the ball and make twenty shots in twenty minutes, and playing football is a way to achieve this goal.

The benefit of setting goals is that if you have set the right goals, you will be much more inspired to achieve them; thus, you will be more productive and time efficient.

Divide big tasks into minor pieces. There is one principle of time management that goes, "To eat a whale, you need to cut it into smaller pieces." If you have a very big project, you might be overwhelmed by the complexities and lack of clarity on how to do it. Divide it into smaller activities, so you will have a clear path of how to get it done. At the end of the day, it may turn out not as big and difficult as you expected.

Unsavory and minor things first. When planning your activities, you should treat the important and unsavory things first. In order for you to remember this time management principle, there is a saying for it: "Eat the frogs first." Starting the day with such activities will make you feel relieved, and the following tasks will be easier. If you don't do the unsavory things first, after doing other activities, you will think of the unsavory ones you left all day and feel bad that you still need to do them.

Also, you should do minor things early in the day as it will feel like you have done much in the first few minutes of the day. These tasks can include calling your companions, checking e-mail, composing a message to a friend, planning some events for the day, and the like.

Keep breaks in mind. You might feel high spirited and productive for a while, but gradually you start losing the vibe, and for the rest of the day, you end up leaving most tasks unfinished. What could be the cause? Simply put, the lack of breaks in your work.

You or your supervisor might be of the opinion that if you don't utilize all eight of the working hours daily, you might do less, but this assumption is wrong. You may be able to accomplish more and be more productive during the day if you take breaks at intervals. It could be as short as a five-minute break for espresso, a breath of fresh air, a simple snack, or a short stroll around the office building. During this period, I advise you to stay away from your laptop and, if possible, your working place so you can relax. Stay away from your phone, social media, etc. Also, take business off your mind.

If you are self-employed or work from home, you may also take a break once in a while. It is not always possible to estimate the amount of rest you might need. You might do a lot according to your schedule or make minor breaks as planned. Once you feel that you are not productive enough, simply take a longer break, changing the task entirely.

Having a short rest, such as a twenty-minute nap, is ideal. If you decide to take a longer rest, you will feel even more tired when you wake. Within twenty minutes, you can have a decent rest and relax sufficiently without falling into a deep sleep, and at the same time, be more productive, hence saving time (you will be more active and productive after taking this break than you would being tired).

CHAPTER 30
WHAT'S WRONG WITH MY CURRENT WAY OF THINKING?

The human mind is simply amazing. Starting with simple, single-cell organisms, in the matter of a short 3.5 billion years or so, nature has developed the human brain! What artifacts have been leftover from this evolutionary process?

There won't be enough space to do justice to the topic of human psychological judgment and decision biases. However, there are excellent, accessible works of psychologists, and particularly the writing by Daniel Kahneman, Thinking, Fast and Slow (2011), will be referred to frequently in this work. However, the topic of human judgment is extremely important to our systems thinking ability. First, humans are the key agents in the systems of interest for business, so we need to have a basic understanding of their psyche. Second, and just as important, we, the system analysts, are human. So, we need to understand something about how our own mind works and where our systems thinking blind spots may be.

To illustrate these blind spots, consider the fascinating Invisible Gorilla experiment by the psychologists Christopher Chabris and Daniel Simons (in their writing The Invisible Gorilla, (2009). In this experiment, subjects are shown a short video of two teams of three players, each passing basketballs amongst the team members. One team is wearing black shirts and the other team is wearing white shirts. Subjects in the experiment are asked to watch the film and count the number of passes made by the team in white shirts. Towards the middle of the film, a person in a gorilla costume walks into the frame, strolls to the center and proceeds to pound their chest, and then walks out of the frame on the opposite side. Thousands of people have seen this video and only about half see the gorilla.

The Invisible Gorilla experiment exposes a fundamental paradox of the mind. On the one hand, the human mind can conceive of theoretical physics, propose the Higgs boson, engineer the Large Hadron Collider at CERN, and find supporting evidence for the Higgs boson. On the other hand, we can't see a gorilla walking across the screen!

Kahneman helps us to grapple with this paradox with his construct of a two-layered (system) mind. In this model, Kahneman uses the idea of the two mind systems working together. First, sensory inputs are fed into System 1. System 1 takes the inputs and makes initial sense out of them. System 1's analysis is then fed to System 2. System 2 is the primary component of what we consider consciousness. The processing by System 2 completes the analysis of information within your mind. Some human actions (like counting passes by the white team) are susceptible to errors introduced by this System 1/System 2 mind. Effective systems thinkers need to understand and adapt to these inherent processes.

The Goal: A New Way of Seeing

What is the goal of this reading? The aim is to arm you with a toolbox filled with systems ideas and then help you to reprogram your System 1 mind to be able to quickly recognize system effects. Is this type of reprogramming possible? The grandmaster has a different way to think about the chess game than his opponents. An idea of the different cognitive processes at work are given by Larry Evans in his writing New Ideas in Chess (2011).

CONCLUSION

Our thinking preferences change based on the cultural and geographical differences.

According to some studies, while Americans perceived people, places and situations more specifically and individually, the Japanese looked at the bigger picture, and they looked at people, places and things in the context of their surrounding objects and their interrelation with these objects.

Two types of thinking are specific thinking or holistic thinking, and these types of thinking are the result of two vastly different perspectives.

Thinking by utilizing your brain's full potential offers multiple benefits:

- A heightened level of awareness
- Increased entrepreneurial capabilities.
- Faster progress in your career.
- Better relationships with family and friends.
- The development of multiple forms of intelligence.

Thinking with full brain involves utilizing the full capacity of your brain as required in any given situation. The benefits of unleashing the full power of your cognitive abilities will help you to improve your life in all areas, be they financial or relational, and heighten your overall happiness.

Most people suffer from the misconception that our thinking abilities depend on our Intelligence Quotient (IQ). But in reality, IQ is a limited parameter of assessing cognitive functioning for academic and work success, but they are not complete.

The general IQ Tests cover only logical-mathematical intelligence, but there are multiple types of intelligence. Howard Gardner described seven different types of intelligence in his writing (as listed below) that determine the success of any individual in different facets of one's life:

- Logical-mathematical
- Verbal-linguistic

- Spatial-mechanical
- Musical
- Bodily-kinesthetic
- Interpersonal-social
- Intrapersonal (self-knowledge)

There are many tests to assess the level of your intelligence, and one of them is the MIDAS test.

Finally, thinking with full brain entails tapping into the multiple intelligences of human beings instead of merely restricting your focus to logical or linguistic abilities.

Many different theories and research studies have been conducted about the brain's physical structure, but we can also examine the brain from an evolutionary perspective.

The two-hemispherical left-right brain concept was propounded by Robert Sperry and led him to win the Nobel Prize in medicine. While the left brain is more logical and rational, the right brain is more imaginative and instinctual.

In the 1960s, there was a study conducted by Paul Maclean; it looked at the brain from an evolutionary perspective and concluded that there are three major brain structures that have developed sequentially.

- Reptilian (instinctual) brain
- Mammalian or limbic (emotional) brain
- Primate or neocortex (thinking) brain

Regardless of whether we are looking at the physical structure or the evolutionary aspects of the brain, thinking in the brain happens in a very complex and non-linear manner.

Our brain is said to have 100 billion neurons, and all thinking is nothing but these different neurons firing with each other and making synaptic connections. These synaptic connections form a neural pathway that determines our thinking preferences.

Our brain is a powerful network of neurons that interact with each other across the brain. A specific type of thinking doesn't result from any specific part of the brain; each individual has different thinking preferences. The more you use a specific part of the brain, the more dominant that part becomes.

Ned Herrmann propounded the concept of the Four Quadrants of Thinking Preference and advocated the view that different people have different types of thinking preferences.

People choose to think in a particular way due to their preference, and it doesn't mean that they don't have the ability to think in a different manner; preference is not the same as competency.

Because of the Preference-praise loop, when people get praised for good work done in their area of preference, they develop that specific thinking preference further.

Understanding the different thinking patterns will help you deal with people of different thinking preferences and can make you a situationally holistic thinker.

Logical thinkers are observing and analyzing phenomena, reactions and feedback, and then drawing conclusions on that input.

You can develop your logical thinking abilities by following the effective strategies listed below:

• Learn to get rid of your confirmation bias and become open-minded. Follow multi-perspective thinking and take a look at the counterargument for every assumption. Look at a variety of opposing views about any specific situation, as that will empower you to make fine distinctions and help you improve your rational thinking.

• Get an outsider's perspective in difficult situations. Learn how an outsider will observe any specific situation; follow the "Revolving Door Test."

• Don't believe something because it sounds reasonable and because it's said by some person of authority. Examine all assumptions critically on your own before arriving at any conclusions or decisions.

• Avoid becoming trapped by the sunk cost fallacy: Don't justify your past mistakes and don't continue to make the same ones merely because it is what you have done in the past. Learn from the past and move forward.

- Learn a foreign language to look at things from a different perspective and get rid of the emotional bias associated with your own language.

- Exercise your mind by using memory-recall techniques. Do brain trainings; switch up your routine activities and engage in healthy debates with individuals who have a different viewpoint than yours on any given topic.

An organized mode of thinking enables you to make plans, create structures, and set up clear processes for doing all the smaller steps necessary to carry out the desired action.

You can use the 4-step process to organize your thoughts. Below are the four steps:

1. Document your thoughts.
2. Sort your thoughts.
3. Reframe your thoughts.
4. Prioritize your thoughts.

Following mind-mapping techniques helps you organize your thinking and enables you to holistically see the bigger picture. You can do mind mapping using simply a pen and paper, or you can use web applications or software to organize the scattered information in your brain, free your brain from clutter, and to perform a better analysis of the information that you have.

Both the compartmentalization and the prioritization of your thoughts are necessary for organized thinking. You can't organize any process or system unless you put them into different categories and assign timelines or deadlines to them.

You need to break the bigger information into small chunks, as they are easier to memorize and handle. You can start more quickly with smaller chunks of activities, and it gives you a good starting point to base your future analysis on.

The way that you organize your workplace or desk directly affects your thinking approach. If your desk is cluttered, you will find it difficult to organize your thinking. A study proved that people who had organized desks were better able to focus more on their work and got better results.

In the age of technology, you can effectively use various online tools and applications to organize your thinking and ideas.

The act of thinking is not merely a rational or logical approach; you need to also nurture the emotional and instinctual side of your brain.

An interpersonal thinking approach empowers you to connect with people more effectively and get results faster. The formula for getting results is as follows:

The higher the level of connection, the less that communication is needed, and the better the results. The lower the level of connection, the more communication is needed, and the results are less than optimal.

The following techniques can be used for developing interpersonal thinking:

Active Listening: You can build trust with the other people by following active listening skills to demonstrate concern using non-verbal cues, brief verbal affirmations, or disclosing similar experiences.

Make curiosity as a habit to develop empathy. Withhold your judgment of any individual, and display curiosity about their behavior.

Widen your circle by meeting new people and more people so that you can understand their concerns. You should especially meet people from other cultural or socio-economic groups than yours.

Reading literary fiction heightens your level of empathy for others, and thus, it develops your interpersonal thinking abilities.

Challenge yourself to have deeper conversations with your colleagues. When you deeply engage in conversation with someone, you understand the underlying emotions and feelings of the other person. You come to know and understand the key drivers or motivators that affect the person's behavior.

Creativity is intelligence having fun, as Albert Einstein said once.

Creative thinking is not limited to only some limited set of people, such as artists, musicians or writers. It's the most essential skill in the modern business world. Surveys taken by top CEOs worldwide show that creativity as one of the top skills that they are looking for in their talent.

Creativity emerges by way of synaptic connections between the neurons in the brain.

Graham Wallas suggested four steps to creativity in his writing, and Ned Herrmann further added two more steps to that. The six steps to creativity are:

1. Interest
2. Preparation
3. Incubation
4. Insights
5. Verification
6. Application

Ideas don't happen in a vacuum. Every new idea extends from the past and travels into the future through the present.

The Medici Effect states that there is an abundance of extraordinary new ideas to explore in the intersection of various fields, disciplines, and cultures.

Asking questions is one of the most effective ways to generate new ideas. You can use the SCAMPER method to direct your questions in a specific manner that will trigger your mind to produce ideas in a targeted way.

You can follow a few other techniques to generate ideas like the Magic Wand technique or the TLC (tempting, lacking, change) technique.

Before we start nurturing ideas, there are multiple idea killers that can stop the flow of ideas. You need to kill these idea killers before they start germinating.

Just like you exercise your physical muscles, you need to exercise your idea muscles as well. Setting up a daily idea quota will force your brain to produce more ideas.

If you want to generate a large number of ideas from a group of people, you can follow the Crawford slip writing method.

PART 2

MENTAL MODELS

INTRODUCTION

Mental models, at their most basic level, are an explanation of the thought process one has regarding the way things in the real-world work. The relationship between the various parts of what is being analyzed, along with one's own actions, feelings, consequences, etc., is taken into account to interpret potential consequences, outcomes, and more.

This is mostly a very detailed breakdown of a process that occurs quite organically and seemingly involuntarily. To keep track of mental models, analyze them, and change them is a very basic part of mastering your mental fortitude and eliminating the barriers that stand between you and what you want in life. When you think about what it is that keeps you from achieving the things you want in life, you will generally find that some combination of your mindset and external circumstances are what prevented success.

Knowing this, we take another step to unravel that mental process. The more factors of which we can take control of a situation, the more likely it is that we'll successfully emerge. That makes a good bit of sense, doesn't it? That's the aim of this writing and the information in it.

A mental model, simply put, is a representation of the simple mechanics on something. This is a very broad statement, but mental models are inherently broad, as you can apply a model to literally anything in life. It's impossible for us to keep every minute detail of everything we encounter in the world, so these models act to simplify the more complex aspects of life into more digestible and organizable units.

The nature and quality of our thought processes are proportional to the mental models we've identified and their suitability for the situation currently at hand.

The more models with which you're familiar, the more likely you are to be equipped to accurately understand and to deal with the situation in front of you. Most of us have a particular focus or specialization for the models we adopt, which is based on our personal and work experience. For example, someone who works in engineering might think of things in more of systematic way, while someone who deals with children for a large part of their day would think in terms of incentives or rewards. By pinpointing the type of mindset, we have and by systematically broadening our scope and arsenal of mental models, we can see things from a more panoramic perspective. By being able to do so, we eliminate the possibilities of blind spots forming in our thought process.

While nothing is guaranteed in life, there is still something to be said for understanding as much as we can about the human thought process, the patterns it follows, and how you can use that to improve your odds of success.

The term mental model dates back to 1943 when Kenneth Craik, in his writing The Nature of Explanation, indicated that children create mental models as a way of understanding the world around them. He further stipulated that humans hold small models of representations of reality that they use to make decisions, reason, and solve problems. Johnson-Laird, in 1983, also suggested that humans create models of their environment and use them in finding solutions to their problems.

Norman, another pioneer in the field of mental models, indicated that the internal representations that people create of the systems with which they interact provide them with an explanatory as well as a predictive capacity for understanding the interactions and systems they encounter. The common concept put forth by these pioneers was that models were an individual's interpretation of their experiences and environment and how these interpretations are applied to facilitate reasoning, explanations, decision-making, finding solutions to problems, and in the prediction of outcomes.

Mental models theory also looks at how mental models influence behavior. Gentner and Stevens (1983) indicated that models are useful tools in the understanding of human behavior. In 1984, Kieras and Bovair stipulated that highly experienced users who had complete knowledge and understanding the model of a device were more adept at using the device compared to those who did not have an associated model. Similarly, Fein, Olson, and Olson in 1993 found that individuals who acquired mental models were more efficient in using complex devices.

In 2002, Sloane reported that individuals with more than one model of internet surfing were found to use different methods to search for another internet. This implied that the more models the person had, the more options and methods they would have at their disposal in accomplishing various tasks. Mental model completeness was found to predict the trust level of users to an adaptive cruise control system in flight (Beggiato & Kriems 2013)

In 2002, Gentner found that the primary prediction method in mental models involved simulation. Simulating a model was found to predict the outcome of the interaction of the user with the system he was in contact with. It was found that by using stored knowledge, people could simulate future states of the particular system in question. These simulations result in the quick execution of actions that are reliant on preexisting knowledge. Using this preexisting knowledge was found to be related to automatic processing of information, which resulted in low effort actions that are predominantly based on procedural knowledge. On the other hand, mental simulations that rely on cognitive knowledge were found to be slow in execution.

The structure of mental models was found to be the basic foundation upon which behavior, beliefs, attitudes, and preferences are built. Wilson & Rutherford in 1989 found that mental simulations and predictions are determined by the structure and content of the mental model. Studies of people in the process of developing mental models have allowed researchers to develop an understanding of the process of model construction. Researchers identified that the construction of a model occurred in multiple stages, these are:

- Identification of the multiple components of the system and all the possible forms each of the components could take.

- Integrating the components into a model based on the relationships between them.

- Testing and running the model.

The rise of the popularity of video games has prompted research into the mental models of video games. Apart from entertainment, video games have been used for educational functions such as training of complex skills, improvement of cognitive aptitude as well as for rehabilitation of physical and mental handicaps. Playing complex games requires the use of procedural and predictive knowledge. Due to the differences in the games, players of multiple games are bound to transfer models from one game to another. The enormous amount of time spent playing video games has been found to result in the construction of a wide variety of mental models both in the experienced and non-experienced players.

However, the models in the experienced players were found to be more developed in terms of the density of networks and the level of abstraction.

There are plenty of writings on this subject on the market, thanks again for choosing this one! Every effort was made to ensure it is full of as much useful information as possible, please enjoy it!

CHAPTER 1
WHAT ARE MENTAL MODELS?

What are these mental models of which I speak? I'm glad you asked because mental models are the foundation of your entire reality. Understanding them is critical to understanding yourself and your life.

Most people take reality at face value. They assume that life is as they see it. But the reality of reality is that it is subjective, based on each person's unique perception and imagination. A lot of factors go into shaping one's reality. The result is that no two people see anything the exact same way.

This leads to a lot of conflict in the world, but it can also lead to people making poor decisions based on limited understandings of the reality before them. Mental models are what you use to read reality and a problematic one can certainly make your life harder because it prevents you from seeing reality with clarity.

A mental model is a representation of the human mind's thought process. Mental models are how we understand the world. Not only do they shape what we think and how we understand situations, but they drive our decisions and feelings. They lay the entire basis for our lives. What makes mental models tricky is that they are not just influenced by reality – but rather, they draw from a series of experiences, biases, and even a person's current mood. Shaped by culture, personal experiences, and background, they are as unalike as snowflakes from person to person. Two children raised in the same household will have two very different mental models, despite having similar backgrounds and the same culture.

Everything that a person sees, hears, and otherwise, senses are represented by mental models inside their minds. Mental models are used as scales by which a person automates decisions and internalizes external stimuli. The Internal scales, as mentioned by scientists, are ever-changing and unstable as the human mind is susceptible to change due to adaptation. They are also variable since every person has a different outlook and thus a different set of models.

Mental models use perception to drive reasoning and decisions. Obviously, this reasoning can be flawed at times. Every bit of reasoning you engage in is driven by your perception, no matter how erroneous it may be, as well as dozens or even hundreds of other factors that you may not be aware of.

For example, you may avoid spending time with someone who has a lot of tattoos because you were raised to believe that people with tattoos are lowlifes, but you are not aware of that bias and you simply dislike someone based on his body modifications. Meanwhile, another person would not have that bias because he was raised differently, so he has no problem hanging out with heavily tattooed people. Your mental model drives you to make a decision about a person that you may not even be consciously aware of.

Furthermore, mental models drive priorities. One woman may consider getting her hair and nails done every few weeks an utmost priority, while another woman does not consider those things necessary at all. Your mental model helps you rate things based on importance so that you can dedicate time, money, and energy to something that you consider worthwhile. Not everyone will agree with your priorities because everyone has a different rating system for importance in life.

Mental models are imperfect because they lack complete information. Obviously, you can't know everything and focus on everything in the world. You can only focus on a few tiny parts that fit into your accepted reality. Therefore, your lens of reality is quite narrow and yet it shapes many decisions that can be quite huge.

Think about this example: You support a certain political healthcare proposal because you recognize a few problems, probably problems that affect you personally somehow, with the current system. You vote thusly. However, other people disagree with your accepted healthcare model because they see different problems with the model that you cannot see from your perspective. Thus, you don't understand why people disagree with you and you feel frustrated.

Your mind will create a small-scale model with the evidence it currently possesses for each situation it encounters. This model will include predicted outcomes of each situation and each decision. Whether or not these outcomes are accurate is hard to say. Sometimes you are right; oftentimes, you are wrong.

Mental models are paradoxical. Some are quite fluid and change with time and experience. That is why you are a different person now than you were ten years ago, and twenty years ago, and so on. Over the course of your life, you begin to change mental models and adapt them to fit what you need from life. Yet, mental models are also incredibly rigid. Some stay with you for life. Others may be fluid, but your mind relies on them so heavily that it applies them to every area of life, even areas of life that don't benefit from the said mental model.

The takeaway here is that mental models can be changed and adapted to become more helpful. However, you must work hard on your mind to undo years of experience that has created the models. You must also perform some brutally honest introspection to uncover the true roots of certain thoughts and actions that you routinely engage in. You must be able to let your ego down for a second and say, "Hey, I'm not doing something right. I need to make a change."

Why is this mental work worthwhile? The fact is that your reasoning is not based on logic or rules, but rather on mental models. So, if you are operated on a bad mental model, you are depriving yourself of the ability to use logic to arrive at the ideal decision. Your decisions are influenced in a direction that may not be beneficial in the long run, even though you think they are great decisions. Learning to recognize mental models and focus on logic instead can help you make the best decisions for yourself.

Also, since mental models vary from person to person, what works for you may not work for anyone else. This is why your decisions can create a lot of negative conflict within your family, your relationship, or your team at work. Learning to depend less on mental models can help you arrive at good decisions for everyone involved. This can help you become a better spouse, parent, and leader. It can also help you remove the emotion from decisions, which in turn can lessen the pain of having to compromise on a decision. Since all relationships contain a lot of compromise, you will do better in life if you are able to accept compromise.

Unforced Errors

An unforced error is basically a mistake or bad decision that somehow harms you. In sports, the mistake is often attributed to your own failure, rather than the talent of the opponent. For example, if you goof at a tennis match, you may blame yourself for not playing the right way when really you were up against a better tennis player.

The fewer unforced errors you make in life, the better off you are. You can avoid making grave errors at work or in your family. You can avoid entering harmful relationships or losing lots of money. Basically, things are great in life when you make wise, informed decisions.

Mental models are designed to help you avoid unforced errors. By using a first bias model, people tend to operate on loss aversion, or basically preventing losses, rather than using their skills for the maximum potential benefit. Thus, most people have a built-in loss aversion model that drives them to make decisions in life, as represented by athletes' decisions in sports. This model is not ideal, however, as using your skills for maximum utility and focusing on making good decisions instead of minimizing losses is a better use of your energy.

Your brain has intuition, and nine times out of ten, that intuition is wrong. Many of our instincts no longer serve us, yet they run in the background, driving us to make decisions that don't make a lot of logical sense. It is wise to use your brain's intuition and mental models as a guide for life, not an instructional manual. If you have an intuitive response to a situation, be sure to check out your intuition with logic before committing to the decision.

Since the brain absolutely loves to formulate predictions, you often think that you know how something will go. You then base your decision off of that assumption to avoid an unforced error. However, life is seldom that predictable. Take your assumptions as hypotheses, not reality.

CHAPTER 2
40 MENTAL MODELS

Your mind has a large series of mental models for different situations. But it tends to resort to a certain one for each situation that it perceives as similar to one it has already encountered – even if the situation is actually entirely unprecedented. Cognitive biases explore some mental models that you default to in certain situations, which can pose challenges or lead to poor decisions.

I remember when I got my first post-grad job. Before, I had only worked in fast food, so my mind assumed my new job would be similar. Of course, I knew I wouldn't be flipping burgers, but I assumed the hierarchy and policies and stress would be the same. I entered the job with the wrong attitude as a result, and I was in for a rude awakening about what corporate life is really like. After the adjustment period, I loved it, but I think it would have been a lot easier had I not entered the job with a fast-food job mental model in my mind.

Here are some of the most common mental models that you use and how to recognize them. Most of these models are helpful in their own ways, though some can be restrictive. Learning to tell when you are using a model and how to adjust the model for maximum reward is crucial to a good life.

1. Inversion

The inversion mental model, though listed under the problem-solving category, is actually one of the most powerful tools in the mental model toolbox. The inversion method blossomed from the mathematical elements of German mathematician Carl Gustav Jacob Jacobi, who worked on elliptical functions. He would solve his problems with the following strategy: man, muss immer umkehren. This means "invert, always invert."

From that thought sprung, the inversion mental model used to show that you can't just look at your problems in one manner. In order to get the entire scope of a project, you have to look at it forward and backward. When you invert someone, it forces your mind to see it in a different light and to uncover truths about the problem or project you have at hand. Obviously, thinking about the exact opposite of the problem doesn't really come naturally to us, but some of the most brilliant people in history have solved problems doing just that.

Don't expect to always invert your problems and magically find the answers; it doesn't quite work like that. What it will do is give you another perspective to draw from, which will allow you to see problematic areas as well as clues toward the path you need to take in order to break through those problems.

Inversion is the process of taking a problem and flipping it upside down in order to see it from a new perspective. Instead of asking "what is the best way to do X?" You could invert the question by saying, "what is the worst thing I could do for X, and how do I avoid that?"

The premise is that it is easier to think about what you want to avoid, rather than what you want to achieve. Imagine you want to lose weight. A traditional goal might be, "I want to lose ten pounds." While this is somewhat specific, it doesn't give a roadmap for achievement. Instead, think about the problem in reverse, what are the things you are trying to avoid? Perhaps you don't want to get tired when playing with your kids, or you are trying to avoid diabetes. By reframing the problem, you can come up with more defined steps to reach your desired outcome.

By saying "I want to lose ten pounds" you have infinite options to get that result. You could do it through many different types of exercise programs, hundreds of different diets, or a combination of diet and exercise. As we covered earlier in the Paradox of Choice, if options are unlimited, they are more difficult to choose, and this makes you more likely to fail.

By reframing the question and looking at it through inversion, clearer options appear. If you don't want to get tired when playing with your kids, you probably need more exercise. Finding a program that will get you in shape for the level of activity you anticipate is far simpler than the all-encompassing goal of "lose some weight."If you are trying to avoid diabetes, a conversation with your doctor can probably provide all the information you need to get started on a healthier path.

When you have any trouble coming up with creative ideas, try doing the opposite. Come up with the worst possible solution, and then think of ways to avoid it.

2. First Principle

Using a first-principles approach to think basically refers to breaking down a process to its basic components and concepts. A first principle is a basic assumption that cannot be broken down any further. It involves looking at a situation at its foundation and starting from the known facts then building from these basics.

When we understand the first principles of a system, we can deconstruct it and then construct it again more effectively. These principles allow us to avoid imitations by not following what has already been created by others but allowing us to build our own systems and conclusion by deconstructing existing concepts then using the core elements to create something new.

3. Second-Order Thinking

Second-order thinking requires us to consider our actions, the immediate consequences of those actions as well as the long-term effects that are bound to arise as a result of the choices you make. The question, "and then what?" directs second-order thinking.

In a hypothetical situation where you are torn between finishing your assignment and going out with friends. When you weigh the options of staying in and finishing your paper or going out with your friends for a drink, going out would seem more gratifying. However, if you ask yourself "and then what" you would be likely to realize which of the two options might have negative consequences.

Thinking beyond the immediate outcome of a decision to the consequences is crucial in making decisions that have lasting positive effects and in ensuring that we are not destroyed from our long-term objectives.

4. Pareto Principle

Also known as the 80/20 rule is the Pareto principle, the law of the vital few and the factor sparsity principle. Ultimately, the rule states that you will see results of 20 percent for 80 percent of the effort exerted.

This principle is translated into a mental model for the use of searching for answers. Facts and information are a vital part of working through any mental model. To be more productive, you are simply searching for the vital few in the vast landscape of the trivial many. Information is almost infinite and might as well be when compared to how much our brains can hold. When searching for the specific information you need, you have to push aside the noise and find the vital few pieces that will help you work through your mental model.

These tasks can be completed for general improvement of productivity and for specific marked tasks. If you have a large project to work on, you can use this productivity mental model in order to get yourself on the right track, to clear away unneeded distractions within a workflow, and to minimize your outgoing tasks to those that bring the largest results.

5. Occam's Razor

Simply put, Occam's razor says that the simplest of answers is always the correct answer. We need to stop racking our brains, attempting to find complex solutions to problems and begin focusing on what actually works for it. This mental model is great for solving problems, but it is also good for drawing initial conclusions before the bulk of the facts or before certain information is brought into the picture.

Arthur Conan Doyle's "Sherlock Holmes," explained Occam's razor. He asserted that if you get rid of the impossible, the thing that remains - no matter how ridiculous, impossible, or even improbable - must be the truth.

Scientifically, studies have been conducted which have proved Occam's razor theory. The principle of minimal energy, a sector of the second law of thermodynamics, merely finds that the least amount of energy is used wherever possible. This concept is utilized in science, business, project management, problem-solving, and many more fields.

William of Ockham, a friar, philosopher, and theologian in the 14th century, didn't exactly theorize Occam's razor, but he was known for deducing, which helped the other writers develop the model.

It is used across the board to prove or disprove specific theories. Below are some examples of how

Occam's razor has been used in the past.

Scientific theories- Scientists use the model to decide whether a hypothesis is genuinely purposeful. If it is easy to be proven or falsified, this is usually a good start. The more complex the hypothesis is, the denser the facts have to become to justify the theory.

Medicine- Doctors use Occam's razor every time they see a patient. They attempt to find the fewest causes for multiple symptoms and the most likely cause of their ailment.

As with any model, always keep in mind that they are not 100 hundred percent fool-proof. That is why it is a process - a discovery through facts and theories - to find the correct answer. Always draw the conclusions you believe will fit best with the situation, and never be afraid to discredit the model if it doesn't fit in with the project at hand.

6. Hanlon's Razor

The principle of Hanlon's razor is built around focusing thoughts on finding solutions to a problem rather than finding fault or someone to blame for the existence of the problem. When we apply this principle to our reasoning and thinking process, we do not attribute bad situations to malice but rather to a lack of knowledge. Devoting energy and time to the paranoid pursuit of people to blame for bad situations means that we do not focus on the solution.

7. Eisenhower Matrix

The Eisenhower Matrix was introduced by Dwight D. Eisenhower. This is an effective time management mental model that was used by Eisenhower during his sensational career. He is best known for being the 34th President of the United States. Eisenhower served two terms beginning in 1953 to 1961.His immense success was attributed to the Eisenhower Matrix box that he often used to manage tasks and time. With this model, one can effectively handle what should be done at the right time.

Eisenhower once pointed out that "What is important is seldom urgent and what is urgent is seldom important." In line with his quote, effective time management centers around knowing how to differentiate between important tasks and urgent tasks.

When using the Eisenhower matrix, you should start by classifying your tasks according to their urgency and importance. In this regard, tasks that are urgent and important should be handled immediately.

Important, but not urgent tasks can be scheduled to be done at a later period. Tasks can be delegated, which are urgent but unimportant. Other people who have the right skills for the job can be employed in these tasks. Finally, tasks which are neither urgent nor significant should be eliminated.

8. The Map Is Not the Territory

We have all used maps at one point in our lives. The basic thing that we understand about maps is that they are a mere abstraction of reality. They are not the reality of what the actual land looks like. So, the map is not the territory. This mental model was introduced by Alfred Korzybski, a mathematician, in 1931.There are certain limitations that a map has. The mere fact that it represents a reduction of the actual territory means that other important details are missing. That's not all, to understand a map, it requires interpretation. This paves the way for mistakes. Another flaw in a map is that it could represent a territory that has already changed.

When you think about this model critically, you will understand that the perceptions you have in your mind are not the reality of how things are. Your mind can take you on a wild ride and create maps of reality. This means that if you believe that these perceptions are true, you stand to suffer.

You will create problems for yourself simply because we are inclined to believe what we think is in line with our beliefs. Therefore, by creating maps of reality within ourselves, we distort our minds from accepting reality. In the end, you will make decisions based on your perceptions and not reality.

The best thing that you can do is to treat maps just as maps. They are not reality in any way. Therefore, they shouldn't define how you think. Using this mental model, you should realize that your perceptions are just mere perceptions and nothing more. Recognize them and learn how to effectively see things as they are.

Evidently, from the discussion of mental models, there are plenty of models that you can use to supercharge your thinking. The best part is that you don't have to focus on mastering one single model. Instead, you should strive to understand how each works to help you think critically. One mental model can supercharge others. This means that your understanding of a particular model can help you gain a firm grasp of how you should think and live your life. In line with this, you shouldn't be rigid to change. Try your level best to find your circle of competence and stick within it.

Successful people are using these models to make their lives easier. This is because they understand that we live in an uncertain world. As a result, the best way of reducing this complexity is by relying on mental models to help you cognize how you should think.

9. Circle of Competence

The circle of competence is not a complicated model in the least. It states that some people have acquired a bank of useful knowledge in certain areas of the world through experience or study. Some of these areas are understandable by almost everyone, while others require a specialty. Buffett believes that you don't necessarily need all the knowledge of a specialist to invest in the more complicated fields. What you do want to do is have a very good grasp of what you are knowledgeable about and stick to that circle. The circle will widen, though slowly.

The circle of competence doesn't just apply to business and investments but covers every aspect of your life. Moreover, if you want to improve that life, find your circle of competence and operate within its walls. One of Buffett's other well-known mental models was the 2-List Strategy.

10. Homeostasis

Homeostasis is also known as "equilibrium," a term coined by Walter Bradford Cannon in 1926. However, the person to initially create the concept was French physiologist Claude Bernard almost 60 years beforehand. Bernard described the problem as such:

Homeostasis is the property of a system in an organism in which a variable, such as a substance's concentration in solution, is actively regulated to remain almost constant. Each of these variables is regulated by a separate regulator or homeostatic system, sustaining life together. Bernard, (1865)

This type of mental model is used in biology on a regular basis.

There are literally hundreds of other mental models out there, but we have highlighted some of the most used models. A few other models include the atomic theory, leverage, power laws, critical mass, relativity, and velocity. While using mental models, you must be thorough and knowledgeable. Sometimes, when in a hurry or in a frustrated mood, a cognitive bias can work its way up to the front of your mind.

11. Evolution by Natural Selection

Mental Model in Biology.

Historical Background

The concept of evolution has long been introduced before Charles Darwin and his fateful voyage to Madagascar. What elevates the theory of Darwin is the evolutionary mechanism called natural selection. Through this, he was able to explain how certain organisms manage to adapt better with their respective environments compared to the others.

Darwin reached his concept of natural selection through the following key observations:

- Offspring are often produced beyond the number that can be reasonably sustained by their environment. As a result, competition arises over the limited resources available.

- Offspring that belong to the same generation vary from one another depending on the traits each has inherited from the parent.

From these observations, Darwin arrived at the following conclusions:

- Within a given population, certain organisms would inherit key traits that would make them more effective in terms of survival and reproduction compared to the other organisms of the same species who did not receive the same set of traits.

- Because organisms with the helpful traits produce more offspring, and because these helpful traits are heritable, there will be more organisms bearing these helpful traits, thus making the traits more common within their generation.

- As time goes by, succeeding generations would be able to better adapt to the environment, making them more successful than their parents were at survival and reproduction.

The model of evolution that Darwin developed allowed him to make sense of the patterns that he had observed during his trip. For example, different species of Galapagos finches share certain traits because they also share the same ancestors. However, if a certain group of organisms became isolated from the rest for several generations, that particular group develops a distinct set of traits that allowed them to survive and thrive in the environment of the island where they can be found. As a result, beaks of different shapes and sizes can be observed among the distinct species of finches that live in different islands of Madagascar.

Over the course of multiple studies conducted on Darwin's theory, experts on this mental model have managed to boil down its prerequisites into the following:

1. Replication - The ability to create new copies with a high level of fidelity with the immediate source.

2. Mutation - The ability of the said copies to change in a slight, but potentially significant ways.

3. Fitness - Copies should be able to persist and reproduce at various rates.

When all three elements are present, you can expect the copies to survive and multiply with a high level of success. Copies that lack any of the given elements are likely going to die off, eventually.

Evolution by Natural Selection in Action

Over the years, Darwin's model of evolution by natural selection has gained popularity and massive support from the different communities. It should be noted, however, that not everything is capable of undergoing this process of evolution. To better understand this concept, there are some common answers of people when asked about the things that can evolve:

1. As evidenced by archaeological findings, homo sapiens has beat out other species, including Neanderthals and apes, among others. Believing that this is an evidence of evolution, however, is inaccurate. Following the three elements required for something to evolve, replication is absent in this particular case. You might counter this by saying that humans replicate themselves by mating and producing children. Again, this is false because parents do not reproduce high-fidelity versions of themselves.

The children will inherit certain traits from the mother and the father, but they will never be nearly exact copies of one or the other.

The correct answer, in this case, is that the human genes evolve. These are the building blocks of human evolution. Genes can replicate themselves over and over – with a small likelihood of undergoing mutation in the process.

2. Biological evolution is often the foremost example that comes to mind for most people. However, when analyzed carefully, cultural evolution also undergoes natural selection. First proposed by Joseph Henrich, the idea that human culture also evolves following similar patterns as genes do seem implausible. Upon closer examination, however, the three elements of evolution by natural selection are present whenever there is a shift in human culture.

In terms of replication, humans are natural at mimicking the behaviors of others, even without fully understanding the rationale behind the said action. By studying the ways of the people they admire or respect, people are able to replicate with high fidelity certain aspects of other people's behaviors. Mutation plays a part because even though humans have high levels of skill when it comes to copying others, it is impossible to be perfect at all times. There are also instances where the initial copy is already wrong in some way, so when it gets replicated, the imperfection is passed on to more people.

The fitness of cultural behaviors is evident because humans only tend to mimic behaviors that they find beneficial or pleasing. Otherwise, the behavior will eventually die down until no one else would ever remember how to do it and why it was done in the first place.

Given these, one can argue that cultural practices are evolving by natural selection. A group's language, rituals, religions, and special tools are all part of the culture, and can, therefore, evolve as they get passed on to the younger generation.

How Evolution by Natural Selection Can Improve Your Mental Models

There are various ways on how you can apply the principles of evolution by natural selection into your day-to-day life. First, you may be able to better assess the likelihood of success and longevity of the system you are creating by examining it against the core tenets of evolution by natural selection. Does your system provide opportunities for faithful replication? Is there an allowance for positive mutation? Does it exhibit signs of fitness? Answering yes to all of these questions is a good indicator that you are on the right track.

12. System 1 and System 2

So, what happens when I ask you what 1 + 1 is? Did you notice that you did not struggle, but the mind just gave you the answer? You did not even think about it. Let us see what will happen if I ask you what is 37 multiplied by 40? Not unless you are a genius, I am sure you need a calculator just like I do. In such a sum, you need to involve your reflective brain. Our reflexive brain is fast and concludes quickly while our reflective brain is slow and needs effort. Daniel Kahnemann names these two models as system one and system 2 for reflexive and reflective, respectively. Our system 1 operates with no effort, and it is quick. System 2 gives effort to the activities that require it and subjects it to concentration. These two do not exist in reality, but they are just models to help us understand our brain. These two systems are awake active every time you are awake; system 1 works automatically, while system 2 is in a comfortable and effortless mode. Our routine actions such as reading, talking are driven by system one, and system two only comes to play when you are encountered with something complex. This arrangement in our brain works well because system 1 does a good job, but on the downside, it is overconfident, and it sometimes does not delegate some decisions to system two, thereby creating errors. These errors are known as biases. Let us look at this diagram and read the words in them loudly.

Did you notice any error? I know you didn't, but it is okay because not so many noticed it. In our first triangle, the word 'the' was written twice; in the second triangle, the word 'a' is repeated twice, and in the third triangle as well, the word 'the' is also repeated. What happened that made you not realize the mistake? Reading is automatic and does not require any effort. Remember, we mentioned that our system 1 is overconfident, and in a hurry to read the sentence, it overlooks small mistakes. If you pay attention, you will engage your system two, and you will perform better because your system two get disrupted if there is no attention.

System 2

System 2 is slow, infrequent, calculating, and effortless. What can it help you to do in life?

- It helps a person to stay ready before a sprint.
- It diverts your focus on the circus clowns.
- It makes you focus on the loud person at a party.
- It is responsible when you notice a woman with grey hair.
- It retrieves a sound from your memory for recognition.
- It helps you to maintain a faster pace than your normal rate.
- It concludes whether a behavior is appropriate or not in a social gathering.
- It is responsible for enabling you to count the letter 'a's' in a specific text.
- It is responsible for retrieving your number from your memory to give it to someone else.
- Do you know how difficult it is to park in a tight parking space? Well, system 2 helps you to do that.
- System 2 boosts of helping you to find out the price and quality ratio of two products.
- It helps you to solve complex calculations.

As we mentioned earlier, system two is the deliberate, rational, and analytical side of your brain. It is glued by the search of logic and more past information obtained through experiments and learning. System 2 processes data slowly and carefully by applying rules consciously, making the procedure to be demanding, but the outcome is better decisions. This system is usually engaged in case of uncertainties, complexities, or when you have ample thinking time, and the outcome has no margin for errors required. As slow and effortful as our system two is, it is not error-free. System two is not reliable when it is being used alone because it may slow down the process. This system relies on experience, which is not mean the outcome will be better performance. After all, experience devoid of feedback can breed faulty thinking.

Cognitive Reflection Test is designed to measure a person's ability to switch to system 2. Shane Frederick explains that in CRT, there are three easy items because they can be understood when explained but to answer the tests, you need to come up with answers that come to mind at once. In this study, he explains that as we proceed to answer questions from the third one, we reduce the use of our intuition. It is also biased because it states that male participants performed better. Judges in the US have used CRT. They are said to use intuition to get clues that lead them to a decision that they later change to logic. This study showed that only two out of three judges gave thought through answers to the three questions. This confirmed that the remaining judges relied on system 1 to make decisions. These decisions are not a general conclusion on how judges make their judgments in court, but it is important to make the judges aware of their thinking and regulate it, especially system two, that can expose their biases.

13. Fight or Flight

Overcoming difficult situations. Everyone is faced with a challenging situation where they have no choice but to act to resolve or mitigate a solution. This can be anything from a tight deadline at work to coping with an unpleasant person or stressful event where we find ourselves in a "fight or flight" response mode. Think of at least three situations where you were confronted with such a situation and how you were able to successfully navigate through it. Getting through such an occurrence doesn't have to be heroic, such as saving someone from a car accident or verbally confronting a bully. It can be as simple as facing fear and using techniques, such as deep breathing, to remain calm until you find inner calm.

14. Opportunity Cost

Accomplishing one thing implies not having the option to do another. We live in a universe of exchange offs, and the idea of chance cost controls all. Most appropriately outlined as "there is nothing of the sort like a free lunch."

Each decision comes at the expense of another. For example, if you choose to send messages after lunch, you can't utilize that opportunity to compose a feature for your blog. On the other hand, if you seek after one huge, leading media campaign, you won't have the data transfer capacity or the hazard resistance to seek after another simultaneously. Always take note of this mind each time you're choosing what to do. Ask yourself what other options you have. On that option, decide if you are willing to let it go.

15. Margin of Safety

An extension may hypothetically deal with as much as 15,000 pounds, yet it is advisable to put a limit of 14,000 for the allowed weight. It would be a significant fiasco if the scaffold wasn't that solid and the hazard isn't justified, despite any potential benefits. What we can say about the margin of safety is that it is simply the possibility that we should leave space for slip-ups or disappointments. For example, when making your site's transformation objectives, you probably won't consider a down-loaded digital writing a lead until they've reacted to a subsequent email or looked for more data from you, just if they alter their thoughts and consider something else. Think about this model as a security net. It's smarter to be charmingly amazed than legitimized.

16. Bayesian Thinking

The Bayesian method is a theory-based on statistics where probabilities express the level of belief in the occurrence of an event. When this principle is applied to thoughts, it involves is a thought considering all probable outcomes and scenarios. When we add new data onto the pre-existing probabilities and update them, we create a more realistic expectation and can thus make decisions based on the expected outcomes. Constantly updating our field of probabilities means that we can create more realistic simulations of scenarios and possible outcomes. We can then use this insight to make decisions that are in alignment with the desired outcome.

17. Entropy

"You can't unscramble an egg."

Entropy says that over time certain irreversible processes happen that cannot be undone. It also says without expending energy, things tend to become more disordered. Dealing with others can be seen through the lens of entropy in several ways. There are ways that you can treat others that can cause permanent damage and are irreversible. If you do something terrible to someone, don't expect them to help you in the future. Keeping this idea in mind can help you avoid potential mistakes. As we all know, the arrow of time only points in one direction, so actions you take now have future consequences.

Maintaining relationships takes energy. Over time if you don't keep in touch, friendships break down and erode. I haven't spoken to my college roommate in over two years, even though we used to live together and were best friends. Without expending energy, the entropy increased.

When relationships break down, they can take more energy to fix if repair is even possible. Understanding that as time progresses, entropy in any system will continue to increase is a helpful perspective to understand your dealing with others.

18. Antifragility

Advanced by Nassim Taleb, the sliding size of delicacy, strength, and antifragility alludes to the responsiveness of a framework to incremental negative inconstancy. A delicate framework or article is one in which extra negative inconstancy has an excessively negative effect, similarly as with an espresso mug breaking from a 6-foot fall, however accepting no harm by any means (instead of 1/sixth of the harm) from a 1-foot fall. A vigorous framework or item will, in general, be unbiased to the extra antagonism inconstancy, and obviously, an antifragile framework benefits: If there were a cup that got more grounded when dropped from 6 feet than when dropped from 1 foot, it would be named antifragile.

19. Newton's Laws of Motion

Isaac Newton has been credited with giving us a term that explains why we do not fall off of the earth. He was able to think critically and develop the reason that we experience gravity. He tested everything and was relentless and rigorous with his testing. As a critical thinker, and a man who was known to test every option, it is safe to assume that there were mental models that he was using in order to make sense of the world.

20. Algorithms

An algorithm is an automated set of rules defining a series of steps or procedures that result in the desired outcome. It is stated in the form of If- then statements. Algorithms are widely used in computing but are also evident in biological systems.

21. Compounding

It has been said that Einstein called a worldly wonder a compounding. He was probably not, but that is a wonder. Compounding is the process through which we add interest to a fixed amount, which then earns interest on the sum before and on the new interest added, and then earns interest on that amount, and so on ad infinitum. It is not a linear or additive effect, but an exponential effect. Money is not the only compounding thing; ideas and relationships do likewise. Compounding is always subject to physical limits and diminishing returns in tangible realms; intangibles can compound freer. Compounding also leads to money's time value, which underlies all modern finance.

22. Thought Experiment

"Consider some hypothesis, theory, or principle for the purpose of thinking through its consequences."

Thought experiments are useful in our everyday lives because by using this mental model, we are able to look at what the consequences are for one decision as applied to different hypothetical situations. Asking ourselves questions that allow us to explore the consequences of our actions is important. When we use thought experiments, some practical applications would include:

- Challenging what is commonly accepted by looking for the flaws in any argument, and to challenge any belief that me being misrepresented.

- To push the boundaries for any fact that has been considered established and could perhaps are incorrect.

- To predict the future or explain past decisions, situations, or events.

- Two bring about a decision, choice, or strategy. This allows you to weigh your options and look at the different information in order to make a decision.

- You use this mental model to solve problems, or you can use it to brainstorm ideas.

- Bring about any success that you had in the past and repeat those same successes.

- And to avoid any past failures in the future.

23. Probabilistic Thinking

This mental model is something that we can use to look at any particular outcome that may happen. This is considered to be one of the best tools that we can have in our mental model toolbox that can greatly improve the accuracy of any decisions that we are making. Our world is one where there is an infinite number of factors that are complex and will affect our decisions. With probabilistic thinking we are able to look at what the most likely outcomes are going to be because of this, we are able to be then more effective with our decisions as well as getting a more precise outcome.

Under this mental model is something called the fat-tailed processes, which simply mean that when the outcomes are distributed, they sometimes have a longer or a larger tale that is going to look at any events that are kind of on the outer edges of the actual distribution? Because the risk can be greater with this strategy, the fact tail is effective to look at the negative side. Our social world is said that tail due to the fact that it is normally attributed.

24. Game Theory

Game theory is applicable to a broad range of relations and is currently used as an umbrella term for the science of logical decision making in people, computers, and even animals. Game theory can be traced back to the 1930s, but the 50s were when it was extensively developed by scholars. In the 1970s, it was put into motion in biology but is now thought of as a very important tool in several different fields of study.

The games must always include specific elements. You need to have a player in the game, the actions available to them, the information available to them, and the payoff for the action. All of these can be internalized and thought about in a strategic mental view.

25. Leverage

Many innovations in engineering have been based on the principle of leverage. Leverage is a principle that is used to identify means by which heavy loads can be lightened and, in effect, make work easier.

26. Maslow's Hierarchy of Needs

Maslow's hierarchy of needs is a concept that was introduced by psychologist Abraham Maslow. According to Maslow, people are more motivated to meet their basic needs as compared to other needs such as safety, self-esteem and self-actualization. With the help of this mental model, people can garner a firm grasp on what motivates people. This theory postulates that people are self-driven because they yearn to meet particular needs.

Maslow's concept is often depicted in a pyramid with the lowest steps showing the most basic needs that will motivate people. Higher levels of the pyramid indicate complex needs. Naturally, people will strive to meet their psychological needs before doing anything else. These needs include food, water, sex, sleep, etc.

The second level of Maslow's pyramid from the bottom indicates safety needs. In reality, this need is more complex as compared to food and water. People desire to live in safe environments. As such, they will work hard to make sure that they are financially stable. Similarly, their safety also touches on their motivation to live healthy lives. As people work to meet these needs, they push themselves to adopt certain behaviors. For instance, they look for jobs, save their money and shift to safe neighborhoods.

On the third tier, you will find love/belonging. This level features social needs, such as the desire to be loved and accepted. Here, human behavior is mainly motivated by emotional relationships. For people to meet their social needs, they want to have friends and family around them. In addition, they will want to be associated with other social groups in their community. Bearing this in mind, meeting these needs helps people to avoid common social problems such as anxiety, depression, and loneliness.

This level in the hierarchy shows esteem needs. Maslow pointed out that people look for respect and admiration. Once people have met their basic and social needs, self-esteem desires begin to take shape. For that reason, people will want their individual efforts recognized and appreciated.

At the top level of the pyramid lies self-actualization needs. These are the needs where people aspire to be the best in their worlds. Accordingly, this need is met when people utilize their talents or any potential at their disposal.

Recognizing that people are motivated by different needs can help us to understand why they choose to behave in a certain way. For instance, some folks will be motivated to meet their love needs. As such, we can learn how to relate to them desirably.

27. Activation Energy

Activating energy is a concept from chemistry, which means the minimum amount of energy needed to initiate a chemical reaction. Often, I don't "feel" like doing something, like working out, but I force myself to do it and I don't need to deplete my willpower to keep going once I hit a certain point.

28. Illusion of Control

The illusion of control is a tendency for humans to believe that they can control or at least influence outcomes over which they have no demonstrable influence.

The predominant paradigm in unrealistic perceived control research has been the 'illusion of control' by Ellen Langer (1975).

29. Parkinson's Law

If you have ever had a school assignment with a deadline in the distant future, you already understand Parkinson's first law.

Cyril Northcote Parkinson was a British bureaucrat in the mid-1900s.His "Laws" are derived from an article he wrote in The Economist in 1955, explaining how the British bureaucracy grew every year, regardless of the amount of work that needed to be (or was actually) done. In addition to the first law mentioned above, he also posited two others:

"Expenditure rises to meet income," and "Expansion means complexity, and complexity decay."

While Parkinson was using these laws to describe giant government functions, they are equally applicable to everyday life. Let's discuss each in turn and how they can be used as beneficial mental models.

The first law shows that regardless of how long you have to complete a task, the task will take all of the available time. In some ways, this is contradictory to Hofstadter's Lawearlier. Assuming the task CAN be completed in the allotted time, then any additional time assigned to it is superfluous.

To take advantage of this law you need to figure out how much time is actually needed for a task, and then assign only that amount. Setting hard deadlines (often before something is actually due to be completed) compresses work time and can yield better results. I can remember college papers I wrote the night before they were due (after ignoring them for weeks) as being some of my best work.

The second law, dealing with spending rising to meet earnings, can be seen anytime a person gets a raise at work. I currently earn much more than I did in my early 20's, but my spending has also gone up to match. One way to combat this is to understand what is happening. If you have a goal to save money, make a rule to put away a certain percentage of any increase in earnings automatically. Since the percentage of the increased pay is never realized in your bank account, it will not be missed.

The third law, "Expansion means complexity, and complexity decay," can be seen as a function of entropy, which we have tackled already. The larger something is, the more complex it becomes. The more complex something is, the more effort is required to maintain it.

This law can be looked at in two ways. First, if you keep adding complexity to your life or business, it will eventually begin to collapse. Or secondly, if you do continue to add complexity, expect to have to invest an equally large amount into maintenance to avoid decay.

Let's look at an example to demonstrate the 2nd and 3rd laws. Imagine you win the lottery tomorrow and you have always wanted to have a giant yacht. You were never able to afford a yacht before, but now it is within your means. You buy the yacht, but it is too big for you to drive, so you have to hire a captain. The engines require constant work, so a mechanic is also needed. You're too rich to wash it yourself, so a crew is hired. Now, in addition to the cost of the yacht, you also have a staff you need to pay in order to use it and keep it in good condition. Your expenses have expanded, and so has the level of complexity. If you suddenly lost all of your money and were unable to sell the yacht, it would quickly fall into disrepair.

Most people never understand that they will take all the time given to complete a task, spend up to (and often beyond) their income, and increase complexity until it comes to the point of collapse. By understanding these simple models, it makes it easier to explain poor allocations of time and financial resources.

30. Scarcity Bias

Human beings have a clear tendency against scarcity. We falsely believe that scarce things are valuable, and that plentiful ones are not.

The human mind is quite funny sometimes. The harder it appears for us to get something, the more we want that thing. Scarcity in economics is a problem of having unlimited human wants in a world with limited resources. This means that society doesn't have enough resources to satisfy human needs and wants.

What fuels scarcity is fear. As humans, we are highly motivated by the fear of losing, more so than the desire to gain. With more than half of the world's population experiencing fear of scarcity, this technique can drive consumer behavior and it may even be the drive behind our love for social media.

The trick here is, how do you create scarcity without waiting for fate to decide in your favor? Let us use the cosmetics provider, Chanel, as an example. By producing a limited number of seasonal colors of its well-known, expensive nail polish, the company has been able to drive more than enough sales season after season.

Amazon, infomercial giant QVC, Expedia, and many others have employed this technique by displaying quantity countdowns ("5 items to go", "only 10 left in stock", or almost sold out"). They even use it in a way that you will be triggered to get it instantly. For example, by telling consumers to pay instantly if they want the product delivered in 24 hours.

This technique is similar to that of the rule of reciprocity. By offering free trials, you will be playing on the loss aversion, which will, therefore, bring scarcity. The customers will be able to see and experience your product and services firsthand. Once they become attached to it, it is more likely for them to pay for the use of that product after a trial ends because they wouldn't want it taken away from them.

31. Social Proof

People are one of numerous social animal categories, alongside honeybees, ants, and chimps, among some more. We have a DNA-level sense to look for security in larger groups and will search for social direction of our conduct. This nature makes a strong feeling of participation and culture, which would not generally be conceivable but rather likewise drives us to accomplish absurd things if our gathering is doing them too.

32. Hyperbolic Discounting

Hyperbolic discounting states that in a way that is irrational, people prefer earnings sooner. If the payoff in the future is greater than the more immediate payoff, depending on the 'time gap' we opt for the more distant payoff. Those more distant payoffs, however, get less weight than should be the case. To put it another way, we tend to trade-off present and future tradeoffs incorrectly.

33. Dunning Kruger Effect

Have you ever met someone who knows everything about nothing? This person may not be a mechanic, but because he performed an oil change once, he fancies himself an expert on cars. Or he may not be a doctor, but because he Googles everything, he thinks he knows better than doctors.

This is the Dunning-Kruger Effect at play. It is a bias where you see things too simplistically when you lack information, so you think that you know everything about the subject. On the other hand, if you know a lot about something, you tend to have less confidence in your knowledge out of caution. It is best to never assume that you are an expert at anything. No matter how advanced you are in a field or a line of work, there is always more to learn. You can avoid making mistakes and looking like a fool by not pretending to know things you don't.

34. The Boiling Frog

Blaming and allowing what someone did in the past to destroy the present is a fast recipe for boiling frog syndrome. Some people say that grudges have a life of their own, but nothing could be further from the truth. In actuality, grudges, like viruses, need to live inside a host organism in order to survive. Unfortunately, in the case of grudges, the host organism is us!

Few things in life suck as much energy from us as holding a grudge. Unfortunately, they are incredibly common. Some grudges last so long that they spread throughout entire families and are passed down through generations – long after anyone can even remember what caused them in the first place. One thing is for sure, though – if you are in a Grudge Match, you are blaming someone else for the problem! A grudge is a sure sign of Blameopathy.

Action Plan

Instead of passing blame ...take responsibility

Truthfully, it's challenging to stop this destructive behavior cold turkey – but here's how. Any time you find that you are pitying yourself and saying, "It's not my fault!" realize that you are experiencing Blameopathy. The lesson is that you have the power to take responsibility for your own actions. Here are some everyday examples.

Instead of blaming slow drivers or red lights for your late appointment:

Admit to yourself that you should have known to leave for the appointment earlier and commit to doing so in another chance.

Instead of blaming your weight on your schedule:

Plan to exercise regularly and eat a healthier diet.

Instead of pinning the blame for a bad day on others:

Realize that you are responsible for thinking positively and making every day a good one. No one has the right to get in the way.

A large part of not blaming others for your circumstances is realizing that many times you may be at fault – yes, that would be you. Get over it.

Instead of dwelling on the negative aspects, realize that you have the power to change too.

If you are involved in a Grudge Match, it is up to you to end it. Make a peace offering. Tell the other person that you want to put a stop to the whole thing and do something nice for them. Take him or her out to dinner or to an activity they enjoy, such as a round of golf or a theatrical production. Apologize – but don't try to rehash the entire event. Don't expect an apology in return. Be the bigger person if necessary. And be persistent. You'll be amazed at how much tension resolving a grudge can take out of your life.

When you have an attack of Blameopathy, change your reaction. Instead of blaming others, take the responsibility (even if it wasn't completely your fault!) Then decide how you will change that circumstance. It's an empowering exercise and a valuable approach to living each day to the fullest. Same goes for putting an end to a "Grudge Match." Unilaterally and blamelessly put an end to it. Don't demand anything from the other party or parties. In time, that hot water will cool way down.

35. Halo Effect

The halo effect is the tendency to judge private properties by a general impression. This cognitive distortion is devotedly explained in the writings of F. Rosenzweig "Halo Effect." Vivid examples of the halo effect are given by sports passion. Suppose a football team lost an important match. The price of one goal is to reach the final of the World Cup. As the game progressed, the team attacked a lot, there were strikes to the post, but the ball did not hit the goal. It is clear that after the game, the thunder of criticism falls on the players, the coach, the leadership of football in the country, the domestic championship, etc. Imagine that the case at this time would be more supportive and the ball would have hit the goal rather than the post. Players turn out to be heroes, the coach is a genius, etc. Losing/winning is not just a halo, it is a thick paint covering a lot of subsequent judgments in black/pink.

According to Rosenzweig, even professionals, researchers of the experience of successful companies, are affected by the halo effect. The success factor becomes a pink halo, painting internal processes and company's market success in good colors – no worse than winning a football team. "Very often the fact that we, managers, journalists, scientists, consider the reason for the company's success, is, in fact, a property attributed to it due to the results shown by it," Rosenzweig concludes.

36. Relativity

This theory has multiple applications in different contexts in physics. The most widely used concept from this law, however, is the fact that an individual is incapable of fully comprehending a system of which they are part.

A person in a plane may not physically feel the motion of the plane, but an observer can observe the movement that is occurring.

Similarly, in personal situations, when a person is in the middle of an event or situation, they cannot judge it from an objective perspective because they are immersed in it and can only see it from one perspective. To objectively judge a situation, we must first remove ourselves from it on a mental level and access it from an observer's point of view.

37. Proximate vs. Root Cause

Let's take a seven-year-old as an example for this mental model. When he tugs at your pant leg or follows you around the kitchen island asking, "Why? Why? Why," until he's satisfied, he's using the mental model Proximate Versus Root Cause. If he asked you why you're hiding in the kitchen instead of hanging out in the living room with the rest of the family, and you gave him a "distal cause," (an answer that's correct but isn't the exact reason why), he will continue to ask until the "root cause" (the exact heart of the issue) is found.

38. Convergent Thinking vs. Divergent Thinking

Convergent thinking is about the convergence of data and facts from different sources and the application of logic or knowledge to solve the problem or make an informed decision. It is about putting various pieces or perspectives of a topic back together in a logical manner to find an answer to the problem. A common example of convergent thinking is deductive reasoning that the popular fictional detective Sherlock Holmes often used to solve mysteries. By accumulating different pieces of information, he could easily put together puzzles and then come up with a logical answer to solve the mystery.

Divergent thinking is about breaking down a topic or pulling it apart to explore different components present within to generate new ideas and solutions. When convergent thinking is often inwards, diverging thinking always outwards, it is a creative process to develop unique and original ideas to find a solution to an existing problem.

39. Anchoring

Anchoring is a cognitive bias that occurs when focusing too much on a single piece of information. You hear one fact and put your blinders on, rendering yourself ignorant to the rest of the picture at hand. Disallowing as much information as possible from entering your problem-solving is a disservice to yourself.

However, if you're aware that you are typically subject to this cognitive bias, you are more likely to recognize when you're putting it into place. It's easily fixable to expand your horizon to allow more information in. Often times, this will also make it easier for you to solve the problem because you can see the entire picture.

Few things are more frazzling than popping a tire and ending up on the side of the road, especially if you lack the necessary tools to change the tire, or even the spare tire itself. In this situation, you could feel yourself slipping into despair, concentrating on how you, stranded by yourself, are going to get this tire fixed.

However, if you just read and remember thinking about the anchoring cognitive bias, you might allow yourself to sit back on your heels and take a breath. You might realize that this situation requires a little bit more creativity and information than you're currently allowing through your blinders.

Before learning about anchoring, you might have walked up the street three miles in your business casual attire and muscled a spare tire all the way back to your car to wrangle it on your own. But now, you hear Munger tsk-ing in your head, telling you that your pride and your thirst for brilliance is allowing more room for failure. Now you are enabled to recognize your cognitive bias and usher in creativity.

Instead, you could take in more information: maybe after inspecting the tire further, you realize it's just a nail. Looking across the street, you realize further that there is a gas station where you could put more air in your tire to get it to the tire shop up the street. Once you're at the tire shop, the mechanics can replace (or maybe even patch) your tire. Another option would be to call a friend or a family member and have them (and all their unique mental models) come to help you out so you can figure it out together. There are so many more solutions when all the information is allowed to come into play.

40. Confirmation Bias

Another cognitive bias that may get in the way of your mental model work is the confirmation bias. This bias is in use when you have a preconceived idea about something, and you walk into the situation to gather the information that will confirm the idea you created before you ever came into contact with the situation.

In other words, you decide what you want to see, and then you see what you want to see. Confirmation bias comes into play all the time in day-to-day life, but the first example that comes to mind is a relational one. Think about the cliché "bringing a guy home to meet your parents for the first time" story. Dad is already convinced the guy's a punk. When your boyfriend comes to the door, Dad, who has it in mind that this kid is bad news, no matter what, takes one look at his untucked shirt and spiked-up hair and thinks to himself, "This guy doesn't even care enough to make himself presentable." Later in the night, the boyfriend shares that he works at the ice cream parlor after dropping out of college, and Dad thinks again, "No good. He's got no future." The night goes on, and more and more, Dad neglects to see all of the good aspects of the future courtship and sees only what he had decided to see before the boyfriend ever approached the door.

Boyfriend anecdote aside, confirmation bias occurs every day. We make assumptions about people based on the color of their skin, the behavior of their children, or the way they dress, and we look for clues to confirm that our narrow-minded stereotypes are correct. You expect the homeless man on the corner to be strung-out, so when he speaks to you with a slur because he's dehydrated and barely lucid, you see intoxication.

You assume that the guy who's always at the office leaves the parenting to his wife, so when he misses yet another recital, you assume it's because he doesn't care about his kids. There is always more to the picture than we expect and operating on the assumption that your first idea is correct and then searching for information to back it up is always going to leave you flailing.

Recognizing confirmation bias will do more for you than making you a less judgmental person. It will make you a better communicator. Even you think you know what your colleague or friend or child is about to say, you might pause and allow them to speak, and be surprised by the ideas that come out. Instead of assuming what a person means by their statement, you might ask more questions and allow them to flesh out their idea, which will earn you respect points and a greater understanding of what they were trying to say.

Recognizing confirmation bias will also inform your decisions at work better. Casting aside assumptions about what a project will look like, or what kind of information you need to complete a presentation will allow you a greater vantage point to receive information that might be ground-breaking. Throwing confirmation bias to the wolves could lead to great success, just like Warren Buffet and Charlie Munger.

Tips for Recognizing Your Cognitive Biases:

- Do your own research. There are hundreds of different cognitive biases other than the ones listed here. They will all inhibit your learning, decision-making, relationships, work, and journey with mental models.

- Once you are familiar with several different kinds of cognitive biases, start to recognize them in your day-to-day interactions, and watch for patterns. Where would you have room to grow if you let go of these biases?

- Realize that this, just like anything else, is going to be a process. Conquering your cognitive biases takes time and is a massive undertaking. Be patient with your growth process.

Are you ready to learn more about these tools that names like Elon Musk, Ivan Pavlov, and Charlie Munger made their fame and their fortune with? These men may all be billionaires or millionaires and huge names in their industries, but don't let that discourage you from thinking that you can't achieve great success, too. Remember that achievements all begin in your mind. Accomplishing your goals and becoming who you were made, to begin with how you think and the way you think.

These big names all started out the same way you and I did. Elon Musk's parents divorced when he was ten. Ivan Pavlov didn't even start in the same school of thought he ended with: he actually began his studies in theology. Charlie Munger and Warren Buffet were just law school grads who, at one point, worked in Buffet's grandpa's grocery store.

They are all normal people who harnessed the power of their minds and trained themselves to use tools like mental models to be more successful than they'd ever dreamed. You can be just like them. You can use your thoughts to get anywhere you want to go. It starts here. Let's talk about concentration.

CHAPTER 3
BREAKING DOWN BARRIERS

Your mental model traps erect barriers in your mind to the best decisions and the most effective solutions. How can you break down these barriers and make better decisions and solve more problems in life? How can you become the best version of yourself possible without mental model traps standing in the way?

The solution to barriers is not always easy or convenient. But it is essential to going far in life and being happier with your decisions. By building more high-quality mental models, you can recognize when you are using a mental model that is trapping you and then switch to a more helpful model with greater utility that you know to fit the situation at hand. You can avoid bad decisions and the experience of being stuck in life. You can achieve things you never thought possible before.

Where Your Mental Models Tend to Go Wrong

While you learned about lots of mental model traps, now let's explore how these traps influence your performance and experience in different areas of life and common life situations. Then, we will delve into alternative ways of thinking that lead to better outcomes.

What You Can Do About It

To overcome these blind spots that poorly constructed mental models create in life, there are a few things that we can do to limit the use of mental models and get our thinking out of traps. Following are some strategies to work around mental models and their traps.

Build Yourself Concept Maps

A concept map can guide you to the reasonable conclusion, regardless of your mental models. As you jot down different ideas and facts, you cannot forget them or ignore them anymore. Everything lays before you. Furthermore, concept maps help you break things down into important points and less important points.

At the very pinnacle of the map, you have your main point or subject. This could be some decision you are grappling with – "Moving" or "Taking a new job." Or, you could summarize a problem – "Boosting test scores" or "Making More Money." You don't want to add details to the point. Just a simple phrase that sums up the basic premise will do.

Then, find the key concepts related to the main idea. If you are deliberating a move, you could consider the key concepts of place, time, cost, and even basic pros and cons to moving. Again, keep the key concepts short and sweet without tons of detail.

Now you can start to get more minutes with each additional step. Under cost, you can list things such as the cost of a U-Haul, the deposit on a new rental, etc. You might add something in there like, "How will I afford this?" Then, under that question, you can list some ideas for raising or saving money to afford this. Do this for every concept, breaking it down into the most minute details you can think of.

The last part is connecting words and phrases that are related. The timing of your move may relate strongly to the cost. You can only move when you have the costs covered. So, you might link the two.

Doing this can be quite therapeutic. It organizes your thoughts and presents them simply. It helps you see ideas that don't even fit into the decision, so you can stop obsessing over them.

Employ First Principles Reasoning

What principles in a logical problem come first and foremost? Which ones can be ignored or abandoned because they really are not important? With first principles thinking, you break things down to the simple core truth and you go from there.

A great example is when I wanted to leave my job. I knew that I was unhappy, but I kept letting various doubts cloud my judgment. "What if a new job doesn't pan out? What if I get a bad reference? What if my boss gets angry when I give him my resignation?" All of these worries and more swirled through my head. I bet you know what that feels like because you have probably done the same thing yourself.

Eventually, I got sick of going back and forth and I knew I couldn't take another year at my job. I broke it down to the first principle – I wanted to quit! So, I figured out each problem that quitting posed and I figured out how to mitigate each problem to come out on top. By the end of the year, I was in a new position and much more satisfied with my life. And my boss wasn't even that mad when I resigned and gave me an excellent reference! I was so scared of something that didn't even happen. I was inspissating the situation in my own mind, supplementing it with my own imagination, and as a result, I was blocking my path to success and happiness.

When you break something down to the simplest truth, you remove a lot of excess noise that confuses you and makes the obvious answer unclear. You let little worries, imagined worst-case scenarios, and the like cloud your judgment. You also tend to accept things as true that are not necessarily true.

Understand that life is different for you than anyone else. Your truths may not be true for anyone else and that's OK. It does not mean you are doing anything wrong. When you try to reason by analogy and apply what someone else did to your own life with slight variation, you will often miss some important fact and do something that doesn't really work for you. Finding your own unique truths and solutions is always imperative.

So, start by breaking a situation into its core pieces. In my example, I wanted to quit, but I was scared of consequences. Identify your vision or goal. It must be as specific as possible. Mine was that I wanted a job I could be happy in. List every obstacle, real or imagined. My obstacles included finding a new job, posting my resume without getting terminated at my current position, talking to my boss to resign, and getting a good reference.

Look at your current assumptions about the obstacles. Then ask if they are real or not. Test them out. I assumed my boss would get angry and refuse to give me a good reference, thus making it hard to get a new job. But when I actually worked up the nerve to speak to him, I found out he was not angry at all. By resigning in a professional manner, nothing bad happened. I was banking everything on an assumption about another person, which I know not to do!

Find the most reasonable and creative solution. Dare to do something unprecedented. My solution was to talk to my boss face to face and explore my options. This was very difficult for me, but it was a creative solution, one I would have never thought of on my own. It worked out in my favor.

Use First- and Second-Order Thinking

First-order thinking is where you make a snap decision to address a problem in the short-term. Meanwhile, you inadvertently create more long-term problems. On the other hand, second-order thinking dives in a bit deeper and ponders the far-reaching consequences of each decision to determine the best one overall.

When I write about this, I think of my niece and a spectacular mistake she made. She took a title loan on a car and became horrified when the 150% interest rate made her few hundred dollars blossom into thousands in a few months' time. So, she traded her car in for another one that was much more expensive, taking on a car loan that she really couldn't afford. Since she couldn't make title loan payments, she definitely couldn't make these more expensive car payments. But since the car dealership paid off her title loan for her, she considered it to be a good decision. Fast forward eight months and she was facing her first car repossession. She did not have another car for years because of the cycle of bad debt she got trapped in. This catastrophic decision-making is an example of a time when second-order thinking really needs to be used.

Absolutely never seize on the first, most obvious, and simplest choice. More testing and thinking are always required. Really consider the long-term implications. Anything that fixes the short-term without addressing the long-term is a bad idea.

We love instant gratification. It is just human nature to want something solved right now and right here. Learning to stave off instant gratification for a long-term reward is a skill that you must develop over time. It hurts almost physically because you feel as if you are depriving yourself, but when you reap the long-term rewards, you are grateful you made such a smart choice.

You Should Ask Why Five Times

When you are facing a problem, it can seem confusing or complicated because of all of the various factors present. Yet when you break it down by asking the question, "Why?" you can simplify matters so much that the solution becomes apparent.

Many people make the mistake of slapping a Band-Aid on problems, so to speak. Instead of addressing the real root of the problem, they solve the symptoms of the problem. The result is that the problem persists. By asking why, you can pare the problem down to its root. When you address the root, you clear up the problem for good.

Usually, it is a human factor that leads to the problem. Human factors can be the simplest to address because they are more under your control than, say, a weather factor. For example, if you ask why you're not doing well in a tennis game, you may blame the weather in a self-serving bias, which is totally out of your control, or you may actually realize what you are doing wrong and correct it. It is easy to rectify what you are doing wrong if you honestly identify the problem at hand. Asking why can get you to that point.

Here Is 5 Why's in Action:

1. Why do I want to move? Because I want to explore a new place.

2. Why do I want to explore a new place? Because I feel I might be limited where I am now.

3. Why do you think you will be trapped in your same home? I can't explore where I am. I want to try new things. New experiences shape life, right?

4. Why can't you go on day trips and explore from your new home? That's a good question... Maybe I could explore the world around me without having to move.

5. Why don't you explore new places now? There is no reason I don't. So, I guess I will! Let me try that before I commit to a big move.

CHAPTER 4
FOCUSING ON THE PROCESS
AND NOT THE OUTCOME

It is anything but difficult to imagine that for you to accomplish remarkable achievement, what you need to do is concentrate on results and utilize these outcomes to quantify your advancement. Anyway, this belief will divert you away from what is important. There's a whole different world to progress than just taking a gander at results without understanding that it's down to your consistency and the procedure associated with taking care of business towards the end of the day.

At the point when you start concentrating and vitality less on the outcomes yet rather on the procedures or the systems included, you find that you adapt quicker, are progressively fruitful and significantly more joyful at the result. By and large, you acquire in life when you center around the procedure instead of the outcomes.

As people, we are not constantly happy with our current conditions. We as a whole have needs and needs that are interminable that we weight accomplishing results continually floating over us. We accept that just through outcomes would we be able to verify a pathway for a superior future. However, such contemplations can be narrow-minded and overpowering when you think about that this stems out of worrying about what others consider us as opposed to what we ought to consider ourselves. Here are a few reasons why individuals who spotlight the procedure instead of results acquire throughout everyday life.

Ability to Deal With the Challenges

Challenges are normal to all of us, as nobody is flawless. The mistakes that you make along the process help you learn and develop throughout everyday life. At the point when you are centered around a particular outcome that you desire, you are less ready to trial or go out on a limb that may simply move you to a superior result than the one you were going for.

They Gain Fulfillment in the Interest

Achievement is a voyage as opposed to a goal. At the point when you are centered around the procedure you truly are amped up for being in the present and getting a charge out of it all the more completely. You are locked in and you need to burrow profound at those chances and roads you can because toward the day's end, it winds up about adapting quicker and picking up understanding.

They Have Fewer Interruptions

Let's be honest, there is the pressure that comes with regards to conveying results. You truly need to demonstrate a point and you are kind of motivated to compromise if your goal is to simply accomplish results. At the point when you center your concentration on the process, you will be able to block what the external environment says. While there, there is minimal pressure. Focusing on the process is not tied in with winning or losing; however, it is tied in with picking up dominance in whatever craving you are seeking after. You are not upset. It isn't generally about fulfilling the outside variables but instead about vanquishing you.

They Are in Control

Concentrating on results places you in the fractional control of whether you arrive at it or not. Things are neutralizing you, time, wellbeing, bolster gathering, rivalry... the rundown is unending. You simply need to convey. In any case, when you don't have the test of getting results floating, you have an interior locus of control that prompts higher confidence, strengthening and all together achievement. This gives you an increasingly important life.

They Determine Satisfaction in Giving Their Absolute Best

There is joy in getting great results out of your reward for so much hard work. That is the thing that concentrate you on the procedure that gives you. Things in life may not turn out how you need to; however, you are cheerful that you committed yourself to the procedure and won inside. There is no reason for predicting your prosperity on just a particular result, this will just prompt dissatisfaction and frustration. Instead of enabling your joy to be dependent upon you achieving a specific outcome, let your satisfaction be subject to the amount you have attempted to arrive at your objective.

There is Nothing Like Pressure, It's All in Our Mind

The pressure we put in ourselves isn't genuine; it's simply the pressure you put on yourself in your mind. Weight is simply the aftereffect of restrictions we put on ourselves to deliver results we don't control. At the point when we center around the result, we start to expect things out of our control, which sets us up for disappointment.

Here's an individual model:

While working as an insurance marketer, I was under a lot of pressure every day to make sales. Everyone I called said they had no interest at the time. My boss was hard on me for not bringing in any money. He threatened to get me fired since I was not adding any value to the company. After many months of this experience, I started to accept a bogus reality: that I could make individuals purchase something if only I said the best thing, correctly, at the ideal time. In any event, that is the thing that my manager asserted. It wasn't until almost 2 years after the fact I at long last quit that dreadful employment and left my manipulative manager that I understood: It is not true. I can't cause anybody to do anything. All that pressure I had been putting on myself was envisioned. I had imagined everything in some wiped out exertion to "inspire" myself. You don't have to put pressure on yourself to contend, to win, to end up as the winner. Since truly, you don't control the result. You don't control anything aside from yourself. The main parts you genuinely have power over are your demeanor, your attitude, and your activities. The rest is out of your control.

There's a statement I heard in my numerous long stretches of treatment and directing: The higher my desires for other individuals are, the lower is my peacefulness. The higher your desires for your activity, the individuals around you, the result leads to lower your serenity. The more you anticipate that things should occur in manners you don't control, the more pressure and weight you'll encounter. This is a hard exercise. I don't anticipate that numerous individuals should get it immediately. I've heard that expression for a considerable length of time and still experience serious difficulties with it. That is OK. A basic mentality shift like this requires some serious energy and time to internalize. If that doesn't bode well currently, don't stress over. Understand that one thing I urge you to consider is that pressure is envisioned. You don't control the result, so don't bother to attempt because it will be just pressurizing yourself. Rather, center around what you can control: yourself, your frame of mind, and your activities. When you comprehend weight is envisioned, nothing can stage you on your way to authority. You can accomplish tremendous objectives without breaking a sweat.

CHAPTER 5
2 TIPS TO IMPROVE DECISION MAKING

Seeing how the brain processes and reacts to data and how this affects our decision making can improve our system execution. Numerous people have invested energy attempting to see how we decide. However, long stretches of research inside brain science, and bolstered by neuroscience, finds that how we approach settling on decisions isn't always sane.

There are two sets of neural frameworks that have a significant effect on our judgment and the nature of decisions we make-programmed responses and intentional preparing and feeling and reason.

Programmed and Voluntary

Programmed responses, for example, perceiving a face, are found out reactions dependent on experience that rapidly realize automatic responses to situations. These are the activities that kick in when a job appears to be well-known and require almost no conscious idea.

Intentional preparing is our cognizant and conscious data director. It is slower to draw in and can help a few assignments at any given moment, while different programmed responses can be made all the while.

Intentional preparing, in any case, appears to represent just a little piece of our general conduct and regularly battles to contend with our programmed responses. Consider it along these lines: our activities and decisions are at first dictated via programmed responses and intentional handling kicks in just when we "delay" since we see that the expense or effect of a planned response might be excessively enormous.

Feeling and Reason

The brain additionally has separate frameworks that help feeling and reason. Opinion alludes to psychological processes that are activated by data that outcomes in a conduct reaction. For instance, a threatening situation, for example, seeing a bear heading for your tent, would trigger the feeling of dread, which may make you flee as quickly as possible, which probably won't be the best game-plan.

Thinking, for example, critical thinking and arranging, is increasingly sound and takes a long haul perspective on the outcomes of our conduct.

Getting the Two Systems to Work Together

Settling on complex decisions whose result is unsure requires both expansive based learning, for example, certainties about the situation, and thinking procedures that spin around objectives, choices for activity, and expectations about future results.

In any case, the rivalry between programmed responses and willful handling can influence our judgment. Similarly, the strain among feeling and reason can change the nature of our decisions. The test, at that point, is to sort out our reasoning and approach and control the various processes that add to our capacity to reason and make them a positive power.

Two systems better equalization programmed and deliberate processes and reason and feeling to improve our decisions.

1. Involving the Right People

This guarantees we incorporate points of view and encounters other than our own and helps fill in applicable information we might not have. Involving people in decisions helps influence the situation for willful preparation and consultation. It guarantees we approach data and points of view that may not generally be accessible to us and diminishes the probability that we will make a move and settle on decisions dependent on our nature. Also, involving people increases decision acceptance, which is necessary to viable execution once the decision has been made.

2. Utilizing a Systematic Process

Utilizing a target, deliberate strategy to settle on decisions guarantees we take a gander at the pertinent data and consider both the advantages and dangers of every option. This can address a significant number of the potential issues brought about by how we take in and process data and settle on decisions. It is an approach to defeat our brain's progressively quick inclination to settle on choices dependent on, and it lessens the negative effect feelings can have on the real idea by guaranteeing there is all the more harmony between the two.

A deliberate methodology additionally makes what is usually an inward point of view increasingly unequivocal and guarantees that the expansive based information about every option is noticeable, which gives a stage after that our individual or group's thinking methodologies can all the more viable work.

The brain is a mind-boggling organ, and decision-production is an intricate action that utilizations numerous individual mental processes. Also, a large number of these processes go after strength and the nature of our decisions are controlled by which ones win out. Attention to this intricacy and the numerous methods that are included increases the likelihood that you will screen your responses to watch that you are not merely settling on decisions dependent on a predisposition or making a well-known move that has been strengthened by involvement.

The test is to guarantee we approach a scope of viewpoints and data that may not generally be accessible to us and increases the probability that we will be increasingly attentive and reasonable when settling on decisions.

Using Sound Judgment, a Habit

Great decision-production doesn't generally fall into place for us, especially inside the turmoil of a commonplace workday. We are inclined to snap decisions and depending a lot on intuition. As pioneers, we need to prepare ourselves to back off, think about who should be included and ponder the possible results. This is more difficult than one might expect, yet we can improve our decision-production with experience and preparation.

In What Capacity Can Graphic Facilitation Improve Decision Making, Vision Association, and Teamwork

What's with practical help that I find so fascinating? Well basic... I discover it is a powerful instrument of correspondence inside a gathering. That is the reason I am persuaded that you should take the time and exertion to comprehend the certified impact of encouraging designs to include yourself in a crisp strategy for correspondence. Maybe like me, you, as of now, locate the standard procedure of gathering meeting help routinely and exhausting. The regular kinds of assistance generally center around the speaker, which frequently can be overwhelming and less compelling. In practical aid, it's a different way. The gathering of people talks, while the facilitator maps everything that is examined inside the collection. Putting the assistance of realistic into a less complicated examination - it alludes to item and procedure. It turns incredibly powerful as it thinks the group as they work, verifying concentration through sorting out and getting their thoughts.

Realistic facilitators had four aptitudes correctly tuning in, thinking, sorting out, and drawing. Every one of the skills is fundamental, so the absence of any can exclude you from winding up one. It is imperative to tune in to the gathering being an outcast, gathering bits of knowledge and subtleties which are altogether examined and mentally acquired. How you consider the nuances and data is fundamental in encouraging a gathering, setting up what is to be incorporated into the realistic chronicle. Then, sorting out the discussions and conversations, giving a development through scholarly reasoning and valuable aptitudes is additionally significant in making a total and coordinated picture. The illustration of images and photographs to structure stories and influence to the enthusiastic and visual bits of the brain as you include more arrangement through groupings, shading, and bolts is additionally significant.

At the point when allowed to take an interest in a discourse that utilizations practical help, I challenge you to see how the realistic facilitator amplifies the reasoning in the sessions. This individual can help you in genuinely delineating your unrivaled rationale, so you and your gathering of people perceive what you are recommending.

I, for one, discover this plan entertaining as it very well may be utilized as a powerful instrument for various exercises. When you use it on your occasions, you will see your thoughts take structure. Mostly, the yields are most full among spatial, orderly, and visual masterminds. It is additionally a valuable apparatus of recognizable proof for everybody. When the occasion is finished, the guide at that point ends up being a report - evidence of the advancement of the gathering just as its course. This helpful guide can be a useful apparatus since groups of people can see its creation in association with its experience. Practical help prompts an insignificant utilization of pictures and words to make a calculated conversational guide.

As should be obvious, pictures are generally passed on abstractly and passionate. Numerous groups of onlookers can undoubtedly perceive or look back to their noteworthy encounters. Practical assistance is undoubtedly a noticeable methodology of mapping conversations in various businesses like instruction, restorative, biotechnology, counseling, protection, sustenance, transportation, innovation, pharmaceutical, and retail.

Boost the utilization of practical help so you can build your concentration and clearness of your work. Keep in mind that when you draw assembled intelligence from numerous vital people, you additionally make better and further considered decisions. Also, when you utilize practical assistance, you make a memory gadget that holds this data on the one page!

CHAPTER 6
MISTAKES OF THINKING

"In the ability to make decisions, we are not as far from our coat-covered brothers as it seems."

- Nassim Taleb

Summarily, it can be said that any difficult problem has a simple, an obvious and a wrong solution.

Decision making is the main work of the intellect. An erroneous judgment is called one that does not correspond to the real object of knowledge, although it is revered according to the reality. Determine the meanings of words, and you will save the world from half of its mistakes.

Complexity is a relationship between a knowing subject and an object. The subject calls the object complex when he is unable to understand and predict the behavior of the object. The situation is aggravated by the fact that, as a rule, a person is forced to make decisions regarding complex systems in the conditions of lack of time and information about them. Thus, the main cause of psychological errors is the un-readiness of the intellect of biological origin to reflect the complexity and systemic nature of the modern social world.

In the irrational nature of our decisions, it is possible to single out at least three factors that are present in varying proportions in thinking errors. The first factor is the participation of the unconscious, emotional-volitional sphere. The second factor is the simplification of reality. Often, to make a decision, a person uses models that are too crude and inaccurately reflect reality. The third factor is associated with overconfidence in oneself and in one's right. One of the manifestations of overconfidence is our painful (if not aggressive) reaction to the criticism of our opinions and actions.

Examples of Psychological Errors

Our judgments and decisions depend on our initial settings; "reference points." We shall take a look at a few of them.

Deviation due to optimism. Reassess the likelihood of desirable events and underestimate the likelihood of unwanted events.

Availability heuristics. It manifests itself in the propensity to make assessments and make decisions based on the available, often insufficient, random, emotionally colored information. (Heuristics is an unconscious thinking process, in contrast to algorithmic inference processes). Making impulsive decisions based on random information is not only a common household one but also a typical professional mistake of many managers. Management decisions should be based on statistically verified data. "Statistical" thinking is one of the leading principles of quality management, Total Quality Management, and ISO 9000 standards were created on its basis.

The retrospection error is manifested in the fact that a person overestimates his own estimates of the probability of a certain event after the event has already occurred. Another manifestation of a retrospective error is retrospective attribution: an assessment of past situations with regard to subsequent events. Knowing the consequences, we unconsciously assign the initial situation of quality, which was not at the time of this situation. Many memories are not copies of the experience that are stored in the data bank of our memory. Rather, we construct memories, fitting them to our current knowledge.

Planning errors. When building plans, people, as a rule, underestimate possible future problems and often make significant mistakes in terms, volumes of work, and resources required.

The need to complete the desire as soon as possible to find the answer to a troubling question, to solve the problem. Man has a pronounced tendency to avoid uncertainty. He prefers a quick and wrong decision over a longer search for the right answer.

Rejection of new ideas. The subjective picture of the world that has developed in man is a tough and uncompromising interpreter of reality and a basis for making decisions. Moreover, a person unconsciously filters incoming information, leaving and accumulating data confirming his initial position.

The tendency to confirm is a deviation close in meaning to the rejection of new ideas. Its essence lies in the fact that a person evaluates as more reliable information that confirms his opinion or his decision compared to information that contradicts this opinion or decision.

Increased self-esteem - a tendency to overestimate the correctness of their beliefs. Nassim Taleb, in Fooled by Accident, described this pheno-menon of arrogance as follows: "We humans are victims of asymmetry in the perception of random events. We attribute our successes to our mastery, and failures to external events beyond our control. Namely - randomness. We take responsibility for the good, but not for the bad. This allows us to think that we are better than others - whatever we do. "

Anthropomorphism is the appropriation of human properties to objects and phenomena of animate and inanimate nature.

Attribution error. Our internal state and what we say and do, depends both on the situation itself and on what we ourselves bring into it. Trying to explain someone's behavior, we underestimate the impact of the situation itself and overestimate the contribution of the person and his attitudes, i.e., we make a mistake of attribution. We often explain our own behavior, referring to external circumstances, at the same time, we consider other people fully responsible for their actions. In relation to ourselves, we usually use verbs that describe our actions and reactions ("It annoys me when..."). In relation to others, we often describe what kind of person this is ("He's a disgusting type").

Projective syndrome - the tendency to subconsciously assume that others share the same or similar thoughts, feelings, values, positions. Well, do not worry about what other people think about you. They are too concerned about what you think about them. An understanding of the existence in our real world of two ethical systems, for example, is neces-sary for a politician, in particular, for a correct prediction of society's reaction with another ethical system to its position and its actions. Conversely, a mirror model, i.e., A priori assumption that he is the same as me, can lead to serious mistakes when making strategic decisions.

The Effect of Observational Selection

This is manifested in the fact that we see, as a rule, part of the picture, but we draw conclusions, implicitly assuming that we see the whole picture. Nassim Taleb in "Black Swan" cites the story described by Cicero. The Greek philosopher Diago, nicknamed the Atheist, was shown images of people who prayed to the gods and were saved during a shipwreck. The implication was that prayer saves from destruction. Diago asked: "Where are the images of those who prayed, but still drowned?" It is not so easy for devout drowned people to express their opinions from the bottom of the sea because they are dead. Taleb calls this the problem of hidden evidence: "Everything that has at least some relation to history is filled with hidden evidence... When you come up with historical theories, it's easy not to look at the cemetery. But we treat things this way, not only with history. We also build models in the same way and collect evidence in any field. We call this the error, that is, the difference between what we see and so on.

In "Fooled by Accident" Nassim Taleb calls into question the widespread view that life's success is entirely connected with personal qualities and talents of a person. This opinion, in his opinion, does not take into account the role of chance and the presence of "hidden witnesses." He proposes to conduct the following thought experiments. Let the business of a large group of people consist of playing Russian roulette imperceptibly to those around them. They twist the drum of a six-shot revolver with one cartridge, bring it to the temple and pull the trigger. After each round of the game, the survivors receive a decent amount of money, and about 1/6 of the group is eliminated. After several sessions of such a game, a small group of rich people will remain and, it is important to emphasize a large cemetery. Can the "success" of survivors be considered a consequence of their talents and abilities? The public usually observes the outward signs of wealth, without thinking about its source. Unfortunately, "no one is watching the bulletproof drum of reality. The naked eye very rarely sees a wealth generator. We observe the values produced, but never the processor (and this makes people lose sight of their risks) and never see the losers. The game seems awfully simple, and we blithely play it further."

CHAPTER 7
INDIVIDUAL AND COLLECTIVE
MENTAL MODELS

Different mental models can motivate different perceptions, feelings, opinions, and actions. For example, for the accountant, a certain result of a company is showing stability, and that should keep its course. For the vice president of marketing, the result proves that the company is stagnant and should start a new advertising campaign. For a board member, it's the "disapproval" of CEO policy. To an investor, it suggests that it is time to sell your shares; for another, it is time to buy. The result is the same; the worldly context is the same; what explains the differences are the different mental models.

Different perceptions, opinions, and actions are not a problem in themselves. They become conflicting, in fact, when each person believes that their way of seeing things (according to their mental model) is the only way of seeing them, at least the only "reasonable." Of course, the idea of "rationality" is an opinion conditioned by the mental model of each person. Everyone believes that their model is the valid model. Instead of using different perceptions to expand their perspectives and integrate them into a common vision, each of the interlocutor's clings to their own point of view. Rather than probing the other's reasoning to understand his mental model, the interlocutors wage a battle to determine who is right, who has the "right" interpretation of reality.

Mental models are also the file that contains routine behaviors. As we have seen, in initiating a practice (such as driving a car, for example), one has to pay conscious attention to making unscheduled decisions. But as time passes, it develops the capacity to act automatically, transferring those decisions to the unconscious and taking advantage of what Gregory Bateson calls "the habit economy." This economy is fundamental to life since, without it, it would be impossible to act with the speed required by circumstances. But it also has a cost: automatic routines are inflexible.

The inflexibility of habit is crucial to operating efficiently in stable contexts. Like the autopilot of an airplane, the habit allows the human pilot to pay attention to other things. But flying with autopilot in the middle of a storm is very dangerous. Lack of flexibility and adaptation to changes in context is one of the main causes of species extinction (such as dinosaurs), crops (such as Roman), companies (99 out of 100 disappear without their first 10 years, and the estimated average of life of Fortune 500 companies is less than 40 years), families (60% of marriages in the world end in divorce) and people (according to recent data, 50% of deaths before age 40 can be attributed to people's behavior).

The filters through which we human beings organize and give meaning to our experiences come from four sources: biology, language, culture, and personal history. These four sources also determine the "usual" response to certain circumstances, programmed in the mental model. Just to throw some more light on the sources we had mentioned briefly before, I will try explaining them a bit further in the following paragraphs:

Biology

The first filter of mental models is the nervous system. We have physiological limitations that prevent us from perceiving certain phenomena with our senses. The reach of the human ear, for example, is 20 to 20,000 vibrations per second, while the dogs can hear shades higher and the elephants, more serious tones. The night vision of the human does not compare with that of the feline, and our vision at a distance is far inferior to that of the hawk. In terms of longitude from where the human being is able to directly see the frequencies that are between 380 and 680 millimeters, that is, a tiny band of the electromagnetic spectrum.

The impossibility of perceiving implies the impossibility to act. While the dog responds to an ultrasonic whistle, the person does not even hear it. While the bat operates in utter darkness, one loses himself. That's why we, humans, invent instruments such as sonar and radar to expand the perceptual reach of our senses and, consequently, our ability to act.

Our interconnection with the world is much more complicated than we think. The objective theory of perception states that the world "out there" creates direct changes and produces effects on the nervous system "in here." Challenging this theory, Humberto Maturana and Francisco Varela argue that the outside world can only produce disturbances in the nervous system. The subject's perceptual experience is much more determined by the very structure of his nervous system than by external disturbance. In The Tree of Knowledge, Maturana and Varela define the nervous system as a closed system. This idea contradicts the traditional notion that it defines it as "an instrument that gets information from the environment and builds a representation of the world, which the body uses to calculate the behavior appropriate for its survival. According to Maturana and Varela", as far as biology and human cognitive structures are concerned, the whole world of our experiences is within ourselves; there is no such thing as the outside experience.

This theory explains why all human beings observe the same image when they look at an object, even when none of them can experience the outside world for themselves. The similarity of our biology allows us to operate in a common reality. Maturana and Varela affirm that what the person experiences is "(reality)" and not "reality." Thus written, in parentheses, "(reality)" denotes the inner experience of the field of energies, external and unknowable, which we call "reality" without parentheses. We live in an inter-subjective (reality), not because the (reality) we see is the real, objective external reality, but because the environment awakens similar responses in our nervous systems.

The second filter of our mental models is language. Language is the medium in which the consciousness of the human being is structured. Language is the space of meaning in which reality appears intelligible and communicable. Thanks to language, we can communicate with ourselves and with others about what exists around us and within us.

The traditional understanding of language is "label theory." According to this theory, we see things in the world as they are and then apply a name, a label. This is the primary use of language: a descriptive system for labeling and classifying preexisting and therefore, independent perceptions. This theory is incomplete and only accounts for a very small function of language. Researchers of cognition, brain, and consciousness have concluded that language categories are not labels applied to preexisting perceptions; on the contrary, they precondition and define perception first: the person does not speak of what he sees, but only sees what he can speak of.

The accountant "watches" on a balance sheet thing that the mechanical engineer does not see. Not that the engineer does not see those same numbers; he does not have the distinctions that the accountant (the language) has to interpret those numbers. The mechanical engineer can "read" a system of differential equations that is totally incomprehensible to the meter. Not that the accountant does not see those same signs; he does not have the distinctions that the engineer (the language) has to interpret those signals. The ability to make distinctions and to order the world into operational categories is what is called "intelligence."

Culture

The third source of mental models is culture. We could consider culture as a collective mental model.

"Here, the decisions are taken by consensus." "Here we buy from the supplier who has the best prices." "Here, the men go out to work while the women stay inside." "Here, the women are independent and make their own lives." "Nature is a resource to be used by man." "Nature is sacred, and man's job is to preserve it."Each of these phrases illustrates a cultural premise. Ideas coalesce into a collective mental model that organizes the (reality) of a culture.

Within any group (families, professions, organizations, industries, nations), collective mental models evolve based on shared experiences. Throughout its history, group members must face challenges. In response, they develop a habitual way (in the sense given by Bateson) of interpreting situations and taking action. This becomes a part of the collective mental model and passes from generation to generation as the "knowledge" of the group. The problem is that with its retrogression in the night of time, such knowledge loses its experiential root and becomes an absolute truth. Instead of being "the way in which our group has effectively responded to the challenges of the past," one now has "the only correct way of responding to the challenges of the present and the future."

Collective mental models are also a double-edged sword, as are individual ones: on the one hand, they help the group structure the effective and efficient realization of their reality based on past experiences, but, on the other hand, determine the range of possible future experiences. This self-validating system helps maintain stability and meaning within a group - indeed, in times of drastic changes, culture (which is always essentially conservative) can turn into a lead lifesaver. Challenges to shared beliefs create anxiety and entrenchment. Changing cultural presuppositions is an extremely arduous process.

Personal History

The fourth force that shapes mental models is personal history: race, gender, nationality, ethnic origin, family influences, social and economic condition, level of education, the way we have been treated by our parents, siblings, the way we started working and becoming self-sufficient, etc. All of these experiences shape the mental model one uses to navigate the world. Just as collective experiences of learning become a culture, personal learning experiences lodge in the most basic strata of consciousness and create automatic predispositions to interpret and act.

There are premises of the mental model that people adopt from their earliest childhood, even before they have any capacity for critical reflection. Throughout life, these unconsciously received ideas underlie the infinity of judgments, attitudes, and behaviors that the person considers "obvious." For example, a girl grew up in a family with an absent father and, as a result, thinks that "men are not reliable to fulfill their obligations." At the same time, the boy from the same family grows up in the opinion that "men are free to do whatever they want."

This is especially dangerous when the mental model is "anchored" in an unresolved historical situation. In such cases, one can get stuck in a repetitive circuit, symbolically recreating some traumatic experience and trying to change its outcome. For example, the individual who explodes in rebellion against his boss may be regressing to childhood in an attempt to complete pending matters with his father. The sign that denotes the regression is the total unconsciousness with which the action is carried out. Back at the house, trying to explain to his wife why he was fired, he says, "I do not know what happened; when he told me to redo all the work, I lost my temper and shouted at him."

CHAPTER 8
WHY YOU SHOULD FOLLOW YOUR INSTINCTS

To start with, we should talk about how the cerebrum functions. The human cerebrum is the most advanced organ on earth and has developed monstrously from the crude mind our precursors had. The cerebrum resembles an onion with layers on layers that have developed after some time. In the cerebrum is the most seasoned part, the mind stem. Correspondingly, out at the front of the mind, or the external most onion layer, is the frontal cortex, the freshest piece of the cerebrum.

The frontal cortex, the best in expansion to the cerebrum, is essentially what's in charge of making people so complex. This frontal cortex is in charge of things, for example, rationale, basic reasoning, learning, and language. This implies, because I have a frontal cortex, I can compose this article, and you can peruse it. This piece of the cerebrum is regularly alluded to as the cognizant personality, given its relationship with rationale and thinking.

The basal ganglia are in the crude piece of the mind, straightforwardly associated with the stem of the brain. It is the spot in the cerebrum where all propensities, sentiments, feelings, encounters, recollections, and senses are put away. This is frequently called the intuitive personality, and it is the place all basic leadership happens, not a few, all. In the frontal cortex is where the learning takes place. Notwithstanding, when this educated conduct turns into a routine, the neurological association in charge of this conduct moves from the frontal cortex to the basal ganglia, where it is put away as a routine.

The purpose of this move is two-overlay. It mitigates the brain from over-thinking for each regular assignment and stalling out in loss of motion. Second, it constantly opens up space in the frontal cortex, so that we can continue to adapt to ideas and take on new experiences. Which is why you don't need to think which shoe to tie first, with which hand to carry your toothbrush, or how to drive to work every morning while in transit. What this also means is that the vast majority of the subliminal personality-the peace of mind that drives basic leadership is developed using recently realized past experiences and skills, which evolved toward becoming propensities. So, when you're settling on a gut choice that feels right, ordinarily, it's not exclusively founded on emotions yet rather on sound rationale and experience. You simply don't see it at the time.

We should take a gander at how this functions in your clients by beginning with an individual model. Have you at any point strolled past an eatery and said to yourself, "Gracious this spot looks great, how about we eat here," at that point continued to stroll in and eat there? Allow me to solicit, what some portion of that choice was levelheaded? Nothing! You had no clue what sort of sustenance the café served, the amount it was going to cost or if the administration would be any great and you had a sum of zero suggestions from companions to get a meal there.

That choice was totally silly. Odds are you were directly about the eatery, the nourishment was great, the administration was amazing, and you'll be back soon. How is this so? All things considered, because premonitions are results of past encounters. Odds are you had eaten at comparable eateries in the past that looked, felt, smelled and had indistinguishable sort of individuals inside from the spot you thought looked great. That is the place the premonition originated from. That is likewise why individuals know inside three or four seconds on the off chance that they like a tune, know inside five seconds of strolling into a store whether they'll purchase something or not and know inside 30 seconds of gathering another person on the off chance that they are pulled in to them or not. These hunches come from past firsthand encounters; they are not only unusual choices.

Presently, we should take a gander at your group. In all honesty, your group is comprised of people as well, and subsequently, their minds work a similar route as your clients. This implies like your clients, they settle on choices dependent on emotions, and instinct, not rational and thinking. At X association, for instance, the group had an extraordinary inward banter about a year prior to whether we should include a component in the application that took into consideration planning conveyances or not. We saw that a greater part of our clients was attempting to plan a pickup, so normally, it seemed well and good that we work in a planning highlight. It simply didn't feel ideal for the group, so we eventually chose not to do it.

All things considered, we accepted that a long time from now, every administration comprehensible will be on-request and therefore, to invest energy and cash working out a component that we'll inevitably dispose of simply didn't bode well. So as opposed to tuning in to our clients the sensible activity - we kept on pushing forward with the on-request administration. Following a couple of months, we found that a large portion of our clients who wanted to plan their conveyances needed to do so, not because they favored planning, but since they needed the security of realizing a driver would be accessible when they required one.

As we developed, and our clients started to believe that somebody would be accessible, they started not exclusively to receive, however, gloat about the on-request administration. Indeed, the vast majority of our accomplice's state it's the element they like the most. When we began, near 80 percent of our clients attempted to plan their pickups, yet now, under 5 percent do. Once more, the group's choice not to offer planning originated from a premonition, not a normal choice to tune in to our clients and rotate. Nonetheless, that this hunch presumably originated from our group's few positive past encounters with other on-request organizations like Lyft, Instacart or Luxe Valet.

Look again at the eatery model, and how it just felt appropriate to stroll in and eat there, even though you had no sensible motivation to help that choice. It felt right because your past encounters at different eateries and choices made about where to eat modified you to accept, with high likelihood, that this eatery would be just as you would prefer. Likewise, all your aggregated information and encounters, from the readings you've perused to the individuals you've met to the spots you've voyage and the interests you've kept or overlooked, were important to the introduction of your vision, which is presently your organization.

Only you had the definite sum and enhancement of encounters fundamental expected to draw an obvious conclusion when that aha minute struck and you stated, "Ah-ha! I have a thought that can change the world." That's the reason, with regards to the real choices about how to maintain your business, you ought to tune in to your gut since it will create better outcomes, but since eventually, the achievement of your business depends altogether on whether you or not you do as such.

In this manner, just by following your instincts, would you be able to enliven your vision for that item, or business, that just comes out as appropriate to you, your group, and at last, your clients. Furthermore, just if your business feels appropriate to your clients, will they eat at your café, wear your garments, or utilize your versatile application.

Accordingly, with regards to settling on significant choices about your organization, do the intelligent thing, think irrationally.

Decisions Are Emotional, Not Logical

When it comes to making a choice, emotions are very important as you make the decision. Truth be told even with what we accept are coherent choices, the very purpose of the decision is ostensibly constantly dependent on emotion.

Think about a circumstance where you had impenetrable actualities, reason, and rationale on your side, and accepted there was positively no chance the other individual could disapprove of your impeccably developed contention and proposition. To do so would be unimaginable, you figured, because there was no other coherent arrangement or answer.

And after that, the other individual delved in his heels and wouldn't move. He wasn't influenced by your rationale. Is it safe to say that you were confounded?

This is like what numerous moderators do when they take a seat at the table to pound out an arrangement. They come outfitted with realities, and they endeavor to utilize rationale to influence the other party. They assume that by heaping on the information and utilizing motivation to clarify their side of the circumstance, they can build an essentially undeniable answer and influence the other state yes.

They're destined to go down, in any case, since basic leadership isn't consistent, it's enthusiastic, as indicated by the most recent discoveries in neuroscience. A couple of years back, neuroscientist Antonio Damasio made a weighty disclosure. He considered individuals with harmed brains where feelings are produced. He found that they appeared to be typical, then again, actually they could not experience feelings. In any case, they all shared something particular for all intents and purposes: they couldn't decide. They could portray what they ought to do in sensible terms, yet they thought that it was hard to settle on even basic choices, for example, what to dress. Numerous choices have upsides and downsides on the two sides will I have the chips or the meat? With no sane method to choose, these guineas pigs were not able to touch base at a choice. Even with what we view as wise decisions, the aim of making a choice is dependent on feeling.

This finding has gigantic ramifications for arrangement experts. Individuals who accept they can assemble a case because of their power of reasoning are arguably termed as poor arbitrators. This is because they do not take the time to understand the factors that have to lead the opponents to make a certain decision. People who base their exchange methodology on rationale end up depending on presumptions, suppositions, and conclusions. On the off chance that my side of the contention is coherent, they figure, at that point, the opposite side can't contend with it and will undoubtedly come around in my mind. The issue is, you can't expect that the other party will see things your way.

What the moderator can and should do, in any case, is making a dream for the opposite side to realize revelation and choice on their part. At last, your rival will settle on the choice since he needs to. Getting him to need to, utilizing the bit by bit philosophy that is a piece of the Camp System, is the activity of the mediator – doing whatever it takes not to persuade him with reason.

You don't advise your rival what to think or what's ideal. You help them find for themselves what feels right and best and most profitable to them. Their definitive choice depends on personal responsibility. That is passionate. I need this. This is beneficial for me and my side.

CHAPTER 9
MOTIVATION

Motivational is tricky but powerful. It's really easy sometimes to get motivated, have you ever noticed that? You can get yourself excited about something, and you get caught up in all of the excitement. Another thing that you know you can be spiraling down a tunnel of procrastination and your motivation has plummeted. Without even realizing why or how it's happened, you want your motivation to slip away as you sit on the couch and do nothing.

Understand that there are several different ways to get motivated. We will discuss mental models that are going to benefit you in increasing your productivity. In the meantime, it's important to understand what exactly motivation is and how it works.

Motivation is the feeling that at some point in time, the pain you feel not to do something is going to be greater than the feel the pain that you are going to feel by accomplishing this task. When it's no longer easier to stay the same, that's when motivation kicks in.

We need to understand that each and every choice that we have is going to cost us something, but when you are motivated, it is easier to take action, then it is to remain the same.

Often times, when you start a new habit or behavior, your motivation is going to follow. The motivation is not going to come before you start this new habit or behavior, but rather it's going to come along after you've already begun. Often time's people are confused, and they think that motivation comes by looking at an inspirational reading or perhaps by watching a video that is supposed to be motivational.

Motivation is not the cause of action, but it is the result of the action. Sometimes the only way to get your motivation going is to start slowly and adopt new habits and small steps.

When you are first getting started with motivation, consider scheduling your motivation. When you set a schedule, you are giving your decision-making process a chance to go on autopilot. The likelihood that you will follow through regardless of your level of motivation increases. Schedule the habit and stop waiting for motivation.

There are many people who are famous and lack motivation. When you do things as a routine or ritual, you are increasing the chances of becoming motivated. Some good suggestions include meditating in the morning in order to start each day with as little stress as possible. Having a routine that allows you to relax before you go to sleep; this is going to allow you to have better, more productive sleep.

You can make motivation a habit. By doing that, there are three simple steps that you can follow.

• Step one is where you have a routine before you are supposed to start. Make sure that the routines include simple steps so that you are unable to say no. Remember that the most important part of starting is actually getting started.

• Step two understands that the routine is meant to get you moving towards the end goal. When you lack mental motivation, it is often because you lack physical movement. When you're depressed, bored, or unmotivated, you are usually not doing much. If you are physically moving and you are far more likely to feel energized and ready to go.

Your routine needs to be as easy as possible, but you need to remember that you need to get physically moving. In order to get your mind and your motivation going, what you need to get your body moving first. Understand that this does not necessarily exercise, but you need to make sure that the habits you are initiating are getting you closer to the end goal.

• Step three makes sure that you are following the same routine every day. When you purposefully get yourself doing the same things every day, pretty soon, they are going to be so tied to who you are that you will not consider skipping them.

How Mental Models and Motivation Are Tie Together?

How you use your own time is also a way for you to weigh the decisions that you're making. There is a cost for sitting on the couch and doing nothing just as there is a cost for choosing to fire an individual from your business.

The mental models included here are going to give you the tools that you need to increase your productivity and increase your motivation will also allow you to look at each and every decision that you are making in a different way. Remember that you are able to use these mental models in every aspect of your life.

Remember that mental models are simply a way that we see our world. When you are trying to increase your motivation or your productivity, mental models are going to allow you to shape the borders and make decisions regarding how you are using your time. Mental models also allow you to determine what is important to you and what is not important to you. When you are using the mental models, you are allowing yourself to weigh each and every decision and looking at the pros and cons of the decisions that you are faced with.

How you use your time is no different than looking at a problem that deals with a business situation. When you are looking at a business situation, you are going to way the cost analysis of each decision.

Now that we've looked at how to get ourselves motivated, we can begin to look at some mental models that are going to help us achieve this motivation.

The Reason Respecting Because of Why

This mental model is useful with motivation simply because it gives you a reason why you should do something. Basically, the premise behind the mental model is that simply adding the word because it will give you a reason, and therefore, you are more persuasive. The model itself is meant to help you persuade other people to do things the way you want them to, however, it is effective when you are looking to get yourself motivated to accomplish either your goals or certain tasks.

Consider the example: if you need to mow your lawn but you are lacking the motivation to start making some lists as to why you need to do this. Start the list I need to mow my lawn because and then from there, simply add each incentive that you will gain when you complete the task.

When finding the motivation to achieve your goals, this strategy is effective as well. You are training your mind to be persuaded simply due to the word because. When you add to your thought processes, it becomes the mental model that is going to help you persuade yourself to take action. I need to complete my goal because my goal for today is to take 30,000 steps by the time I go to bed because and then list the reasons you need to do this and what you will gain by accomplishing this goal. The key is to make sure that you are giving yourself enough incentive to keep you going.

Motivation is tricky because when you are trying to motivate yourself oftentimes, you can talk yourself out of doing anything.

CHAPTER 10
CASE STUDIES THAT ACTUALLY WORKED!

The Big Dreams Garage

Another type of group that we are going to take a look at is the Big Dreams Garage. This one is all about startups that began in the backyard garage. This could be a real garage, a car boot, a college dorm, a sitting room couch, a bedroom, or somewhere else that is small and that you would not expect a business to start out, much less see success. It is basically going to be some kind of unconventional space for a business. Even some startups were able to establish themselves from a food café or something similar.

This is going to be a type of mental model is all about utilizing the free space that is available to start up your venture. First off, it can be cost-efficient because you do not have to worry about paying business rent to a startup. You just need to have a little space. This one is all about the sheer passion that comes from doing this whole process, rather than the sophisticated space from where you started the business. Some examples of people who fit into the Big Dreams Garage mental model will include:

Bill Gates

Staying along with the same idea with this one, we are going to move over to the start of Bill Gates and the Microsoft company. Bill Gates, with the help of his college friend Paul Allen, saw an advertisement in the magazine known as Popular Electronics. This advertising was looking for someone who could work with the Altair 8800 programming language.

Bill Gates and Paul Allen saw this as a really big opportunity for them to get ahead, and they decided to go straight for it. At this time, Gates dropped out of Harvard University to pursue his dream venture. It was a matter of urgency now. This shows us that if something is not that urgent, and it is not so pressing to you, then it is time to just kick it out and not pay any attention to it any longer.

Richard Branson

Branson started from the streets as a kid hawker who sold Christmas trees. Eventually, though, he rose up and established a magazine business from the Churchyard. Branson is the most famous for his enterprise brand, known as Virgin Group. Under this enterprise, there are a few different options, including:

Virgin Atlantic: This is an airline company.

Virgin Galactica: This is a space technology company.

Virgin Records: This is a well-known record production company.

Just like what we saw with Elon Musk, Branson's Virgin Group was able to break out of its core and cut across a lot of diverse fields in the process. At this point, Branson owns almost 400 companies under this umbrella group, and not all of them are going to be in the same field either.

Ivan Pavlov and Classical Conditioning

If you have any interest in Psychology or were forced to take a general education requirement at some point, the name Ivan Pavlov might ring a bell. Pavlov was a Russian physiologist that made a serendipitous discovery that changed the world of mental models and psychology forever. His experiment wasn't on people, though: Pavlov was studying canines when this epiphany struck.

The year was 1890, and Pavlov's lab room was overtaken by dogs and dog food. His theory was that when a dish of food is placed in front of a dog, it will stimulate a response: salivating. He would have his assistant place a dish of food in front of the dog and then measure the amount of salivation produced in the dog's cheek. After time went by, though, Pavlov realized something was occurring that he didn't expect.

Fascinated, Pavlov began another series of experiments. He played the metronome (similar to the rhythm of his assistant's tapping feet) for the dogs. Not surprisingly, hearing the metronome by itself didn't make the dogs salivate. Then he began the learning process, which he calls conditioning. He played the metronome just before the dogs were fed.

After repeating this procedure over and over again, he played the metronome on its' own, without giving the dogs any food. At this point, however, the dogs had learned that the sound of the metronome was supposedly linked with eating time. Even without being presented with food, this time upon hearing the metronome's tones, the dogs began to salivate just as if their food were right in front of them.

Simply put, an unconditioned stimulus is something that is already present in your life and produces a response from you without any learning or conditioning needed. When the unconditioned stimulus is presented to you, you have a natural response to it. If you already like chocolate (unconditioned stimulus), your response when you eat it (joy!) doesn't have to be learned. Eating chocolate (unconditioned stimulus) elicits joy (unconditioned response). For your purposes, choose an unconditioned stimulus, or reward, that really motivates you to get something done in order to enjoy it! Still with me?

Plato's Virtuous Mental Health Model

According to this model, the soul has three main parts – the rational part, the emotional part (thumos), and the appetite. Thus, to be able to have a healthy living, one must first of all, be able to understand that the soul is a tripartite entity. Furthermore, one must be able to understand the relationship between the three parts and how this relationship affects one's health.

Plato asserts that in order to lead virtuous mental health, the rational part, aided by the emotional part, must reign over the part of the appetite. Yet, the rational part must also rule over the emotional part. Thus, the rational part must have sovereign authority over the tripartite.

In this regard, the part of the appetite is that part responsible for the human's primitive desires – both positive (such as love, affection, etc.) and negative (such as lust, greed, etc.). Without the sovereign authority of the rational mind over the appetites, virtuous health gets lost (such as when a human being gets engulfed by lust, greed, jealousy, and such other vices). This negatively affects one's mental health.

The most optimal situation is when the rational part is in control, yet there is harmony among the three parts. Contrary to this, chaos abounds and thus mental sickness (loss of virtuous mental health).

While this model looks great, it has its own body of critics. This criticism is largely due to Plato's analogously equating lack of virtuous mental health with madness... and in essence, associating madness with loss of virtue. This implicitly accuses mad people as having lacked virtues. Obviously, this is not the case as most mental diseases are a result of a biological malfunction of the brain rather than immorality. Nonetheless, with the exception of the 'erroneous' assumption of madness being caused by immorality, Plato's model does attempt to ventilate on the relationship between psychological health and mental health.

Warren Buffett, Charlie Munger, and Mental Models

Warren Buffett is well-known for his prowess as an investor, though his business partner Charlie Munger is given less credit. Munger is more out of the financial spotlight but is known for his extensive work in organizing mental models. One of the most famous speeches regarding mental models was given by Charlie Munger at USC Business School in 1994. Even though the speech was intended to discuss his business philosophy and investment, he also talked about a general framework for wise decision making. It is this type of decision making that sets success apart from failure. Business partner Warren Buffett had also used these mental models, which allowed both to become learning machines. They took the time to attack problems from different angles before choosing a solution, which allowed them to make the wisest and most effective business decisions. The models used by people like Buffett and Munger are rules of thumb that create a truth that can be generally accepted by the majority. Therefore, any information that can be put into a specific mental model lets the problem evaluated from a certain angle. With several mental models available to analyze any given problem, a person can reduce the amount of uncertainty in their world and feel assured that the decisions they are making are those that are going to yield the best result.

In a way, mental models make a person smarter. This is not merely a collection of knowledge or ideas, but the way that knowledge and ideas are applied to the decision-making process. People often take the complexity that exists around them for granted, never truly realizing the impact that it has on their lives. People are generally focused on 1-2 factors and the results that it will produce. In reality, however, there could be billions of variables that affect a single situation. People see surface-level results because they do not account for these extra variables. However, the solution isn't to account for all those variables. There are so many variables that can influence a situation that it may be impossible to know which of these variables to focus on to sway the outcome the way you are hoping. Additionally, it would be impossible to sway every single variable that comes into play in a situation. Instead of overburdening your brain with these minute details, people rely on mental models. Even though there is no single perfect model, perfection is not necessary for a mental model to work. They are merely a tool that makes all those complex variables that surround a decision easier to account for.

According to Munger, it is essential that a person looks for mastery of mental models across different disciplines. Some of the areas Munger has studied and learned the principles of include accounting, physics, psychology, finance, economics, architecture, medicine, mathematics, history, geography, sociology, biology, and chemistry. The reasoning behind this is that there are elements of every discipline that can contribute to a person's collection of mental models. Even though people agree, there are some mental models that are more helpful than others and more easily able to be applied to life, not all of these mental models exist within the same academic department. People's mental models are often flawed because they specialize in a single area. For example, businesspeople make decisions according to certain principles that they use to evaluate risks and benefits. Someone who is a researcher or scientist may use hypotheses or experiments to solve problems. It is not necessarily a bad thing; however, it limits a person's ability to see the full scope of possibilities when problem-solving and decision-making.

Something else to keep in mind is that the same mental models do not work for everyone. It would be nearly impossible to master dozens of disciplines to the extent needed to handle some of the more complex mental models. Fortunately, the most useful models are those based on simplicity rather than complex ideas. You do not have to master a discipline to master some of its basic principles. Even a basic foundation in different disciplines allow you to view problems and decision-making from new angles, giving you a greater range of options and a better chance of success.

CHAPTER 11
PUTTING MENTAL MODELS INTO PERSPECTIVE

Even though mental models are undoubtedly useful, they are not the 'keys to the kingdom' on their own. Mental models are meant to give you a clearer picture of reality. Unfortunately, many people distort this picture based on their own experiences. While storing information about the experiences we have is important, it can also create bias. To properly use mental models, it is important that these biases are identified and accounted for. Otherwise, the mental model is as flawed as the bias that is influencing it, and it becomes harder to accurately predict outcomes.

Here you will understand what mental models are and what they are not, which will help you decide how they can be best applied in life.

"We all have mental models: the lens through which we see the world that drives our responses to everything we experience. Being aware of your mental models is key to being objective."

- Elizabeth Thorton

Mental models are not foolproof in their ability to map the world. They are subject to human error and rarely detail the reality of the situation. However, once you become more aware of the mental models you use and their likelihood of yielding either satisfying or dissatisfying thoughts, you can begin picking and choosing the mental model that will work best in the situation. In order to do that, it is important to be aware of each model's strengths and where it falls short.

For example, imagine that you were solving a complex math problem. You could go through hundreds of equations, but unless the right equation was applied to the problem, it would not yield a satisfying (or accurate) solution.

Cause and Effect in Problem-Solving

In many ways, the human mind is a double-edged sword. Even though it quickly evaluates cause and effect, this quick evaluation often causes the mind to overlook important variables. This isn't to say that you must think of and evaluate the billions of elements that come together when faced with a problem or decision. However, it is important to account for different factors that will significantly impact the result.

The major benefit of this quick cause-and-effect evaluation that the mind does is that it creates order in the brain and lets you draw conclusions in a logical way; in a way that makes sense. Unfortunately, even though the brain's own cause-and-effect is similar to a mental model in its usefulness, it is also similar to a mental model in the way that it is flawed. Cause-and-effect relationships are a shortcut, and it is not uncommon for these shortcuts to be misguided or wrong. They are based on instinct and subconscious thought rather than the rationalities (or lack of rationalities) in the situation.

Blind Spots and Mental Models

Among Munger's theories regarding mental models is the idea that people can limit the risks or potential downsides of a situation by avoiding mistakes instead of focusing on coming up with the most brilliant solution. Even solutions that take many factors into account expose a person to some harm. Eventually, regardless of a person's brilliance, their tendency to take risks is going to result in poor luck. It is not a matter of intelligence, but of statistics and the reality that there is no single person that is right all the time. People naturally develop blind spots. These are connections, factors, and other elements that are easily overlooked, whether a person ignores them, or they do not have experience with them.

Once a person acknowledges the blind spots that exist in the mental models they use in day-to-day lives, they can learn to identify and account for these blind spots. For example, people often experience confirmation bias, which means they have a tendency to choose evidence depending on what supports their ideas rather than looking for the truth. When a person recognizes this bias, they can take a more critical look at the information and thus create a more accurate and effective mental model.

Mental Models Can Be Useful or Limiting

One of the biggest struggles when examining the tools in our toolbox is having a limited view of the world. For example, someone who works as a divorce lawyer may overanalyze the relationships they try to have because they see divorce everywhere. While this is good insight when it comes to identifying problems in a relationship, it can also cause the person to look for problems. If the divorce lawyer is constantly looking for problems in their personal relationships, especially problems that have ultimately caused the end for many of their clients, they will always struggle to be happy in a relationship. They may find it hard to be committed since they see so many commitments failing day in and day out.

Essentially, for mental models to work well, they have to be used in a way that is beneficial. With the divorce lawyer, if they are always nitpicking problems as a means of an end, rather than recognizing problems and using their insight to handle them, they are ultimately choosing to have an unsuccessful dating life. The key to using mental models properly is to use them in a way that provides the greatest benefit with the lowest risk.

If you put a business executive and an environmental expert in the same room and ask them to discuss what to do with a plot of land, chances are the options will be vast and it will be difficult for the pair to come to a conclusion about anything. The business executive is more likely to focus on the habitat in terms of what it can do for development or how it can turn a profit in some way, while the environmental expert might be focused on improving the natural habitat or the quality of the living environment.

The two would likely come to a head because of what is known as mental models. Put simply, mental models are representations of the world. People use mental models to solve their problems. These mental models are developed over a person's lifetime as they learn new things and recognize patterns in their lives.

Mastery of mental models is a good thing; however, it also has the potential to be someone's downfall. People who rely on a small group of mental models or ways of thinking are ultimately limiting their ability to see the true potential of the situation. It becomes impossible to choose the best possible outcome because they cannot clearly see the reality of the choices in front of them.

It is natural to favor certain mental models, especially when you have become accustomed to thinking in a specific way. Unfortunately, the more you favor any single mental model, the more likely it is that the model will be your downfall. It is easy to get caught in the trap of favoring the mental models most familiar to you. When you are solving problems or making decisions, however, the most desirable outcome is not always what is most familiar to you. If you allow familiarity to dictate what you do, it will be nearly impossible to make the changes that are often required for success. Remember that while expertise can be a good thing, particularly when you are establishing your authority in an area, it can also be a limitation.

Removing Bias from Mental Models

Mental models are incredibly subject to bias. Like with the divorce lawyer, they saw only the bad side of the problems instead of looking for opportunities to fix them. The easiest way to remove bias is to consider only the factual information that can be proven. This is challenging, especially in personal relationships, because it can be hard to remove emotion. This is even true in the workplace. For example, imagine that a person has the opportunity to go away on a week-long trip with work that has the potential to advance the career. However, the person in charge of the trip is someone that they do not get along with at work. They may be biased in their decision of whether to go or not because they might allow their personal relationship with that person to get in the way of accomplishing greater things in their life. However, they are punishing themselves rather than punishing the other person and choosing a path that ultimately leads to a lesser degree of success.

Furthermore, to be truly successful in life, it is critical that you are open to new opinions and ideas. One of the biggest mistakes that people make when sharing ideas with others or having disagreements is that they do not listen. Rather than listening to the other person's ideas and using it to gain a new perspective, they may shut the idea down before it comes to fruition because they do not want to hear anything that contrasts their own beliefs.

In order to successfully use mental models, these fallacies must be overcome. Learning is a critical part of using all the mental models at your disposal. As you make connections of the principles across different disciplines, you gain a greater understanding of the knowledge available and different methods of thinking. Rather than running from this, it is important to embrace it and remain open-minded to new ideas and new perspectives. After all, with a greater number of outcomes, there is a greater chance of success.

What Mental Models Are Not: A Constant

Mental models do not represent a constant, as they can change as new information or sequences are introduced to the model. The purpose of a mental model is to create a simulation or a representation of what is in front of you. Often, mental models are visual in nature. By adding information into the 'matrix' that is a mental model, the results of the model change.

Even though mental models are used for decision-making and mental processes, they are not definitive by any means. Mental models have limits, such as the information available at the time, a person's unique perception of the situation they are in, and limits based on the mental model itself, as there is no single mental model that can be used to draw conclusions and make decisions – it is a matter of picking and choosing the mental models that can be best applied to the situation at hand.

It is not uncommon for terms like if, and, or to be used to create conditions within a mental model. These conditions allow the scenario to be played out in full and for firm conclusions to be drawn. These terms also help account for deficiencies and problems within the mental models.

CHAPTER 12
THE FUNDAMENTAL MENTAL MODEL OR FMM

The first model that we are going to take a look at is the Fundamental Mental Model. The primary power and role that comes with the FMM is that they are going to determine how we think and what we can or can't think about, what is possible, and what is not possible. We will find in our study of FMM that there are two primary types to focus on and these will include:

1. The FMM is going to advocate for OR and EITHER. But not for AND WITH. The keyword for this model is going to be OR.

2. The FMM that is able to advocate for AND WITH, but not for EITHER and OR. The keyword that is used with this one will be AND.

The FMM OR model is only going to be able to switch between two possibilities, so that is all that you can work with. For example, me OR you would show us how this model works. Whenever this FMM OR is showing up, it is going to have the power to create exclusivity, separations, and some divisions, so be ready to see some conflict show up with this one over some of the others. It is going to be pretty egocentric with power as well.

It is going to be the OR mental model that will show us more about individualism and will allow the individual to be above the nation, above society, and any other grouping form. It is going to place the personal individual identity above the crowd, and it doesn't like to share the limelight. You will find that with this one, you become an abominable presupposition, especially when it comes to things like ownership, possession, privileges, and rights.

The OR model is going to create a type of world view where things are always black and white, with no areas of grey to go along with it. There is true or false, right or wrong, and good or bad in this kind of world. While the OR model is going to be good in that it advances the individual, personal effort, and lots of creativity, it can also be negative because it could include things like loneliness and greed in the process.

The World of OR

Collective MM is not necessarily devoid of the FMM OR. When a group of individuals coalesces against another group, these are going to be collective actions that still have individualism, identity ego, and some of the other attributes that we could see with the FMM OR. Collective MM in the world of OR can be seen as those in collective OR entities, including regional, national, and religious, along with anything else that would promote a configuration that is US vs. THEM.

When economics claims the power of money, politics are going to claim the power of the law, science will step in to claim the power of knowledge, and religion will finish it out with some claims to the power of truth. When these groups do actions like this, they are doing manifestations of the Collective MM within the world of FMM OR.

This does not mean that a collective MM is only going to exist hand in hand with the FMM OR. It just means that you can find some of the collective MM inside of this mental model as well. Not all collectives are going to see the world in the view of us vs. them, but some of them will.

As we have seen, lots of different groups can be a Collective MM within the FMM OR world. These entities are going to attain a unique identity that will help them to stand out from the rest of the world. For example, one religious entity could claim to be the one that holds onto the absolute truth while claiming that some of the other religious entities are only spreading falsehoods. As such, this kind of religious entity is going to be able to identify itself back to God, while claiming that the other religious entities around can only have 'gods' instead.

Nationalities are often going to claim exclusive ownership of a given territory, and then they would issue National Identity Cards just to those whom the political system within that nationality is going to identify as citizens. Those who are seen as the non-citizens are not going to get the National IDs and they will have to get things like a passport or a visa before they can temporarily reside, pass through, or even enter that identified territory.

We can see this happen when we work with a political system. You may have one kind of political system that claims to be the only one that has any civility, while it brands the other competitor as backward, barbaric, or primitive. As such, it is able to pass laws that will grant itself the power to do what it would like to rule over, settle, and invade while grabbing from nations that it claims are from the backward system. This is something that has been seen with neo-colonialism, colonialism, and slavery.

These are just a few of the examples of what can happen with the collective mental model. It can definitely be more than one person who steps in and takes control like this to get what they want. They may have a good message attached to it, but the basics that it comes down to will be the idea of US vs. THEM and that we are better than others.

In the name of Identity MM, millions of people have ended up losing their lives, millions in Europe during the world wars, millions in the Soviet Union during the Bolshevik Revolution, and so on. The world of OR, whether it comes from individual MM, identity MM, or collective MM has the power to breed a lot of brutality, wars, and conflict if it is not used in the proper manner.

This, of course, doesn't mean that the FMM OR is going to be bad or dangerous all of the time. It is going to be based on the person and on the truthful reality that they decide to focus on. Individual power is not always a bad thing, and if it is used in the proper manner, it can be a really good thing too. There are a lot of benefits that we are able to see with this individual power. For example, individual power is going to enable someone to:

- Be right and fight off any wrongs.

- Avoid having other people control us all of the time.

- Avoid looking bad, by learning how to look good.

- How to avoid being dominated while dominating ourselves.

The important thing to remember when we are working with the FMM OR mental model is that the world is not going to be just black or white. The extreme of any of the above mentioned can, of course, be dangerous, this is why this kind of mental model needs to be measured out. This is why we need to bring in some of the other mental models in order to ensure that there is always a healthy balance present to work with.

The World of AND

Now that we have had a chance to talk about the world of OR, and what can happen when that individuality and that it can become a bad thing when it is taken too far, whether by the individual or by a group, it is time to switch gears for a moment and look a bit at the world of AND.

As you can imagine, learning how to shift away from the FMM OR can be a good thing. This is because some of the hallmarks that end up with the FMM AND are going to include things like mutually beneficial collaborations, peaceful unity, and genuine partnerships. It is only from this kind of context that the collective MM is going to craft a powerful and sustainable team spirit.

This does not mean that you have to give up your individuality. But it does mean that you see that the world is not about you vs. them. Both parties can benefit, and live in more peace and harmony when we view the world through the lens of the FMM AND.

With this kind of worldview, we are going to see that the world can provide us with a WIN-WIN outcome in each scenario. This doesn't mean that there won't be times when it is difficult and when things are not going to always work out the way that we would like. But it does ensure that we keep an open mind during the process of communication and that both parties will be open to hearing the other side, making some compromises, and coming up with solutions that are the best for both.

It is only in this kind of world where we are going to see that the ceiling for development will be removed and that the sky is no longer a big limit for us to reach with others. Instead, the sky becomes one of our milestones along the way. True education is what will open up all of the different possibilities so that we end up with a world of more FMM AND.

Now, there are benefits that work with the OR and the AND world view. The best mental models that are out there will be able to hide the negatives while balancing out the benefits that come with FMM AND along with the FMM OR. It is a mental model that is able to optimize the benefits that come with both worlds, the idea of collectivism and individualism.

This is not always going to be easy. When you do this, you will pretty much be working on a nice balancing act that can hardly stay perfect all of the time, thanks to our ever-changing world. As such, it is going to be a journey, not a final destination point that is going to include a lot of improvement, change, discovery, and exploration along the way.

Creating the best mental model for you and for those around, you can be tough. You want to make sure that you are taking care of yourself and not getting others to walk all over you. And there is certainly nothing wrong with having an individual spirit and wanting to stand strong against others at times. But we can see what can happen when the OR MM goes too far.

We need to be able to combine both the OR and the AND model together in order to allow us to get some of what we want in the process, while also taking care of the other person in the mix, and not causing them a lot of harm in the process. And while this may seem like such a monumental task right now, we are going to take an even closer look at the different mental models, and how you can do exactly that, as we go through this writing.

CHAPTER 13
START THINKING DIFFERENTLY

The ultimate aim of learning all these mental models is to implement them in your life. So, for that, you also need to start thinking differently and challenge your current mental model in order to achieve the change that you want. This will help you take every challenging situation in your life as a learning opportunity. And when you are practicing this kind of mindset, you will also be increasing your effectiveness as a leader.

There is so much change and competition in the world out there, that you are bound to feel challenged at all times. Everyone is facing some increased amount of responsibilities in their life and so the number of complex situations has increased more than ever. Levels of urgency and uncertainty are also more than they were before. So, you need to be able to adapt and accept everyone if you want to grow in life. Thus, learning how to manage change becomes extremely important and essential.

So, here are some ways in which you can challenge your existing mental models:

Disorient Your Dilemma

Relying on intellectual capabilities has become a habit of modern-day people. They are always craving for some new innovation, creativity or learning and no one loves to stick to a routine. The need for you to come up with a flexible mindset is of utmost importance and specialists all over the world stress on this issue. The rate at which a person can adapt, or change is one of the determining factors of a leader. There can be several challenging situations in your life and even in your workplace, for example, outplacements, downsizing, financial crises, and mergers and acquisitions as well.

All of these crisis situations can create a dilemma in people, which can definitely destabilize you, but in that situation, you should see the good and take the opportunity to learn. It will be a type of transformational learning since major changes will be made to your existing mental model. Thus, in short, facing disorienting situations in your life can also produce you with a scope to learn as well. All you have to do is be ready to take the lessons that are being given.

Self-Examination

Self-examination or self-reflection is one of the most powerful things to practice if you want to bring some major changes in your mindset. This may be a very simple act, but it can impact you in major ways. In fact, self-examination is what differentiates losers and winners. All the experiences that you are having in your life mean something. So, if you do not take out time from your busy schedule and try to analyze these situations and figure out their meaning, you will never be able to make any considerable change.

But winners are those who indulge in a tremendous amount of soul-searching. They start placing a perspective on all their experiences in life. This, in turn, helps them make the wisest decisions. Thus, in short, they are able to tweak their course of action from time to time just because they take out time to analyze everything that is happening. Self-examination can be quite an empowering ritual. You can optimize your skillsets whenever you think back about what is happening in your life and what you can do to make everything better.

Assess Your Assumptions

People develop some really unhealthy thinking habits just because they assume the harshest things about everything, including themselves. So, you can start by making a list of all the assumptions that you have in mind for achieving a certain goal. Now start from point number and argue its validity. If you want to make this exercise more valuable, then you can try doing it with someone who is not related to the goal in any way at all but has some basic knowledge in that field. This will show you whether your assumptions match with what other people think or whether they are biased or completely unrealistic.

People often force themselves to operate in a certain way in all situations and this is what solidifies those assumptions even more. So, you need to stop seeing everything from the same perspective. If there are questions in your mind, then you need to question your questions as well. Sometimes, the assumptions are also the result of your past. You need to make yourself understand that what happened in the past is gone and now the circumstances have changed, so it also calls for you to change your course of thinking.

Know That Others Have Undergone a Similar Change

Do you consider yourself as a misfit in your environment? Well, the first step to overcoming that is to understand that you are not the only one in the world who has gone through a similar situation. You may be discontent with what you are doing. It might be your current situation in college. You might be thinking that you want to increase your grades, but then you might be feeling that you are way too behind others and that it is impossible to catch up. This is the type of thinking that you need to change. You need to remind yourself that every year there are students in the same position as you who worked hard and did pull up their grades. All you have to do is believe in yourself.

Recognizing the fact that your sense of misfit is not only your own but is shared by others as well often works as a catalyst in helping you transform your mental model. You can also try speaking with someone who was once in your position but ultimately rose from there and got better achievements in life.

Try on New Roles

It is not mandatory for you to love the same thing consistently over the years or to have the same goal that you had over five years back. People change and so do their dreams and aspirations and there is nothing wrong with that. You might have been happy with that you were doing a year back, but now you might be feeling stressed. You might not be willing to put the same amount of effort you used to. If all of this is making you frustrated and see everything in a negative light, then it is time for you to change roles.

When you began your endeavor, you were hoping to reach the endpoint, but now you might be feeling that you have lost your way. It is simply that you are no longer interested in the same purpose. If what you are doing doesn't excite you or doesn't make you want to wake up every morning, then my dear, you are doing it all wrong. This is not a life of contentment or happiness and it is time for you to step out of your old perspective and see things differently. It is time for you to adapt to a new mental model.

Plan Your Course of Action

If you want to change your way of thinking, you also need to figure out the course of action you need to follow. That is the key to adapting a mental model in your life. If you want to change your current model of thinking, it won't happen in a day. It will take patience from your side to make it happen and you also need to follow a path steadily. So, you need to decide what your goals are and then you need to figure out the steps you need to adopt to achieve those goals. You can create your own schedule so that you follow all the steps diligently. Make these steps your micro-goals and reward yourself for every small victory you achieve.

Change Your Self-Talk

The way you talk to yourself influences a lot of things and changing your self-talk can definitely have huge impacts. If you constantly keep reminding yourself that you are not good enough for what you are doing or that you will never be able to achieve the things you want in life, it will impact you in such a way that you will stop putting the effort to make any changes whatsoever. Remember that your reality is created by the thoughts you are having and so you need to alter your thoughts accordingly.

Your self-talk is also the direct reflection of your self-worth and self-worth plays a big role in enhancing your level of confidence. So, if you want to make the right decisions in life, you need to be able to believe in yourself and engaging in positive self-talk can help you with all of that. It might sound a bit cliché, but you need to remind yourself that it is okay to fail once or that it is okay and you have got it.

Determine the Mental Model You Need

Now that you know that you need to change your existing mental model, you also need to figure out what other mental models you need to adapt. If you do not know what to adapt, you will be wandering aimlessly without any purpose as such. So, if you have gone through the topics, then you must have come across various types of mental models to choose from. Figure out what thoughts you are having. Maintain a thought diary where you can write your thoughts down for analysis. When you see what you are thinking, it will trigger deeper levels of analysis in your brain and you will be able to think clearly.

So, once you jot down your thoughts, it is time for you to figure out the problems in your thinking. This, in turn, will help you determine which mental model will be helpful for a growth mindset.

Stop Being a Pessimist

In order to truly change your mindset, you need to first adopt the thought there is still something good that you can do. If you believe that everything has gone wrong and that there is nothing that you can do, then you are being a pessimist. A pessimist can never adapt to any changes or start thinking differently because they are stuck in that same cycle of negative thinking that takes them down.

Start being an optimist and stop wallowing in your own misery. Some people think that they are born unlucky and that no matter what they do, success will never come to them. This is a kind of thinking that can cause your downfall. There is no such thing as being born unlucky. So, you need to work on that and start creating your own positive affirmations that will lift you up from your lows in life.

CHAPTER 14
TRAIN YOUR BRAIN FOR MENTAL TOUGHNESS

Train your brain is necessary to stay calm under pressure. It helps you to increase your mental toughness. In case of any disaster, it helps you to look beyond what happened. It gives you prudence to observe the elements of disaster with a new lens, revisit your thoughts, get the shortcomings, recompose the actionable parts in a new frame and get the work done seamlessly. However, life does not always follow an easy-going road, and everyone has to face failure. So, do not worry about your failure or do not feel sad due to failure. Your mental strength is actually your true friend who always stays with you like your shadow. It stays with you in success and as well as failure. So, it is always with and all you need to strengthen it more.

Know the Difference Between Ruminating and Problem-Solving

Like any other person, you also recall the past event of your life and reflect your behavior in a present event, which is similar to the past one. This is common to all. You must remember that while understanding your experience in one incident helps you to make more informed decisions on a similar occasion in the future.

However, on many occasions in which it is seen wandering in the past creates a situation more complex than the past situation and people shatter in the present occasion. This happens because people like to travel in the past and try to find out the answers to too many questions from the failure of the occasion. Ultimately, they fall into the trap of chewing the cud of past events. They even do not try to explore the abilities they have to solve the problem in the present situation. Additionally, they reflect their experience and relate the same in the present occasion. This way they force themselves to run into the harsh and unpleasant cycle of rumination. This creates an immense negative impact on their mindset and prolongs for a considerable time. As a result, they immerse themselves in a deep depression and even get detached from their close family members and friends.

Now, how can you get to know if you are engaging yourself in an adaptive self-analysis of the past event to solve the present problem or in a maladaptive rumination? Possibly the answer is within you. So, the best way is to ask yourself if your thought process is helping you to solve the present problem or, in fact, it is challenging your potential ability to handle the present situation. Asking yourself this question is very important to you because when you ruminate an issue, you only focus on your critical thoughts. This is the thought process that prevents you to come up with the right solution in the present situation. Although you might have tried to solve the problem you still become unable to find out an effective solution because of your mindset that has been trapped into a vicious cycle.

Different studies have made to understand the link between a rumination condition and the difficulties in solving the problems. The studies revealed that the persons who fell under a rumination condition were less able to handle their present problems. On the contrary, those who could divert the experience of failure to adopt in the present situation were more able to solve their present problems. So, it is always suggested when you fall under rumination, immediately take a break from the situation. Divert your concentration on other things. Read a humor manuscript or participate in entertainment with families or friends. Refresh your mindset. Then analyze your present problem. Find out your abilities to solve the problem.

Practice Meditation

It has been proved time and again that meditation can improve the level of mental toughness you have. Even soldiers who are about to go on a mission or are being trained for combat are advised to practice meditation and for a good reason. They do not become too emotional in their career or in other words, their mental toughness is improved.

In the world of mental toughness, there are usually three types of people. The first one is the marshmallow. As the name suggests, these people are very soft, both inside out and so any little amount of pressure on them can cause havoc. They have a soft inner core but a hard shell. They are obviously tougher than marshmallows, but at times, even they can buckle up after a prolonged period of stress. The last group of people is the rocks, who can literally handle everything that is put in front of them. They are not only hard from the outside but also from the inside.

When a person learns to adopt a lifestyle that includes a regular time set aside for meditation, then he/she eventually starts developing a growth mindset. In this mindset, people do not see their failures or obstacles as negative things but rather learn from their mistakes and events of life. You will learn to harness the power of meditation and then use that energy to stay positive throughout your day. Your idea of mental toughness will be elevated to a whole new level with this new routine of meditation.

At an average, a person has over 70,000 thoughts in a day. What meditation does is that it helps you seek that quiet place inside your head that is present but is hidden under the pressure of all those thoughts weighing you down. But people often confuse meditation with mindfulness. Mindfulness is a different thing and you can say that it is a type of meditation. But with the help of meditation, you will be able to analyze so many thoughts that got buried in your subconscious and you will be able to do so without being judgmental at all.

The first way in which meditation promotes mental toughness is that it helps you enter a state of calmness. When you are calm, you have the time and concentration required to judge which thoughts are worthy of your attention and thus, you can invest your time in them. You will also learn a rational way to respond to anxiety in your daily life. Moreover, with meditation, you can distinguish between noise and static. Your recalling power will increase, and you will also learn how you can control your mind so that you do not get affected by any distractions. In short, meditation can improve your capacity to handle stress and thus enhance your level of mental toughness.

Don't Beat Yourself up for Things You Cannot Control

There will always be things in your life that are beyond your control and this is the ultimate truth. If you cannot make peace with this fact, then you will have a tough time on this planet. When people cannot get over the fact that they can't control everything, they end up becoming control freaks.

Thus, if you want to train your brain to have mental toughness, then you need to stop picking fights on every small matter that comes your way. Frankly, you need to understand that everything is not worth it to waste your energy fighting over it. There will always be some troubling times that you have to face in your life. But don't fret or don't give in to depression just because you cannot control the situation. The simple fact is that the situation cannot be controlled. And when something goes wrong, don't beat yourself up for something that didn't happen because of you.

Yes, you can influence people, but you can never or rather, you should never force your will upon others. For example, you can do everything you can to make the party good, but you cannot do anything to make the people have fun. It is their own decision and choice. Sometimes, the feeling of being a control freak intensifies even more when you have the tendency to jump to catastrophic outcomes, which might not even happen. So, judge your thoughts and think whether you are indulging in such a practice or not. If you are, then think about what is the worst that can practically happen. Usually, it won't be as bad as you are thinking it to be.

You also need to have a stress management plan. As already mentioned in the past point, you can practice meditation, or you can also do something you love. Practice anything that is stress-relieving to you. You can even go out and have a good time with your friends if that is what you want. Create your own positive affirmations that you can tell yourself in a situation of stress. For example, if you are thinking 'Important members of the board are going to be present at the meeting,' then you need to tell yourself 'I can handle it.'

Engage in Third-Person Self-Talk

Do you often remember all the saddening or painful experiences of your past? Then, self-talk from a third-person perspective can be really helpful in such situations. Moreover, psychologists have stated it as a crucial method of self-regulation. Everyone has anxiety-inducing contexts, but third-person self-talk can help you combat them. When you are speaking to yourself in third person, you are actually distancing yourself from your own mind and this can help you judge yourself less emotionally. Every emotion has its own perceived intensity, but all that can be lessened if you try seeing it from a third-person perspective.

If you want to solidify your long-term emotional, cognitive and behavioral goals, then indulging in positive self-talk can help you achieve that. Now, if you are wondering how third-person self-talk is done, then you must know that it is quite simple. The usage of first-person pronouns like I, my or me is restricted. Rather, you should be using pronouns like 'she,' 'he,' 'it' or your name. In some way, a third-person self-talk session can promote you to think in a way that you do about others. In short, you will be viewing yourself just like you view others. And so, this will, in turn, promote self-control by giving you the much-needed emotional distance.

You can practice this form of emotional regulation if you are someone who is coping with some intense feeling or is trying to control your emotions or anxiety or even depression for that matter. Thus, third-person self-talk can come in quite handy and it is something that you should add to your mental tools arsenal because it can not only increase your level of mental toughness but also help you cope with a lot of problems that can come your way.

CHAPTER 15
UNDERSTAND INNER WORLD

Four Temperaments

What is my temperament mix, and how does it affect the way I think and act?

The concept of temperaments goes way back to the time of Hippocrates (around 400 BC). The modern adaptation is the Keirsey Temperament Sorter (KTS), which is closely associated with MBTI.

In a horizontal plane is the extroversion-introversion spectrum, while in a vertical plane is the emotional stability spectrum. Cross plotting these two aspects gives us four unique quadrants representing the four temperaments.

· On the upper right plane is the phlegmatic temperament, a stable introverted nature. It is calm and passive, like flowing water.

· On the lower right plane is the melancholic temperament, an unstable introverted nature. It is thoughtful and anxious, like the rigid and quaky earth.

· On the upper left plane is the sanguine temperament, a stable extroverted nature. It is lively and loquacious, like the whistling wind.

· On the lower left plane is the choleric temperament, an unstable extroverted nature. It is active and restless, like roaring fire.

To know your primary and secondary temperaments, you can take a free online test. Why is it important to know our personality type?

Similar to MBTI, this model of personality is not meant to be a standalone guide to understand your inner world. It is best to use it vis-à-vis other personality models. Connecting your various personality classifications can yield richer models to understand yourself better.

Johari Window: How Do I Expand My Self-Awareness?

Aristotle once said: "The more you know, the more you don't know." Or perhaps it was Plato or Socrates. We don't really know who said it, but the important thing is that it was said, and it captures the complexity of the mind, the self, and the world. Johari Window is a model that tackles what we know and don't know.

Cross-plotting what you know and don't know about your own self vis-à-vis what other people know and don't know about you yields four windows.

On the upper left quadrant is what you know about yourself and what you like to reveal to others. This is your open or public self. Talking about these things is like stating the obvious.

Meanwhile, on the upper right quadrant is what you don't know about yourself but what others know about you. These are your blind spots, and you can be cognizant of these if you listen to feedback, whether solicited or unsolicited, whether positive or negative, whether constructive or otherwise. This quadrant decreases in size, the more you build and nurture trusting relationships with people who openly give you constructive feedback, both positive and negative.

On the lower left quadrant is what you know about yourself but conceal from others. These are your secrets. This quadrant decreases in size, the more you disclose yourself to people you trust.

Lastly, the lower right quadrant is hidden both from yourself and from others. This is your hidden or unconscious self. From time to time, your unconscious sends signals to your conscious self, usually in the form of dreams. It is up to you to interpret these signals that rise to the surface.

You can also expand your self-awareness by exploring hidden aspects of yourself through introspection, meditation, reflection, psychoanalysis, hypnosis, and other methods that let you go into the deep.

Uffe Elbæk's Web of Traits: How do I Define My Dichotomies?

The world is full of dichotomies or opposing characteristics. You would see this even in the natural world. As physicist Isaac Newton said, for every force, there is an equal and opposite force. So, we have light and dark, hot and cold, north and south, wet and dry, rough and smooth, tasty and bland, clean and dirty, full and empty, big and small, fast and slow, light and heavy, strong and weak, shallow and deep, black and white, and all the gray areas in between.

Even deep within us are dichotomies, and what makes each of us unique is how we fall into different spectrums. For example, where do you fall in the introvert-extrovert spectrum? Are you more of a team player or individualist? Is your mind or your body more dominant? Do you value form or content more? Is your mindset more local or more global?

Perhaps you have a ready answer to these questions, or perhaps you need more time to reconcile aspects of yourself. Or maybe you have other spectrums in mind that you would like to examine.

The first step is to think of five spectrums or axis. The model above is more corporate, political, and group-oriented. You can choose the axis you want to plot. You can even plot MBTI and the other mental models earlier.

Second step is to determine where you are in this spectrum. To help you, think of the axis as having 10-point scale on each side, and you need to determine where you are leaning more. Just note that the points on each side must sum up to 10. In the example below, Body is 4 and Brain is 6. You cannot rate yourself 10 on both aspects.

Repeat this process for all the other axis. In the end, you have a web of your different characteristics. You can compare your web with your loved ones or with people you deal with. Or perhaps you can ask a loved one or colleague to fill it up for you, then compare how you view yourself versus how they view you. You can even do this periodically to check how you change over time.

State of Flow Model: Am I in a State of Flourish or Anguish?

"I felt energy running through my veins. At that moment, the world stopped, and I just flowed, like a crystal-clear river running down its course." This is the state of flow or zone described by Hungarian psychologist Mihály Csíkszentmihályi.

In this state of flow, you feel ultimate happiness and a profound sense of satisfaction. You may also find yourself losing track of the time and everything else when you get so immersed in what you are doing. You would often hear this from artists and athletes, but the state of flow can be achieved by anyone from any discipline.

What is preventing you from flowing and flourishing? Maybe the challenge is harder than you anticipated. Maybe you need to learn a new skill or sharpen your current skill set. Maybe it's not the path for you to flow. Maybe you do not have a clear objective, or you lack feedback mechanism. There are many possible reasons and many possible routes for you to overcome your energy blocks.

CHAPTER 16
WHAT IS YOUR MENTAL MODEL?

There are numerous purposes behind clash, yet they eventually can be refined into the way that we as a whole have diverse mental models of how the world works. These mental models are both useful and frightful. From one perspective, they are unbelievably helpful in the way that they disentangle our lives and spare us the vitality of reexamining every viewpoint we have each time we are gone up against with a circumstance.

These models are on the whole relevant. We have various models for every feature of life, from who we choose to be friends with, to what sort of music we tune in to, to the kinds of nourishment we eat and the make of vehicle we drive.

Your parameters and mental model for restaurant selection may be that the restaurant use just privately developed produce and have a veggie-lover selection at sensible costs virtually. Your friend may have a mental model that directs they dine in higher-end restaurants that have the best wines and choicest cuts of meat. These are the furthest edges of the range, and there likely isn't a lot of a trade-off for the general population at either end in finding a spot they can dine together (for example, the money related perspective alone is generally a deal-breaker if you're not willing to move).

Or on the other hand, take, for instance, your decision in where you live. One individual needs to live in a metropolitan zone encompassed by movement, shops, theater, restaurants, displays, and assorted variety and their accomplice needs to live in a rural or community atmosphere where there is grass in the middle of the houses and one-stop sign around the local area.

We donate truly see deliberately that these mental models are in real life until we face somebody who has contradicting mental models. If you are among similar individuals in a detached atmosphere, you can stay away from the information of correctly understanding different models of the world that are conceivable. It's not that you don't understand these different convictions are out there, nonetheless, because you know contrasts of confidence are out there at any rate as per TV, motion pictures, and the web.

Issue emerge when we are not aware of our mental models. We can stall out and be obstinate and think our own is the primary way. I've witnessed this with more established people in my family - there's a correct way and an incorrect way, and that is how it is. Enough said. They believe that there is just a single way for the world to work, and the issues of the world lay in the resistance of everybody who doesn't share their world view.

That would be a fantastically substantial weight to be the attendant of the truth concerning how the world works. How does this fit into influence? Indeed, this falls under the heading of knowing thyself. When we reveal our mental models, we can reverse engineer where things aren't working, or if they are working, we can reverse engineer to perceive how we've turned out to be so fruitful at what we show.

The Second Discipline of Learning Organizations

My supervisor never tunes in to anything I need to state. He'll request my supposition at that point do precisely what he intended to in any case. Why trouble?"

"My employees don't generally think much about their work. The main thing that appears to rouse them is the week's end. Speculation I'll need to do it without anyone's help."

Sound well-known? Those are two different views of a similar situation. They are mental models in real life, and they strengthen a negative example of behavior that is, at last ruinous to an organization from multiple points of view.

CHAPTER 17
EXPANDING YOUR SET OF MENTAL MODELS

Based on our fields of expertise or area of specialization, we tend to developmental models that are rich in a particular area and lacking in other disciplines. The key to excellence of thought is developing interdisciplinary mental models that have multiple and varied applications and utility in different spheres of life.

Understanding the major models in key disciplines such as Biology, Physics or commerce will enhance your ability to understand systems better. Most of our thoughts, belief systems and perceptions are deeply embedded in our psyche. We make assumptions and make conclusions without really thinking about it at a conscious level.

The key to controlling our thoughts is first becoming aware of them. Once you can identify the beliefs and thought patterns that are dominant in your life, you can then seek to change your perceptions. We can alter our view of the world by analyzing our deeply held beliefs and looking for ways to expand, deconstruct or discard them depending on the impact they have on our objectivity.

We can develop new thought patterns by:

a. Looking for Evidence That Discounts Your Beliefs and Assumptions and Challenging Them.

Our deeply held beliefs are influenced by emotions, past experience, preconceived notions, and our reasoning. It is, therefore, difficult to alter our beliefs because they are deeply embedded in our personalities and, to a large extent, constitute our personal identity.

· To deconstruct our deeply held beliefs, we must first look for evidence that they are not always accurate. When your belief of something is in a certain way, you will be bound to see only the facts that reinforce and conform to your assumptions. This gives you blind spots when assessing situations and, in effect, causes impaired judgment because you lack the benefit of having all the facts.

To discount our beliefs, we do not need to disprove all of them. Since most of our beliefs are linked in chains leading from one core belief to another, disproving one core belief will break the links and create room for questioning and discrediting our assumptions. For instance, a core belief that you are not intelligent links to a belief that you can only handle average tasks that do not require a high cognitive aptitude. Discounting the first belief will automatically remove the mental limits you have placed on your abilities.

Taking a step by step approach to changing our belief systems is the most effective way to do it. When you deconstruct your beliefs concept by the concept, it becomes easiest to change our underlying mentality. Concepts and perceptions that we have in our minds are usually interlinked and hence creating breaks in the links will deconstruct the foundation of our beliefs and cause us to build new ones.

b. Adopt New Mental Models to Enlarge Your Perspective.

In much the same way that familiarity breeds comfort, our preferred thought patterns, and mental models give us a comfort zone from which to operate. In our comfort zone, we think and act in the same way without venturing outside of what we are used to.

A mental jail that limits our cognitive abilities to a certain set pattern is every bit as restrictive as a physical jail. If you can only see things in one way, your behavior, experiences, and outcomes will undoubtedly remain the same, creating a cycle of predictable decisions which in turn, result in the same outcomes that are characteristic of your decisions.

Opening yourself up to new opportunities and experiences requires that you first adopt new ways of thinking and perceiving situations. Acquiring new mental models will not only increase your understanding of systems and the world in general, but it will also broaden your view of life. Varied mental models give you different perspectives with which to interpret and understand occurrences and systems.

Developing a better understanding of situations will enhance your decision-making process, which will, in turn, better outcomes. Through a well-developed mental model structure, we can develop better decision-making skills and increase our ability to solve problems and identify opportunities.

Accumulating mental models and creating a latticework of inter-disciplinary models is instrumental in improving our thinking capacity and our ability to see situations from multiple perspectives. When we rely on a fixed number or set of mental models, we, in effect, limit our range of thought, our capacity to generate new ideas and the aptitude for finding solutions to problems.

To improve ourselves through behavior, change, we must first change the way we think and how our thoughts influence our actions. This is only possible if we are willing to expand our set of mental models and set aside our belief systems. Our attitudes, values, beliefs, actions, and behavior are shaped by our thoughts. To achieve something, we must first conceive it in our minds before we can bring it into reality.

The importance of mental models can thus not be stressed enough. Not only do they affect our personal growth and development, but they also influence our interactions and experiences with others and our effectiveness at the workplace and in other intellectual pursuits. Looking at the world through the perspective of one subject or body of knowledge leads to a limited and biased perception of the world and limits our ability to adapt our thoughts to reflect reality.

Our education system mainly focuses on creating experts in specific bodies of knowledge such as biology, physics, geology, and many other specialist disciplines. To be exemplary thinkers, we must be willing to break out of the mold of our fields of expertise and pursue liquid knowledge. Liquid knowledge is the knowledge that encompasses multiple fields and has utility across various situations in day to day life.

Liquid knowledge facilitates the formation of interlinked concepts within the mental model. It forms co-relationships between related concepts establishing similarities and areas of interactions across different fields of knowledge and expertise. These linkages within the mental model are important in creating opportunities and innovative ideas that would otherwise be missed if we limited ourselves to just one area of expertise.

Mastering the fundamental principles of each discipline will open up your view of the world and enable you to perceive situations from multiple points of view and enhance your understanding of the world.

CHAPTER 18
ABOUT REALITY, BELIEF, AND PERCEPTION

The reality, belief, and perception are all elements that are connected with one another. Determining their individual definitions, their purposes, and how they interact is a great step to determining what needs to be done in order to achieve the goals you have. Let's break down each of these components and start with a definition.

Reality

This one seems self-explanatory because it is simply what is. It's the current state of affairs, regardless of opinion, bias, preference, or anything else. In very short terms, this is the way things are. Dealing only in the way things are can give us a rather short-sighted approach to things. This is not to say that there is anything wrong with a pragmatic approach to your goals. Being realistic and methodical is a great way to ensure progress is being made, contingencies are being kept, and things are going the way they should.

However, when you're looking at things specifically from the standpoint of the way things are, it can open the door to a measure of pessimism. Have you ever had a conversation with someone about wanting to achieve a goal, but it's like talking to a brick wall? For instance, you tell your friend Calvin that you want to be a writer who is wildly successful. Calvin hits you with a heavy dose of "reality" and starts throwing out statistics of the likelihood that a new writer will have huge success.

Yes, okay, the odds are small. That doesn't mean that those odds are not subject to change, it doesn't mean you can't be that change, and it doesn't mean that you have any less of a right to be excited or passionate about your pursuit. Being realistic certainly has its uses when it comes to being aware of the obstacles you need to overcome. After all, it's impossible to overcome barriers you didn't even know were there, right?

Let's take a look at another aspect of reality and where it can hamper success. When analyzing the statement, "I want to succeed," we'll find a few things to be true. The first is that we're establishing a desire for a situation that is currently not in place. This is the very beginning of a provision for the future. So, where does that leave me in a current sense?

If I want the future to differ from my current situation by containing success, this tells me that my current situation does not contain success. This is where we begin to get into the subject of perception. How do we determine what indicates success and what intrinsically signals success? Let's take a look at what perception is and how that could figure into our plans for future success!

Perception

Perception is the personal interpretation or mental impression of a circumstance or situation. How we react and how we conduct ourselves depends fairly heavily upon what our perception of things turns out to be. If we perceive that everything is fine, we take a more relaxed approach to going about things. If we perceive that things are not going well, we may adopt a more tense or problem-oriented approach.

Perception can really change your entire worldview and the way you respond to everything you've ever experienced. In Hamlet, William Shakespeare wrote, "...There is nothing either good or bad, but thinking makes it so." Think about this with me for just a moment. If we take an event that is seen as sad, like your dog running away from home. Dogs are great companions and losing one has been known to be very unfortunate. However, you hold off on being sad for a day or so and you put up posters. Someone calls you and tells you they've found your dog!

You meet up with this person to get your dog back and hit it off with them really well. Now that person and you are friends! What a joy. Sometime later, you find that your new "friend" stole the dog in the first place. Well, now, how are you supposed to feel? You're being jerked around by your perception of the intrinsic meaning and emotional baseline for each of these events.

By taking each of these moments as they come, and by refraining from automatically assigning an emotional response to them, you gain more control over your response to things as they happen. You'll be in a position to ask yourself, "How do I want to feel about this?" From here, you can respond accordingly.

When you keep yourself reserved from feeling an automatic emotional response that's dictated by societal perception of events, it can lead you to a line of thinking that might be less than appealing. Emotions and feelings are the essences of life. If you don't feel anything, what's the point of living? Emotions are equal to meaning. If the things we go through have no meaning, why live?

This is, funnily enough, partially the point of this. Emotions are not equal to meaning. An event or occurrence can mean the world to you, but you dictate your response to that meaning. In addition to this, the circumstances you cannot control in life will no longer own you. You will have the freedom to experience what life has to offer without being subject to the emotions that supposedly "come with" them.

Once you have the power over your response to the events that are happening around you, you'll find a strength to keep going in the face of staunch adversity. To do this is, in essence, to flip the entire narrative of your life. Go from being the person everything happens to, to being one of the first people to bounce back from the worst that life has to offer.

Belief

A belief is a conclusion that one holds as applicable to a number of different circumstances and factors that are based on faith, trust, or confidence in something. This means that we have been given a reason in the past to believe that something would occur a certain way, whether or not we have discernable proof which directly supports the immediate situation at hand.

So how do these three things coalesce or intermingle with one another, relate to each other, differ from one another, and relate to our personal triumph over the circumstances or situations in our immediate environments?

It's true that the things we believe to be true will color the way we interpret the things to happen around us. In addition to this, we tend to behave and respond to stimuli, situations, and circumstances according to those beliefs.

What sorts of things affect the beliefs you have? Let's break them down.

Past Experiences

What you've been through in life will leave you with conclusions that you've taken from your experience. For instance, if you go to the DMV at 9:00 in the morning on a Saturday and the line is wrapped around the whole building, you will probably learn that 9:00 on a Saturday is the absolute worst time to go to the DMV. This is a belief you now hold, regardless of the DMV location, weather, nearby holidays, popularity of that location, and several other factors that might affect wait times. It's important to consciously make those conclusions after your experiences, so you can be sure you're not making any without taking everything into account or doing so erroneously.

Knowledge

Knowledge is the component that allows us to form new conclusions that are based in fact. These allow us to consciously create beliefs that we can use to our advantage in defining and achieving our goals. If we take the belief that was created above, we can use knowledge to amend that belief, so it's most useful. Did you know that most business chains and establishment chains have listings with Google? If you do a search for a particular location, you'll see a little graph for each of the days they're in business. Each graph will tell you when they're the busiest.

Your knowledge now tells you that you have that resource and that you can use it to achieve your goal of getting in and out of the DMV with the lowest possible wait time!

Events

Occurrences in our lives that bear a lot of weight, whether they're joyous or quite negative, can cause us to adopt beliefs on a subconscious level. Try to think of something that happened in your life that had a large emotional effect on you. This could be the birth of a family member, the loss of someone you care about, the day you got a job you really wanted, the day of a tragic public incident, or anything that caused you to feel a profound emotional effect. Did you decide to do anything differently as a result of that occurrence? What was it? Has it helped you or has it held you back?

Environment

The environment around us can have a profound effect on a large number of aspects of who we are as people. It had often been said that we are a product of our environment. This does not have to be the case if we are aware of our surroundings. In fact, if we choose only to adopt the changes, beliefs, mannerisms, conditions, etc., bestowed on us by the environment that serves us well, we would find ourselves in a position to control our destinies much more readily.

Outlook and Prediction

Our view of the future is largely painted by all the factors mentioned. That being said, this mechanism can easily go both ways. The way you see something going (because of the factors above) can easily paint a picture of a future that strongly validates every conclusion, belief, etc.

Because of this, it's very important to maintain an open view of things to come, while continuing to strengthen and validate the conclusion and beliefs that have served us well.

Being aware of the aspects that impact these factors can help you to see them coming from a mile away. When you can see them coming and you know the potential they have for forming your opinions, conclusions, beliefs, etc. Your chances of changing those opinions, conclusions, and beliefs into more positive and beneficial ones.

CHAPTER 19
DECODING THE EMPATH

Characteristics of Mental Models

1. Mental Models Are Incomplete Representations of Reality and Are Constantly Changing

Mental models are context-based. Our perception and interpretation of the situation are dependent on our beliefs, attitudes, and preferences. We base our understanding of the world on our experiences and the knowledge we are exposed to. As our environments and experiences change, and we acquire more knowledge, our view of the world evolves to incorporate the acquired information. Mental models are, therefore, constantly growing and evolving to adapt to our learning curve and experiences.

2. Mental Models Are Not Factual Representations of Reality

Perception is unique to individuals. Two people looking at the same thing will see and focus on different aspects of it. Our perceptions and understanding of the world around us differ from person to person because our experiences, views, and beliefs differ. We each construct our mental models to explain and interpret our own view of how the world works. A mental model is thus not a collective view of reality but a personal interpretation that we use to facilitate thought and our decision-making process.

3. Mental Models Simplify Complex Knowledge

A mental model is used to interpret complex concepts and situations. They explain the relationship between things, how they interact in the larger scheme of things and how they function. In different fields, there are mental models that enhance our understanding of how things work in that particular system.

If you are in business and need to understand how much product to put in other markets at any given time, then the law of supply and demand helps you understand that if supply exceeds demand, you should expect a fall in prices. Conversely, if demand exceeds supply, prices will undoubtedly rise.

Understanding models in different fields enhance the level of knowledge and comprehension we have regarding different subjects. This knowledge is instrumental in making sound decisions, coming up with ideas and in solving problems.

4. Each Mental Model Represents a Possible Outcome

Mental models are predictive in nature. We use them to create mental simulations of different scenarios and infer possibilities and probable outcomes. In business, we can predict or forecast sales based on experience, market trends and acquired knowledge. We can, therefore, use mental models as planning tools when making decisions and developing objectives and goals.

Mental Model Construction and Development

Mental models typically contain different types and levels of knowledge. The functions of system components, knowledge on how these systems interlink to produce the desired effect as well as procedural knowledge to operate the system to achieve a particular outcome are all contained in the structure of the mental model.

The structure of a mental model forms the basis on which behavior or reaction towards an experience or occurrence is formed and developed. This means that how we behave towards a situation or an experience will be based upon our interpretation and understanding of the experience regardless of whether our perception is factual or imaginary.

The organization of knowledge in the structure of a mental model is comprised of networks of knowledge and concepts that are interlinked. This organization of information is important not only for the creation of mental simulations and predicting outcomes but also for recalling procedural knowledge that we tend to use repeatedly on a daily basis.

Research has shown that organized knowledge is easier to recall than random concepts. When we form a mental model of how a particular system works, how its components are interlinked and how these components function within the system, this knowledge becomes entrenched in our minds and we can execute tasks related to this model quickly and with little additional mental effort mainly relying on recollection.

The structural characteristics of mental models differ based on levels of experience. Mental models in individuals with high levels of experience or experts are better developed in comparison to the mental model of individuals with little to no experience. These differences in the structure of these two types of mental models are evident in the;

- Networking of the mental model.
- Procedural set up of the mental model.
- Level of language in the mental model.
- The level of abstraction. Of the mental model.

Networking of the Mental Model

The mental model in an amateur or a person with little experience in a particular field or system typically has few links between components of the concepts in question. This is because only has a surface understanding that has not developed into identifying the relationships between the components of the concept.

On the other hand, when an individual is highly experienced in a certain field, the associated mental model will have many networks and links between the components of the concept because they have a deeper and thorough understanding of how the system works. The higher the level of experience a person has, the higher the level of networking of their mental model will be and in effect, their understanding of the system in question will be much better.

The Level of Abstraction of the Mental Model

When a person is highly experienced in a certain field, the mental model they create will be derived from abstract concepts as well as conceptual features of the system and the relationships between these concepts. In amateurs, the mental model structure is conceptualized based on the surface features and tangible objects in a system.

Procedural Set Up

Mental models associated with low levels of experience or in amateurs have concepts that are not necessarily linked or tied together to create a procedure. In highly experienced people, concepts are linked to a sequence to create procedures.

Language

At an amateur level, the connections in the model are based on the meaning of words in the natural language. However, at an expert level, the connections are based on the meanings of words in the language of the domain of the system in question.

The knowledge and concepts that make up the basic structure of mental models evolve as we gain more knowledge and experience with a particular system. The greater your experience is in a particular field, the more comprehensive the mental models you create are going to be. To enhance our understanding of a system, we need to acquire more knowledge on and develop experience in that field so that our mental models are comprehensive and well structured.

Mental models influence and shape our thoughts and actions daily. It is important to understand how these models are formed and developed and how they evolve with time. From simple everyday tasks such as driving, cycling, using a computer or learning, to more complex activities such as flying a plane or treating a patient, we are constantly using our mental models to direct our thought process and guide our actions and behavior. Understanding how mental models are constructed and developed will enhance our thought process, ability to make sound decisions and overall productivity.

Mental models help guide our perception and views of experiences and systems by enhancing our understanding. They are vital thinking tools that filter knowledge and simplify complexities to equip us with the knowledge we require to understand life and explain occurrences. Mental models help us in making decisions, generating new ideas and solving problems.

Well-developed and interlinked mental models improve our clarity of thought and level of perception. This, in turn, will impact positively on our ability to generate ideas, predict outcomes and on the ease of solving problems. By using varied mental models to base our judgments on, we develop an objective and multi-dimensional view of a situation and, in doing so, increase our capacity to identify opportunities and generate new ideas and adapt to our environment.

A mental model is generally a framework that a person carries in their mind to help them interpret concepts and occurrences and explain the world around them. A person's thoughts will be limited and biased based on the set of mental models they choose to rely on as their thinking tools. Developing and using as many mental models as we possibly can give us a broad view of the world.

The wider our world view is, the greater the opportunities we will be able to see and have access to.

The most useful mental models are the ones with a broad range of utility that we can utilize across different situations and systems. The construction of a mental model typically occurs in three main stages. The initial stage involves identifying a system and its components. This is then followed by integrating the components based on their connections and interactions with each other within the system.

The final stage of the construction of the mental model is testing the model. Building a latticework of interconnected mental models is done by taking a set of useful concepts from different disciplines and tying them together to form a greater concept which is composed of smaller interlinked concepts.

The complexity of the structure of a mental model increases proportionately as our knowledge increases.

When you are a child, you learn that your heart is an important part of your body. As your knowledge in biology grows, you learn that good heart health is essential for longevity and this knowledge will probably influence your nutrition choices and lifestyle. From a simple understanding of a concept, you learn more and more, and this knowledge shapes your actions and behavior. This is the power of mental models. By structuring knowledge in a way that you can infer the consequences of your decisions, they guide your thoughts and decision-making process.

Regardless of our field of expertise, acquisition of more knowledge and experience leads to better developed mental models. Better developed models, in turn, yield better thoughts and better choices. These all play a role in our quality of life by influencing our behavior and adaptability. Clarity of thought enables you to focus on your goals and make decisions that further your agenda.

Mental models take our experiences and acquired knowledge and organize these data in a format that is easy to comprehend and memorize. The points of reference created in a mental model are based on experience; hence a person is able to make inferences based on past situations. To properly develop our mental models in any particular field, we must continuously commit to learning and gaining more knowledge on the subject.

Learning is the acquisition of new knowledge. This knowledge can be classified into declarative knowledge and procedural knowledge. Declarative knowledge represents people's beliefs in terms of processes, relationships, acceptable behavior, and cultural norms. Declarative knowledge occurs on a conscious level and it is contained in the beliefs people have about different concepts. Mainstream education and professional training are typically focused on the acquisition of declarative knowledge.

Procedural knowledge is predominantly composed of modes of action or processes that are triggered automatically from memory without additional mental effort. Knowledge such as cycling, driving and other repetitive tasks form part of procedural knowledge. Procedural knowledge becomes committed to memory and can be recalled and used automatically.

Declarative knowledge contained within the framework of a mental model requires the construction of increasingly complex mental representations to accommodate the increasing data. The more knowledge we acquire, the greater the complexity of the mental model that is required to filter and arrange this knowledge into simpler understandable concepts.

CHAPTER 20
DIFFERENT AREAS OF MENTAL MODELS

There are several areas that mental models are created and can be changed. Here, we will explore the different areas and start to understand how we develop mental models and why. Changing mental models is a process and will take time. Some models will be easy to change, and some will not. Understanding how they work for us or against us is essential. If we are aware of the mental models, we can change them. Improving these areas will enhance your life and give you new insight into changing the mental models you need to change in order to provide you with the amazing life you want.

There are different things you can do to improve your memory and thinking process. Eating a healthy diet and drinking plenty of water fuels the brain and helps it function properly. Getting enough exercise will help you release stress and "clear your mind."Helpful chemicals in the brain will be released, and new connections will be made. Meditation has been proven to quiet the mind and bring peace and balance to the person that is using it. The list for improving your brain and your health are endless. Find something that works for you and continue to do it. If after time that doesn't seem to work for you anymore, then decide to try something new. It is not set in stone what is the right or wrong way to bring peace to your mind.

Memory and How It Works

There are different areas of memory.

The long-term memory will store, retrieve, and organize memories. Short-term memory is information that hasn't been decided to dismiss or store into long-term memory. Explicit memory is a long-term memory that you will have to concentrate on remembering them. Recalling a certain memory. Implicit memory is remembering from repetitiveness, subconscious "auto-pilot." Autobiographical memory is a memory you can recall more vividly than others.

Long-Term Memory

For memories to become long-term memories, it will have to impact you in some way. Big or small, you will remember it for years to come. You can recall it and may remember all of it or just a few segments of it. These are what we base our future upon. These memories are gathered and organized, so when a situation comes up again, we will be more prepared for it. The thought of getting on a roller coast may make you instantly recall a memory of you getting sick on a roller coaster when you were twelve. The mind will remind you not to get on the roller coaster because last time you felt ill. Long-term memory will store everything that happens to us.

If we didn't have long-term memory, we would not be able to continue to have relationships or have a conversation. The long-term memory is what retains all the information that allows us to do these things – the schooling we have had and everything that we have learned from our parents or teachers. Thinking about the things you do on a daily couldn't be done without long-term memory. It is the life behind all that we do. The long-term memory is critical to maintaining the life we have created.

Short-Term Memory

The mind takes in so much information on a second by second bases – some of the information we need and some we don't. Short-term memory is where we take in all of this information. Our brain decides if we need to dismiss it or if we need to store it into long-term memory. Working the memory muscle will help you strengthen your mind now and help ward off Alzheimer's later in life. Studies have shown that practicing brain games will increase new connections and boost your brain to stay healthy.

Short-term memory is how the waiter at your favorite restaurant takes your order and doesn't write it down. They are exercising their memory muscles. The short-term memory can only hold a limited amount of information for about 20 to 30 seconds. That is why repeating the information will help you retain it better. When you first met someone, Hi Connie. I am glad to meet you, Connie. Doing this will help you remember the person's name.

Explicit Memory

Explicit memory is recalling a memory and intentionally remembering the memory. You try to remember vivid details when you think hard enough about the memory. This is the memory you have when you smell apple pie, and you think of your grandmother's house at Thanksgiving time. There are two different types of explicit memory. One is episodic, which is your memory of your name, childhood, and family relationships. The other is semantic memory, which is random knowledge, like the capital of Kentucky, is Frankfort. When remembering a memory, if two or more senses are recalled, the memory will be easier to recall.

Implicit Memory

Implicit memory is a memory that we don't have to think about it. The subconscious memory takes over. The repetition of this task just happens. We don't have to think about it. It is the route we take home. We know this route so well we sometimes forget if we stopped at the stop sign before entering the neighborhood. Assembly line workers use implicit memory daily. Missing parts or a defect will send a red flag in the brain, letting the worker know it isn't right because it will look different from the last 300 parts, they have seen that day. The subconscious mind will take over and let the conscious mind think of other things.

Autobiographical Memory

This memory you can recall better than other memories. Autobiographical memory falls in with explicit memory, but what makes it different is you can remember it and feel like you are there right back where you were in the memory. Autobiographical memory is highlighted with more than one sense. Trent remembers working on his grandfather's farm when he smells wet hay and sees a field of horses. Vividly remembering is autobiographical memory.

Critical Thinking

Critical thinking is looking at an issue or situation with the facts and coming up with a conclusion or solution. There are five skills we use when talking about critical thinking. The first is analytical. Analytical is when we ask questions to find out more information to create a decision. We use data and facts about the situation or event to determine how we see the world. A person will ask questions to find more information in order to help make a decision. Communication is essential to relay your idea or answer to others in a way that they can understand and understand your point of view. It will help get information and give information to make the decision for the situation. If your conclusions are relayed clearly, others can understand what is being said, and that can help them make their own decisions.

Creativity is a way of looking at a problem and finding a new way to solve it. Creativity promotes curiosity, imagination, and new thinking. When critical thinking uses an open-mind, it is able to set aside emotions, assumptions, and judgments. A decision is made based on facts and data. The decision or solution will be fair and unbiased.

Problem-solving contracts the facts and data that the analytical brain has gathered and organizes that information to understand the problem, based on that information, the brain can start to solve the problem. Decide on the best way to handle the situation. Problem-solving will make clarifications and have a conclusion.

Analytical Thinking

In this stage of the problem-solving dilemma, the brain gathers the information that will later give us the tools to create a resolution to the problem at hand. It is always seeking information. The information coming into the brain starts to be organized and shuffled to make sense of what the outside world is doing. At this stage, mostly what is happing is just getting the information, assessing the situation, and looking for an answer to the problem.

Analytical thinking uses the sense to gather information. A person has been transported to a hospital after a severe car accident. The emergency room nurse will start to evaluate the person and ask questions to gather information to help improve the patient's health and current situation. Watching vitals and how the patient is responding to different evaluations will determine how the nurse will take the steps needed to save this patient's life. Analytical thinking gathers the information in the world so the brain can determine the solution to the current problem.

A great way to create a stronger analytical thinking skill is to practice. Walkout in the world and just observe the surroundings. Be aware of what is going on, look at details, and notice what you are interested in. Create questions about how things work and understand the concept. Games are another great way to improve the analytical mind. Research online and find brain games that will help you improve your brain function. When resolving a problem, look at the pros and cons of the issue. Be intentional in your decision making and recognize the consequences of your decision.

Communication Skill

This is important in all aspects of your life. In relationships and in problem-solving. If you have discovered a link or resolution to a problem and need to relay the information to someone else, your communication skills should be clear and direct. The tone we use to say it will also help understand the information. If you are able to share information effectively and use terminology that your audience can understand, it will be a benefit to you and the audience. Having excellent communication skills with verbal as well as written, will help you relay critical information.

Jason has a great idea to change the kitchen so that it will flow and be more efficient. In relaying this idea to his wife, he has to be clear on where the table, appliances, cabinets will be placed. Jason created a diagram that showed where everything will be set and what walls need to be taken out or moved. Having clear information, you and the person can have a better understanding of the problem.

A great way to improve communication skills is to talk to different people with different views. Get new perspectives on the issues that mean the most to you.

Find yourself a pen pal and start to write or email friends and explain the ideas that you have. Make communication a priority each day. Learning a new word, a day and use it throughout the day. Check on the internet for games that will enhance your communication skills.

Creativity Skills

Creativity is in everyone; there are lots of ways to express it. Some people are creative in an artistic way, like most people think about painting, sculpture, drawings. But there are other ways to be creative. Being creative is looking at the world in a different way than what you usually see it. Creativity skills are fueled by imagination and curiosity. Creative thinking may also be called "thinking outside the box."This way of thinking will help create solutions to daily human problems. Asking questions of why something is working or not will help start your creative thinking.

CHAPTER 21
WHY DO WE MAKE POOR CHOICES?

Sometimes poor choices are just because we do not have all of the information. Some call its stupidity, but in reality, you increase the odds of having irrational thought processes because of physical and environmental concerns. These concerns include lack of rest, intense focus, being hurried, being distracted, working within an ineffective group, or working under someone who is a self-proclaimed expert.

Other times we make because we do not have the correct information available to us. When we make assumptions or decisions based on poor information, it stands to reason that this information is going to cause us to fail. Sometimes, this can be our fault, and other times, we have no control over the information that we are given. One way that this is true is in today's world, and we are often given false news. Without mental models, we are unable to decipher what is fact and what is fiction, and therefore, our decisions and our thought processes are affected.

The mental model that we use is the wrong one, and often, this will affect the quality of our decision-making process. The quality of our thinking also suffers when we use mental models that are not appropriate, that are incomplete, or that are untrue. Remember that not all mental models are true based on facts, but rather, they are based on what we believe is factual. This is often seen when we are working outside of our knowledgeable area. If you are trying to be a teacher, it stands to reason that performing delicate work like a doctor is not going to be within your knowledge base. If you act on circumstances that need you to perform as a doctor, and you do not have the appropriate background, you will fail. When you use the wrong model, the odds of failure will increase.

Sometimes we do not learn from our mistakes. An example of this would be a person who refuses to learn from mistakes and continues to make the same behavior. When we don't understand the way that we learn, the mistakes that we make are going to look the same, be the same, and be repeated over and over and over again. This is why mental models are so important. When you learn from your mistakes, if you are able to change the outcome, then and become more successful. By opening your mind, and learning new mental models and techniques, if you are giving yourself the gift of learning from past mistakes.

In some cases, the choices that we make are a reflection of how we wish to be perceived by other people. Not having a strong sense of who we are, and we are constantly seeking validation from other people, or we are trying to avoid consequences or punishment for our behaviors, we tend to make poor choices. Our decisions are affected by our motivations, and if we are motivated by trying to look good and keeping up a certain appearance, our decisions are going to suffer.

The best way that we are able to open her mind is to a team to truly know what the world is. As we expand our worldview, we are able to correct our thinking processes then. But how do we understand the world as it truly is?

We need to understand first that when we are trying to learn new things, this can be very intimidating. Looking at the toolbox that we have in our mind, we need to understand that it is only as good as the tools that we have available. You cannot do something if the tools that you have are not meant for the job. Consider a plumber who comes to work and does not have the tools that he needs six pipes. His job is going to become more difficult because he lacks the appropriate tools that he needs.

You need to understand that the tools that you need are not something that you can purchase online or in a store. When you use mental models, we store them in our brain, and we acquire them by learning. In order to use them properly, we need to think of or mental models as tools. We also need to learn to use these tools to help us make better choices when we are confronted with this situation.

Another point that we need to understand is the latticework of our brain is meant to hang the mental models from. We need to understand that there is a framework that shapes the way we see the world and understand how it works. The framework that you have is going to allow you to make better decisions, pry yourself out of situations that are bad, and allow you to think about the problems that you are facing critically.

When you are trying to understand reality, you need to look at situations from many different vantage points. Changing your perspective is going to allow you to understand the world better.

CHAPTER 22
MINDSET OBSERVATION DEVELOPMENT

Many people perceive the universe without ever having the clearest of truths. Their eyes and ears are impeccable devices, their nerves pass on reliable information, but the psyche's analytical resources fail to monitor and interpret the faculty's study. Especially, they see and hear, but the faculties 'reports are not being studied or noticed by them; they mean nothing to them. We can see many things, but then see not many things as yet.

Besides the fact that one is to a great extent supplying fair information based on generated discernment, however, one's prosperity additionally relies tangibly on similar tools. The successful man in business and expert life is usually he who created discerning forces; he who has figured out how to see, listen, and remember. The man who sees and makes mental notes of what's happening in his life is the man capable of understanding things when such knowledge is needed. Right now, we find that "manuscript teaching" is not nearly as perceptive as those children who had to rely on observation powers for their insight. In an hour, the young Arab or Indian will watch more than the socialized youth will watch in a day.

Life in a world of writings appears to weaken the powers of perception and understanding, most of the time.

Observation could come about through training. Begin by paying attention to the things you've seen and heard in your regular strolls. Hold the brain's eyes open all the way. Note individual essences, their walk and their attributes. Look for things that are fascinating and strange and you can see them. Seek not to live life in a dream but look out for interesting and worthwhile stuff. The most natural stuff will reward you for the time and effort of looking at them in-depth, and the experience picked up from these undertakings will prove important in your recognition progress.

A position comments that not many people, even those living in the country, know whether the ears of a bovine are above, below, behind, or in front of its horns, nor whether felines fall trees first head or first tail. Not many residents in their neighborhood will identify the leaves of the different forms of commonplace trees. Relatively scarcely any person can represent the house they reside in, in any event beyond the broadest highlights – the subtleties are obscure.

Houdin, the French seer, had the choice of walking through a shop window, seeing every item in it, and then rehashing what he saw. In any case, merely by constant and steady practice, he procured this aptitude. He himself opposed his aptitude and promised that nothing contrasted with that of the common lady who could move through another lady in town and "take in" all her clothing, from head to toe, at one glance; And "have the choice not only to represent the design and essence of the objects but also to state whether the ribbon is real or only made of a computer." A former Yale chief is said to have had the option to look at a reading and browse a fourth page at once.

Any test or profession that needs investigation may increase the discernment sensitivity. Subsequently, on the off chance, we're going to break down the things we see, settle them into their parts or components, we're going to build up the powerful tools similarly. Making note of them on a piece of paper is a good exercise to look at any little article and seek to identify any number of different objectives of discernment as would be required under the circumstances. If painstakingly checked, the most identifiable element will yield rich returns. Should two people take part in such a challenge, the soul of contention and rivalry will enliven the forces of perception. Individuals who have had the patience and steadiness to rehearse this kind of operation effectively say that they find a steady change from the very start.

Nevertheless, irrespective of how one does not feel compelled to rehearse right now, it would be discovered conceivable to begin paying attention to the subtleties of items that one observes, the appearance of people's faces, the subtleties of their clothes, their way of speaking, the essence of the goods that we treat, and the specifics that are especially easily missed. Observation, similar to analysis, follows intrigue; in any case, however, by studying their subtleties, eccentricities, and attributes, suspense may be generated in stuff.

The best information one picks up is that from his very own appreciation afterward. There is a familiarity and genuineness in what one knows right now is lacking in what he believes only on the grounds that he has perused or experienced it. One can make a piece of himself of these knowledges. The knowledge of one is not solely subject to what he does, but his very identity often derives from the identity of his experiences. The condition's effect is extraordinary – and what state are objects seen around one, however? It's not so much what lies outside of one, as what aspect of it gets through observation inside one. By directing one's attention on attractive posts, and seeing them as pretty much as possible, one truly willingly creates one's own character.

The world needs great "perceivers" in all the different backgrounds. It finds a lack of them, and is requesting them uproariously, being happy to address a decent cost for their administrations. The individual who can deliberately see and watch the subtleties of any calling, business, or exchange will go far in that employment. The instruction of youngsters should take the staff of recognition into dynamic thought. The kindergarten has made a few strides right now, there is substantially more to be finished.

The Memory

Clinicians class as "agent mental procedures" otherwise regarded as creative mind and memory, respectively. The expression "portrayal" is utilized in brain research to demonstrate the procedures of representation or introducing again to cognizance that which has some time ago been introduced to it yet which a short time later went from its field. As Hamilton says:

"The general ability of information essentially requires that, other than the intensity of bringing out of obviousness one part of our held information in inclination to another, we have the workforce of speaking to in cognizance what is accordingly evoked."

Memory is the essential agent workforce or intensity of the psyche. Memory is relied on by the creative mind as its material, just as we see when we think about issues generally. Each psychological procedure, which includes the recognition, memory, or portrayal of a sensation, discernment, mental picture, thought, or thought recently experienced, must rely on memory for its material. Memory is the extraordinary storage facility of the brain in which are put the records of past mental encounters. It is a piece of the incredible intuitive field of mental movement, and most of its work is performed beneath the plane of cognizance. When the results and outcomes are passed into our perceptions, do we know and have the field of cognizance. We know memory just by its works. Of its inclination, we know close to nothing, albeit sure of its chief laws and standards have been found.

It was a standard to class memory with the different resources of the brain, however later brain science never again so thinks about it. Memory is currently viewed as an intensity of the general brain, showing regarding each workforce of the psyche.

It is presently viewed as having a place with the incredible intuitive field of mentation, and its clarification must be looked for there. It is totally unexplainable something else. The significance of memory can't be overestimated. The character and training of a man does not depend necessarily solely on it, but his psychological nature is bound to it. In case there was no memory, man would never be able to progress mentally beyond the infant darling's psychological state. Despite comprehension, he will still be unable to gain. He could still not picture simple discernments. He will still be unable to make judgments about purpose or structure. For information, the thinking procedures rely on the memory of past encounters; there can be no knowledge of this information missing.

Memory has two significant general capacities, viz.: (1) The maintenance of impressions and encounters; and (2) the propagation of the impressions and encounters so held.

This was believed in the past that the memory retained only a portion of the experiences and interactions which it initially recorded. The current theory, in any case, is that it retains every perception and experience which it observes. The facts suggest that a large amount of such experiences is never duplicated in cognition, but attempts will usually indicate, all things considered, that the records are still in memory and that proper and sufficiently strong boosts will carry them into the field of consciousness.

The marvels of insomnia, dreams, mania, insanity, approach of death, and so forth show that the subliminal psyche has a huge amassing of evidently overlooked realities, which irregular improvements will serve to take a look at again.

The intensity of the memory to replicate the held impressions and encounters is differently called recognition, memory, or memory. This force shifts physically in different people, yet it is an aphorism of brain research that the memory of any individual might be created and prepared by training. The capacity to look back relies, all things considered, on the clearness and profundity of the first impression, which thus relies on the level of consideration given to it at the hour of its event.

Memory is additionally enormously supported by the law of affiliation, or the guideline whereby one mental actuality is connected to another. The more realities to which a given certainty is connected, the more prominent the simplicity by which it is recalled. Memory is additionally enormously helped by use and exercise.

Like the fingers on our hands, the cerebrum's memory cellular parts become master and effective by use and exercise or weakened and wasted by lack of the equivalent. Notwithstanding the maintenance and proliferation periods, there are two major memory cycles, i.e.: (3) Recognition of recurring impression or experience; and (4) restriction of impression or its relation to a fairly unmistakable time and place.

The subconscious is increasingly aware of the experience being examined as it becomes conscious of the sensation. At that point, it similarly perceives the connection between the impression and the first one as it understands the connection between the sensation and its article. Especially critical is the containment of the impression examined and interpreted. Regardless of how we understand the experience examined, it would be of almost no use to us except if we can consider it as if it happened yesterday, a week ago, a month ago, a year ago, ten years ago, or earlier; and as if it happened in our office, in our home, or in such and such a place on the lane, or in some distant location. Without the intensity of confinement, we should not be able to interface and partner with the recalled certainty of time, spot, and people with whom it should be set to be useful and incentive for us in our way of thinking.

CHAPTER 23
ROLES OF SCHEMAS IN YOUR DAILY LIFE

Schemas, regardless of their accuracy, completeness, and level of detail, are ever-present among humans from all walks of life. It is not only a tool that young children use to get a better understanding of the world. Adults frequently rely on schemas as well in the following different aspects of their lives, sometimes without even realizing that they are doing so.

Acting like filters, schemas can either enhance or subdue the qualities of a person, object, or situation. This makes it easier for people to classify information, like when an employer pigeon-holes a job applicant for his educational background.

Schemas can help one predict what will happen after a particular event has transpired. For example, if a student fails to submit his assignment on time, he is likely expecting to receive at the end of the class a note about his recent poor performance from his teacher to his parents.

Many people use schemas to enhance their level of information retention and recall. Color-coding your possessions and your roommate's, for example, makes it easier for both of you to remember which towel belongs to whom.

Schemas are useful for filling in the gaps when the knowledge you have about a certain event or issue is limited. For instance, a news report about a woman missing for several days does not specify whether the investigators have found evidence about whether or not the missing woman is still alive. Based on your current knowledge about cases like this, you might automatically assume that the woman is likely dead at this point.

A type of schema called the "multiple necessary cause schema" allows a person to come up with two or more probable causes for a particular outcome or event. These probable causes have varying degrees of likelihood, depending on the context of the situation, and may usually be confirmed when one of these schemas has been determined as the correct cause.

Because schemas are typically shared among those who belong in the same culture, using these mental structures serves as foundations for communication shortcuts. This means that most words could have an attached schema to them based on their respective cultural connotations. Schemas are formed based on one's life experiences. Unfortunately, even when faced with opposition and contradictory information, established mental models can be quite difficult to change or entirely remove.

Therefore, the human mind is hard-wired to create its own version of reality and how things work, and even if this said version becomes inaccurate or unhelpful, people are inclined to keep on using them. That is why one's experiences during the earlier phases of human development are critical of how that person would turn out later on. The schemas that have been formed during these stages are carried on to adulthood, impacting not only one's perception of the world but of himself or herself as well.

Examining Yourself for Poor Schemas and Weak Mental Models

As mentioned earlier, people have a tendency to hold on to old beliefs. The effect of doing so influences your attitudes and behaviors, even without your prompt. The way to ensure that your schemas still serve you well be to examine yourself for mental models that need to be improved upon. After all, awareness and recognition are the first steps of almost every effective self-improvement program there are.

To guide you on this, here is an activity that would help you identify the schemas that are governing your thought processes. Follow these steps and carry them out as you go along.

Step 1: Get Yourself a Piece of Paper or Journal

This would serve as your personal log of your progress in your endeavor to improve your mental models. As you continue reading this, keep that piece of paper or journal on hand so that you can refer to them when you have to reflect on how the concepts that would be mentioned and apply to your personal experiences and goals in self-improvement.

Step 2: Think About Your Beliefs That You Have Had for as Long as You Can Remember

Regardless of whether you have come up with these beliefs on your own or you have just adapted from somebody else, list them down in a concise but sufficiently descriptive terms. To make your list more comprehensive, think of at least five believes you have that would fall under each main type of schema:

a. Personal Schemas
b. Social Schemas
c. Self-Schemas
d. Event Schemas

Step 3: Reflect on the Beliefs You Have Listed Down For Each Category of Schemas

Without learning yet the makings of a weak mental model, analyze your personal views about the beliefs you are holding on to. As a guide, ask yourself these questions during your self-reflection:

- "Is this belief still accurate?"
- "Am I being limited in any way by this belief?"
- "Does this belief strengthen me as a person or not?"

For example, you believe that eating fast food products is a way of treating yourself well since doing so allows you to enjoy your favorite comfort food without the hassle of cooking it yourself. Ask yourself if this is actually a valid self-care method. Do you feel good about yourself after eating fast food items? Does it contribute anything else to your life?

Write down your reflections on your journal so that you will not have to come up with them again later on. After you have gone through the succeeding segments, check back on your responses on these questions and see anything has changed on how you view your beliefs.

At this point, you are not likely aware of how to effectively change some of your long-held beliefs for the better. That is perfectly alright since you still have a long way to go. Just keep in mind that you do not have to see the world as you have always done. Change can be good when you have good intentions, and it is managed properly. Furthermore, what is true in the past does not mean that it will always be true. Similarly, even if you have learned how to do things in a certain does not mean that you have already learned how to do it best. Your current schemas might be dictating how you think and act right now, but you can regain control over them once you have fully understood how to build and maintain stronger mental structures.

CONCLUSION

A mental model is a collection of methods and values chosen to explain a sure meaning, based on a less conscious framework or worldview.

Context is something of a slippery term, but think of context as all the things that include the teaching environment to our intent. Nowadays, there is growing criticism of the traditional conceptual model of how teachers cope with the learning situation.

This is nothing new as there have usually been great debates more than educational methods. Nevertheless, we today have something new to think about - stylish scientific research on the way the brain learns. While not conclusive, this particular research supports the task of the conventional "teacher tell" strategy.

As a consequence, instructors and teachers in most educational venues are experimenting with various techniques of educating learners. Nevertheless, instructors are adopting new techniques without also analyzing their belief systems about what constitutes good training, particularly and the way the community in general functions.

If you feel a world with no structure and order results in chaos, how committed are you very likely to be too flipping over a whole workshop to team conversation strategies, role plays, and simulations?

You may think learners need some say in what it is they considered but feel caught by the leader's guide you have to stick to when doing a workshop.

If perhaps your worldview doesn't include freedom in offering with structure and order every so often, how likely have you been to search for solutions to integrate pupil involvement in the current framework?

It is likely to change one's brain design, but if you initially considered what it is. If you are in an atmosphere where in a focus on student-centered learning makes you feel as if an outside onlooker to the procedure, you may want to think about altering your mental model regarding good learning and the teacher's job.

For one factor, if you believe teachers have to offer order and structure to a learning atmosphere, check out the writings of the father of progressive training, John Dewey, and you will find, and so did he.

Nowadays, how about following a hybrid type - one that includes the best of the demand for order and structure with the best of effective involvement from the learners.

If perhaps your leader's guide has many role-plays and simulations, allow the participants to select the people they think suit them best. If perhaps time permits, break individuals into discussion groups and allow them to build their very simulations and role-plays.

Read again whatever lecture notes you have with an eye toward energetic student participation. Time is surely a useful enemy in an innovative classroom, but look for chances to pepper your lectures with anecdotes and function examples drawn out of the happenings of the pupils. Search for the right opportunities to disrupt the lecture with open-ended, thought-provoking questions.

To sum up, before rejecting or accepting an instructional technique, examine your beliefs about the correct job of both the teacher and the student in learning.